# International Studies in Entrepreneurship

## Volume 98

**Series Editors**
Zoltan J. Acs
George Mason University
Fairfax, VA, USA

David B. Audretsch
Indiana University
Bloomington, IN, USA

More information about this series at http://www.springer.com/series/6149

Niklas Elert • Magnus Henrekson •
Mark Sanders

# The Entrepreneurial Society

A Reform Strategy for the European
Union

Springer Open

Niklas Elert
Research Institute of Industrial
Economics (IFN)
Stockholm, Sweden

Magnus Henrekson
Research Institute of Industrial
Economics (IFN)
Stockholm, Sweden

Mark Sanders
Utrecht University School of Economics (USE)
Utrecht University
Utrecht, The Netherlands

ISSN 1572-1922      ISSN 2197-5884   (electronic)
International Studies in Entrepreneurship
ISBN 978-3-662-59585-5      ISBN 978-3-662-59586-2   (eBook)
https://doi.org/10.1007/978-3-662-59586-2

This book is an open access publication.

This Springer imprint is published by the registered company Springer-Verlag GmbH, DE, part of Springer Nature.
The registered company address is: Heidelberger Platz 3, 14197 Berlin, Germany

# Preface

Launched in 2015, project FIRES (Financial and Institutional Reforms for the Entrepreneurial Society) endeavored to analyze the conditions required for smart, inclusive, and sustainable growth in the European Union, in line with the Commission's "Europe 2020" growth strategy. At the heart of the project was the dual recognition that the Union suffers from an innovation emergency affecting its economic growth and social equality, and that this challenge could be overcome if Europe were to become a more entrepreneurial society.

Ample academic research supports the hypothesis that more entrepreneurial regions and countries innovate more and see greater economic growth. Moreover, entrepreneurship provides opportunities for a great many people and is instrumental in shaping a country's transition to a more sustainable future. Research has also shown that institutions, i.e., the rules of the game in a society, go a long way towards explaining the differences in quality and quantity of entrepreneurial venturing across countries and regions. Rather than adding to this already vast literature, the chief aim of FIRES was to translate the insights of some three decades of entrepreneurship research into actionable institutional reform proposals. In June 2018, the program officially ended after yielding a host of reports, scientific articles, and books that addressed the question of how to make the European Union (EU) more entrepreneurial and innovative from numerous perspectives. FIRES concluded with a seven-step procedure, which, if followed, would tailor a reform strategy to the needs of a country or region:

- Step 1: Assess the most salient features of the institutions of a country or region and trace their historical roots.

- Step 2: Assess the strengths and weaknesses of the institutions and flag the bottlenecks in the entrepreneurial ecosystem using structured data analysis.
- Step 3: Identify using careful primary data collection among entrepreneurial individuals, the most salient features characterizing the start-up process, and the barriers that entrepreneurs face.
- Step 4: Map the results of steps 2 and 3 onto a menu of evidence-based policy interventions to identify suitable interventions for the region or country under investigation.
- Step 5: In light of the historical analysis under step 1, fit the proposed reforms to the existing local, regional, and national institutional setup.
- Step 6: Identify the relevant policymakers and procedures, i.e., who should change what and in what order for the reform strategy to have the greatest chance of success.
- Step 7: Experiment, evaluate, and learn—and return to step 1 for the next iteration.

This book centers on the second half of this list. Its purpose is to present a menu of evidence-based interventions aimed at creating an entrepreneurial society in Europe (Step 4) and to assess who should change what and in what order (Step 6) for the reform strategy to have the greatest possible chance of success. As such, its purpose is one of synthesizing and finalizing previously acquired insights and creating a road map answering the question: Where do we go from here?

The present volume is the work of three authors, but we are indebted to and draw inspiration from practically all prior FIRES output and the academic literature beyond. Some previous contributions, however, merit explicit mention here.

First, we would like to draw attention to *Institutional Reform for Innovation and Entrepreneurship: An Agenda for Europe,* a book published in the spring of 2017. Written by Niklas Elert and Magnus Henrekson, also coauthors of this volume, as well as Mikael Stenkula, the book was an early attempt to identify the institutional preconditions for entrepreneurship across Europe and to shortlist the reforms needed to promote a more innovative Union.

Second, we acknowledge the report *Identification and Assessment of the Legal Implications of an Entrepreneurial Reform Agenda,* by Andrei Suse and Nicolas Hachez (in collaboration with Axel Marx). They made Elert et al.'s book more concrete by offering a comprehensive account of which level of government (the European, member state, regional, or local level) had the competencies and mandate to implement the suggested reforms.

Finally, we wish to highlight the contribution of *Financial and Institutional Reforms for the Entrepreneurial Society, Part I*, authored by Mark Sanders, scientific coordinator of the FIRES project and coauthor of this volume. This volume was written towards the end of the project and served as a pertinent summary of all (or most) of the reform proposals discussed and investigated in the project.

In the following, we expand on these and many other sources, creating a new and original work in the process.

Stockholm, Sweden                                                     Niklas Elert
                                                                     Magnus Henrekson
Montpellier, France                                                   Mark Sanders
April 2019

# Acknowledgments

The authors thank Marcos Demetry for his excellent research assistance and Luca Grilli, Friedemann Polzin, Per Skedinger, and Rens van Tilburg for their useful comments and suggestions on earlier drafts. Niklas Elert and Magnus Henrekson gratefully acknowledge financial support from Jan Wallanders och Tom Hedelius stiftelse and from the Marianne and Marcus Wallenberg Foundation, and Mark Sanders thanks Montpellier Business School for their hospitality while drafting the manuscript during his sabbatical in the first half of 2019. Finally, financial support for open access publication of this book was provided by the European Commission under the Horizon 2020 project Financial and Institutional Reforms for the Entrepreneurial Society (FIRES), Grant Agreement Number 649378.

# Contents

# About the Authors

**Niklas Elert** has a Ph.D. in economics and is a Research Fellow at the Research Institute of Industrial Economics (IFN) in Stockholm, Sweden. He defended his Ph.D. thesis *Economic Dynamism: Essays on Firm Entry and Firm Growth* in 2014 at Örebro University, Sweden.

His research focuses on economic dynamism, the relationship between entrepreneurship and institutions, and the effects of entrepreneurship education and training efforts. His book *The Challenge of the Human Ape* (Timbro 2014; in Swedish) deals with the relationship between economic growth and the environment. He is the coauthor of the book *Institutional Reform for Innovation and Entrepreneurship: An Agenda for Europe* (Springer 2017). He has also worked as an editorial writer at the Swedish newspaper *Expressen*.

**Magnus Henrekson** is a professor and president of the Research Institute of Industrial Economics (IFN) in Stockholm, Sweden. Until 2009, he held the Jacob Wallenberg Research Chair in the Department of Economics at the Stockholm School of Economics. He received his Ph.D. in 1990 from Gothenburg University with his dissertation *An Economic Analysis of Swedish Government Expenditure*.

Throughout the 1990s, he conducted several projects that aimed to explain cross-country growth differences. Since the turn of the new millennium, his primary research focus has been entrepreneurship economics and the institutional determinants of the business climate. In this area, he has published extensively in scientific journals and contributed several research surveys to *Handbooks* in the entrepreneurship field.

In addition to his academic qualifications, he has extensive experience as an advisor, board member, and lecturer in many different contexts, both in the business sector and in the public sector.

**Mark Sanders** is an associate professor of economics of transition and sustainability at Utrecht University School of Economics. He received his Ph.D. in 2004 from Maastricht University with the dissertation *Skill Biased Technical Change: Its Origins, the Interaction with the Labour Market and Policy Implications.*

When Mark joined the Max Planck Society Institute for Economics in Jena, Germany in 2005, he shifted his research focus to entrepreneurship economics. When he joined the Utrecht School of Economics, he added finance to his research repertoire and began to investigate the role of entrepreneurship in shaping energy transition. Mark has bridged and combined these topics and published extensively in international peer reviewed journals. He is also a founding member of the Sustainable Finance Lab at the Utrecht School of Economics and was scientific coordinator of the FIRES-consortium 2015–2018.

In addition to his academic qualifications, Mark has been an active member of the Dutch liberal-democratic party D66.

# 1

# Introduction: Why Entrepreneurship?

In 2005, Harvard professor Benjamin Friedman published the book *The Moral Consequences of Economic Growth*. His message was depressing in its simplicity: economic stagnation is a threat to liberal democracy, as it ushers in xenophobia and political populism of all colors. Today, amid sluggish growth and rising inequality, populism is on the rise. The liberal political and economic order of the EU, which Fukuyama (1989) suggested was a more likely candidate than the communist utopia for "the end of history," faces what may be its most formidable challenge since the rise of communism.

This book is written to help address this challenge. In line with the view expressed by Karl Popper in his book *The Open Society and Its Enemies* (1945), we believe that a healthy society is a contestable society. Contestability ensures opportunity, freedom, and progress. From that perspective, growth and innovation are as much a manifestation of freedom as they are a precondition for a sustainable liberal democratic order. Europe needs an optimistic and compelling new perspective if it is to regain its legitimacy among large parts of its population. In a stagnant economy, people no longer see the opportunities for improvement and turn to strong leaders who blame outsiders and promise to make things right. In a truly entrepreneurial Europe in which all are empowered to participate, their simplistic recipes will lose much of their appeal. Reforms enabling smart, inclusive, and sustainable growth across the entire EU could, therefore, offer a way out of the present, perilous situation. The academic consensus on the importance of an economy that innovates in a

© The Author(s) 2019

N. Elert et al., *The Entrepreneurial Society*, International Studies in Entrepreneurship 98,
https://doi.org/10.1007/978-3-662-59586-2_1

sustainable direction and offers opportunities to all lends urgency to our agenda.[1]

Economic stagnation in Europe arguably relates to a lack of innovation, which the EU itself acknowledges: when the European Commission launched the "Innovation Union," a flagship initiative of the EU's 2020 strategy, it simultaneously stressed that the EU was "facing a situation of 'innovation emergency'" (European Commission 2015b).[2] This stark conclusion followed the observation that European member states were gradually slipping out of the top positions in global rankings on innovation. In Table 1.1, we present recent rankings of the top 20 countries according to the most commonly used measures for innovativeness. As can be seen, the USA consistently ranks higher than European countries, as do the Asian Tigers Singapore and Hong Kong. Nonetheless, half of the top 20 countries in all rankings are European; in particular, Nordic and Western European countries continue to do well. By contrast, southern and eastern EU member states are virtually absent in the rankings, hinting at Europe's well-known core–periphery pattern.

In view of this evidence, it is troubling that a key term is missing from the Commission's statement warning of the Union's innovation emergency. Despite acknowledging that "[w]e need to do much better at turning our research into new and better services and products if we are to remain competitive in the global marketplace and improve the quality of life in Europe," the authors do not mention the word "entrepreneurship" once. One is reminded of economist William Baumol's (1968) lament 50 years ago that economics without the entrepreneur is like Hamlet without the Prince of Denmark. Since this statement was made, the economics profession has come to acknowledge the importance of the entrepreneur; the same does not seem to be the case for the EU's top policymakers.

Our starting point when tackling Europe's innovation emergency is that entrepreneurship—broadly defined as the act of challenging the status quo by introducing novelty into the economic realm—must be a central theme of such a strategy. While entrepreneurship is a multifaceted concept, we are convinced that particular emphasis must be placed on what has come to be called Schumpeterian entrepreneurship: the kind of entrepreneurship that intro-

---

[1] As the reasoning suggests, macroeconomics is not a part of this book. Instead, we believe that issues related to fiscal and monetary stimulus and the survival of the EU serve to distract from the structural transformation the EU must undertake in order to achieve sustainable growth. Åslund and Djankov (2017, pp. 5–7) develop this argument in more detail.

[2] See http://ec.europa.eu/research/innovation-union/index_en.cfm?pg=why.

**Table 1.1** Country ranking according to the five most commonly used measures of national innovativeness, top 20 countries for the last available year

| Rank | IMD world competitiveness ranking 2018 | WEF global competitiveness index 2018 | Global innovation index 2018 (INSEAD, Cornell, WIPO) | No. of triadic patents per capita 2013[a] | R&D spending as a share of GDP 2016 |
|---|---|---|---|---|---|
| 1 | USA | USA | Switzerland | Switzerland | Israel |
| 2 | Hong Kong | Singapore | Netherlands | Japan | South Korea |
| 3 | Singapore | Germany | Sweden | Germany | Sweden |
| 4 | Netherlands | Switzerland | UK | Sweden | Japan |
| 5 | Switzerland | Japan | Singapore | Denmark | Austria |
| 6 | Denmark | Netherlands | USA | South Korea | Germany |
| 7 | UAE | Hong Kong | Finland | Austria | Denmark |
| 8 | Norway | UK | Denmark | Netherlands | Finland |
| 9 | Sweden | Sweden | Germany | Israel | USA |
| 10 | Canada | Denmark | Ireland | USA | Belgium |
| 11 | Luxembourg | Finland | Israel | Finland | France |
| 12 | Ireland | Canada | South Korea | Belgium | China |
| 13 | China | Taiwan | Japan | France | Iceland |
| 14 | Qatar | Australia | Hong Kong | Luxembourg | Netherlands |
| 15 | Germany | South Korea | Luxembourg | UK | Norway |
| 16 | Finland | Norway | France | Norway | Slovenia |
| 17 | Taiwan | France | China | Ireland | UK |
| 18 | Austria | New Zealand | Canada | Canada | Czech Rep. |
| 19 | Australia | Luxembourg | Norway | Australia | Canada |
| 20 | UK | Israel | Australia | Italy | Italy |

Sources: *IMD World Competitiveness Yearbook 2018*; World Economic Forum, *Global Competitiveness Report 2018*; *The Global Innovation Index 2018—Energizing the World with Innovation* (INSEAD, Cornell University and WIPO); *OECD Factbook 2015–2016: Economic, Environmental and Social Statistics*; OECD Statistics
[a]Triadic patent families are a set of patents filed at three of the major patent offices: the European Patent Office (EPO), the Japan Patent Office (JPO), and the United States Patent and Trademark Office (USPTO). Patents included in the triadic family are typically of higher economic value

duces new products and technologies and serves as a conduit of knowledge to generate innovation and growth (Schumpeter 1934 [1911]).[3]

The evidence is clear that innovation promotes the further diffusion and creation of knowledge and ultimately drives economic progress (Romer 1986, 1990; Aghion and Howitt 1992; Grossman and Helpman 1991; Jones 1995,

---

[3] In Schumpeterian terms, innovation is the creation of new combinations, generally of (old and new) knowledge, resulting in a new product, a new method of production, the opening of a new market, the conquest of a new source of supply, or the carrying out of a new organization of industry (Schumpeter 1934, p. 66; OECD 2010).

2005). Crucially, Schumpeter saw the entrepreneur, the agent responsible for introducing such innovation into the market, as the *primus motor* of economic growth. However, finding suitable empirical proxies for such entrepreneurship has proven difficult.[4] To this day, a fierce debate in the literature continues to confuse Schumpeter's clearly defined theoretical concept and the inherently imprecise proxies for entrepreneurship provided by empirical data. In our view, the empirical definition of entrepreneurship is less relevant. What matters for our purposes are the qualitative aspects of entrepreneurship; empirical evidence taking these aspects into account suggests that an economy that fosters high-growth firms and high-impact entrepreneurial firms grows faster than an economy with high numbers of small- and medium-sized enterprises (SMEs) or a high self-employment rate (Shane 2008; Henrekson and Sanandaji 2014, 2019). But for this growth to be inclusive as well as innovative, others have emphasized the importance of a broad base of active "everyday entrepreneurs" (Welter et al. 2017).

Table 1.2 presents four measures of Schumpeterian entrepreneurship together with the self-employment rate for Western Europe, Eastern Europe, the USA, China, and East Asia. While the self-employment rate is considerably lower in the USA than in Western Europe and East Asia, the number of US billionaire entrepreneurs per capita—a measure indicative of successful Schumpeterian entrepreneurship—is three times greater. The other approximations of Schumpeterian entrepreneurship reveal a similar picture: total venture capital (VC) investment as a share of GDP is five times greater in the USA than in Western Europe.[5] Furthermore, the number of large firms founded by entrepreneurs since 1990 is more than three times greater in the USA despite Western Europe's much larger population, and the number of unicorns (privately held start-up companies valued at over USD 1 billion as determined by private or public investment) per capita is almost seven times greater.

Western Europe trumps East Asia only in terms of the number of unicorns and is on a par in terms of VC investment as a share of GDP; it scores clearly below East Asia based on the number of billionaire entrepreneurs per capita and the number of large firms founded by entrepreneurs since 1990. Eastern Europe, meanwhile, scores below both East Asia and China on all four measures and has the highest rate of self-employment (partly reflecting its sizable

---

[4] As Acs et al. (2014, p. 476) state: "In spite of years of research, entrepreneurship is a fiendishly difficult concept to pin down". Anderson and Starnawska also (2008, p. 224) note: "more than two decades of concentrated endeavor have failed to produce a universally acceptable definition of entrepreneurship".

[5] However, this may also be related to the strong path dependency and complementarities in institutions, particularly financial institutions, to which we return below.

**Table 1.2** Entrepreneurship in Europe, the USA, and East Asia

| | Population in million | Per capita GDP in USD | Billionaire entrepreneurs, # | Billionaire entrepreneurs per million | Unicorns, # | Large firms founded since 1990, # | Venture capital share of GDP, % | Self-employment, % |
|---|---|---|---|---|---|---|---|---|
| USA | 316 | 52,000 | 432 | 1.37 | 115 | 60 | 0.30 | 6.8 |
| China | 1358 | 11,600 | 228 | 0.17 | 47 | 22 | 0.06 | 12.1 |
| East Asia | 213 | 37,700 | 118 | 0.55 | 8 | 19 | 0.06 | 16.3 |
| Eastern Europe | 104 | 23,000 | 14 | 0.13 | 1 | 2 | 0.01 | 21.0 |
| Western Europe | 412 | 39,700 | 194 | 0.47 | 22 | 18 | 0.06 | 15.8 |

Note: The country groups are defined as follows:

East Asia: Japan, South Korea, Taiwan, Singapore, and Hong Kong

Western Europe: Germany, France, the UK, Italy, Spain, the Netherlands, Greece, Belgium, Portugal, Sweden, Austria, Denmark, Finland, Ireland, Luxembourg, Switzerland, Norway, and Iceland

Eastern Europe: Bulgaria, Croatia, Czech Republic, Estonia, Hungary, Latvia, Lithuania, Romania, Slovak Republic, Slovenia, and Poland

Nordic region: Denmark, Finland, Iceland, Norway, and Sweden

Source: Henrekson and Sanandaji (2018b)

agricultural sector) among the five regions compared. In conclusion, all regions show a relatively small number of truly transformative entrepreneurs and also differ significantly in the width of the base from which such ventures grow.

Overall, the data suggest that contemporary Europe has a comparatively less fertile "ecosystem" for Schumpeterian/high-impact entrepreneurship than the USA, and in some respects even relative to China and East Asia (O'Connor et al. 2018). In Eastern Europe, much of the self-employment is marginal necessity-driven entrepreneurship, whereas in Western Europe the base of self-employment may be broad, but opportunities to grow into the global competitors of the future, in particular, seem limited. These shortcomings, we believe, explain the EU's innovation emergency and are the most significant impediments to the Union transiting to inclusive and sustainable growth; developing a broad reform strategy starts from acknowledging that Europe has a long way to go in this respect.

We should stress that a more entrepreneurial EU would benefit all strata of society and not only the few exceedingly successful Schumpeterian entrepreneurs—the latter are, more than anything else, an important measure of *ex post* success. In addition, of course, "the good life" cannot be achieved through material consumption alone: as highlighted by Nobel Laureate Edmund Phelps in his book *Mass Flourishing* (2013), individuals find meaning through flourishing as producers of offspring, goods, and services, and as actors who solve problems, face challenges, and discover, create, and act upon opportunities. Moreover, as people naturally have a strong sense of justice (Binmore 2005), these amenities in life should be open to all. Hence, while outcomes matter, the processes that lead to these outcomes matter as well.[6] Part of what it means to be an entrepreneur—facing challenges and discovering, creating, and acting upon opportunities—is also part of what it means to aspire to a good life. This holistic emphasis is in line with evidence that the self-employed typically report greater job satisfaction and happiness than do employees, despite working longer hours (Blanchflower and Oswald 1998; Benz and Frey 2004).[7] And the entrepreneurial process, where success and reward follow taking risks, working hard and competing on a level playing field, is perceived as both open and just. Thus, entrepreneurship not only holds the key to the future economic welfare of Europe, but is also a major ingredient in creating

---

[6] Frey et al. (2004) refer to this as "procedural utility."

[7] Similar findings are reported by Csíkszentmihályi (1990), who even found that most people were, in fact, happier at work than at rest.

"the good life" for its citizens, which should be the ultimate goal of policymaking.

How, then, is the EU to become a more entrepreneurial society? In answering this question, our starting points are threefold. *First, entrepreneurship does not occur in a vacuum*; instead, it is the result of several crucial skills coming together to create value in what we term a collaborative innovation bloc. The flesh and blood actors who possess these skills are both incentivized and constrained by society's rules of the game: its institutions (cf. Welter et al. 2019).

*Second, institutions are path-dependent and complementary*; this means that introducing US-style institutions or any other one-size-fits-all reform strategy across Europe is destined to fail. A reform strategy is more viable when policymakers tailor it to the historical preconditions of an individual region or country or to a group of similar countries. To design such a strategy, the focus must not be on the institutions per se but on the *functions* these institutions perform in a well-functioning entrepreneurial ecosystem.

*Third, entrepreneurship contributes to prosperity by challenging the status quo in an open market economy*. Entrepreneurship thrives when open institutions create open societies where vested interests and incumbents can be challenged on a level playing field, enabling fair competition, and new ventures fail or succeed based on the value they provide to their customers and society at large.

We outline the gist of this argument in the remainder of the present chapter, in the process providing a framework for our vision of how to make the EU more entrepreneurial and innovative.

## 1.1 Entrepreneurship as a Source of Growth and Inclusion

It is a rare firm that always behaves as entrepreneurially as Schumpeter envisioned.[8] But one should not dismiss less Schumpeterian entrepreneurs out of hand: Baumol (2010, p. 18), for example, distinguishes between Schumpeterian entrepreneurs and replicative entrepreneurs, who start firms that are similar to existing businesses. Replicative entrepreneurs play a crucial role during the stage of economic development that follows innovation, when a more general adoption and diffusion of new knowledge occurs (Braunerhjelm 2011; see also Baumol et al. 2007).

---

[8] In fact, Schumpeter himself argued that successful entrepreneurs will at some point turn from challengers into defenders of the status quo, and they will venture to limit competition and contestability as soon as they have conquered a strong position in their market.

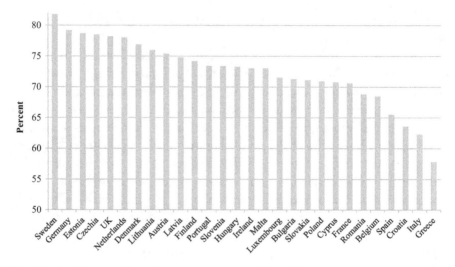

**Fig. 1.1** Employment share in 2017 among people aged 20–64 in EU countries. Note: There are no data for the USA for the 20- to 64-year olds. However, in the OECD data, which reports employment rates for 15- to 64-year olds, the US employment rate was 70.7% in 2017, compared to 76.9% in top-ranked Sweden and 53.5% in Greece, which has the lowest employment rate among 15- to 64-year olds. Source: Eurostat

Replicative entrepreneurs also help explain why few entrepreneurs capture a large share of the value they create; Nordhaus (2004) estimates that the original innovators and entrepreneurs capture, on average, a mere 3% of the value they create. This premium is so small because the existence of challengers, or the mere possibility of being challenged by new entrants, forces incumbent firms to invest continuously in innovation. Consequently, the bulk of the innovative surplus accrues to consumers in the form of lower prices and better products. Contestable, open markets are therefore a precondition for the creation of economic prosperity. Moreover, as open and contestable markets create opportunities for all and reward merit (a combination of talent, luck, and equal access to resources), the resulting wealth (re)distribution is usually perceived as equitable.

The need for more replicative entrepreneurship and more contestable markets is particularly acute in Southern and Eastern European countries marred by high levels of non-employment. Figure 1.1 shows the considerable EU cross-country variation in the need for job creation, captured by the employment rate; it ranges from 58% in Greece to approximately 82% in Sweden.

As we shall see, a great deal can be done to improve the contestability of EU markets, but this is scarcely enough to create an entrepreneurial society. Nor can one achieve this goal by merely ticking off the items on the usual institutional laundry list—stable property rights, the rule of law, and so on. Although ensuring that opportunities exist is crucial, it is also not enough; ideally, institutions should also ensure access to essential resources on equal terms irrespective of social background and personal wealth, thereby empowering entrepreneurs to act on these opportunities.[9]

European institutions did not evolve spontaneously to ensure such equitable resource access, nor have they been designed to achieve that goal. A broad range of institutions are therefore in need of reform: much broader, we argue, than the range entrepreneurship scholars and policymakers typically feel comfortable discussing. To better appreciate the scope of this challenge, we now turn to outline the ecosystem on which entrepreneurs depend to be able to innovate successfully. We label this the collaborative innovation bloc.

## 1.2 The Collaborative Innovation Bloc

Entrepreneurship scholars have long understood that entrepreneurial venturing does not occur in a vacuum. For example, the Swedish research tradition labeled the experimentally organized economy [EOE; see, e.g., Eliasson (1996) and Johansson (2009) for a synthesis] recognizes that the entrepreneurial process is inherently collaborative: to pursue their innovative projects, entrepreneurs need to cooperate with several actors whose complementary skills and resources drastically increase the probability that an innovation-based venture will be successful. The actors, skills, and resources are drawn from several sources, together forming what we call a *collaborative innovation bloc*. This perspective is useful for understanding how innovations come about

---

[9] This view echoes that of John Tomasi, a philosopher who promotes what he calls market democracy: a hybrid view combining insights from progressive liberals such as John Rawls and classical liberals like Friedrich von Hayek. The Rawlsian aspect of Tomasi's (2012) theory is that social justice be used as a standard to evaluate a society's institutions. In other words, inequality is only acceptable if it benefits the least well off. The classical liberal aspect is that economic freedom be considered one of citizens' most important rights, since it is necessary for self-authorship, a Rawlsian term that Tomasi describes as (2012, p. 40) "the capacity to develop and act upon a life plan (whether that plan be individual, collective, or otherwise shared). People are life agents and their agency matters. As responsible self-authors, they have the capacity to realistically assess the options before them and, in light of that assessment, to set standards for a life of a sort that each deems worth living." This view is shared by, e.g., Deirdre McCloskey (2010, p. 74): "The economic history of innovation ... fulfils the so-called difference principle of the philosopher John Rawls ... that a change is ethically justified when it helps the very poorest. Markets and innovation did."

in a modern economy and how the institutional framework of that economy ought to change to achieve more innovation and prosperity.[10]

An economy's institutional framework is commonly conceptualized as "the humanly devised rules of the game" that determine people's incentives to acquire, utilize, and share their resources (North 1991, p. 97). An implication of the EOE perspective's actor and resource complementarity is that institutions have a more substantial effect on innovation and growth than an analysis focusing on any one actor would suggest (cf. Phelps 2007, p. 553). The mobilization of actors and resources in the collaborative innovation bloc is a daunting task for the entrepreneur in the best of circumstances.[11] Generally, institutions must enable the emergence of a minimum critical mass and variety of skills and resources before innovation-based venturing can have a high probability of success. The number, variety, and character of actors determine the shape and intensity of the competition between collaborative teams for the scarce resources at hand, as well as their incentives to learn, experiment, and collaborate.

When employed successfully, the entrepreneurial meta-skill of gathering and jointly combining these skills and resources makes it possible to turn an innovation into a good or a service that is produced and sold on an industrial scale in competition with innovations created by other collaborative teams and the older technology offered by incumbents. When economic institutions interact with such meta-skills, they shape the exchange and collaboration that ultimately determine access to such skills and resources (Spigel and Harrison 2018). Competition between various collaborative teams will bring about an evolution of collaborative innovation blocs in the entrepreneurial ecosystem. Since the resulting innovations drive out, or at least challenge, incumbents, this process generates aggregate economic growth in the experimentally organized market economy (Elert and Henrekson 2019) and drives the process of creative destruction as conceptualized by Joseph Schumpeter (Aghion and Howitt 1992; Caballero and Jaffe 1993).

---

[10] The EOE perspective shares many features with the more recent literature on entrepreneurial ecosystems (Stam 2015; Autio 2016; O'Connor et al. 2018) and the national system of entrepreneurship approach (Acs et al. 2014), but we can trace its roots back to the works of Swedish economists Johan Åkerman and Erik Dahmén; see Erixon (2011) and Dahmén (1970). While these other perspectives offer valuable insights, they seldom make a clear distinction between actors and institutions, and "the institutional variables that are used, such as technology absorption, gender equality, R&D spending, and depth of capital markets, are not institutional variables; they are outcomes resulting from the evolution of the economic system in a given institutional setup" (Braunerhjelm and Henrekson 2016, p. 101).

[11] For one thing, knowledge is often tacit (i.e., difficult to transfer to another person by means of written documentation or verbalizing it) and non-communicable (Hayek 1945). Moreover, labor contracts are necessarily incomplete and access to finance for early-stage ventures is limited.

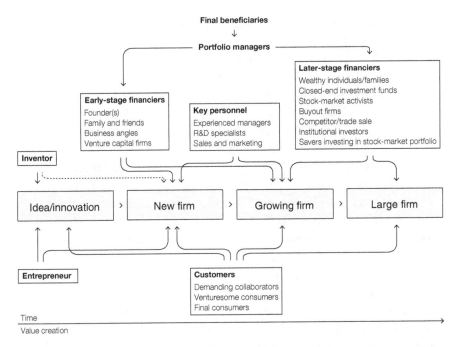

**Fig. 1.2** The collaborative innovation bloc—an overview. Note: Financing by founders (using their assets or retained earnings) and by passive individual and institutional investors (in either phase) is not included in the diagram. Source: Elert and Henrekson (2019)

Figure 1.2 provides a schematic overview of the structure and resources required for a new idea to transform into a growing firm that eventually reaches maturity [as described by, e.g., Fenn et al. (1995) and Gompers and Lerner (2001)]. The agents and resources in the collaborative innovation bloc fall into six categories: entrepreneurs, inventors, key personnel, early-stage financiers, later-stage financiers, and customers. Below, we draw on Elert and Henrekson (2019) to briefly describe the six categories.

1. *The entrepreneur.* Treating the entrepreneur as a collaborator is not a new approach; in fact, Schumpeter (1989 [1949], p. 261) argued that the entrepreneurial function "may be and is often filled cooperatively," and several perspectives on entrepreneurship acknowledge this fact (e.g., McCloskey and Klamer 1995; Cosgel and Klamer 1990; Lazear 2004). In the EOE perspective, entrepreneurs create new collaborative teams, both searching for and attracting the skills and resources they perceive to be necessary to realize their projects. In this role, they benefit from existing collaborative blocs and also create new blocs and help existing blocs evolve. Consequently,

the institutional infrastructure supporting entrepreneurship often emerges as a product of a critical mass of entrepreneurship in an industry or a set of related industries (Stam and Lambooy 2012).

2. *Inventors*: Entrepreneurs generally have an excellent overall understanding of how to exploit an opportunity but may lack specific knowledge regarding relevant technologies. Conversely, while inventors can be involved in founding teams, there is no reason to assume that they have a comparative advantage in bringing new ideas to the market as a good or service. In fact, Schumpeter (1934 [1911]) distinguished between inventors and entrepreneurs, but the nuance was lost when modern growth models (e.g., Romer 1990; Aghion and Howitt 1992) collapsed invention, innovation, and commercialization into one decision (Acs and Sanders 2012, 2013).

3. *Key personnel*: While much has been said about the market's Hayekian knowledge problem—the fact that knowledge of the particular circumstances of time and place is dispersed (Hayek 1945)—such a problem is consistently present *within* firms and increasing with the size of the organization (Foss 1997). In times of rapid firm growth and development, key personnel such as professional managers, skilled specialists, production staff, and front-line personnel may contribute skills that are essential to an entrepreneurial venture (Sautet 2000).[12] They will only be able to do so if they are allowed to act upon the knowledge only they possess to promote intra-firm learning and local discoveries (Foss 1997; Pongracic 2009). Detailed evidence on the sequence in which ventures typically draw on such resources suggests that founder teams and employees grow more rapidly for radical product innovations than for incremental service innovations (Held et al. 2018b).

Determining the relative importance of the different skills that key personnel contribute is challenging. While much of the mainstream entrepreneurship and economics literature sees R&D teams and technical specialists as key to innovation (Audretsch et al. 2006; Chandler 1990), turning high-level ideas into commercially viable products seldom involves much in the way of high-level R&D. As Bhidé (2008, pp. 150–151) puts it, "the commercial success of innovations turns not just on the attributes of the product or know-how, but on the effectiveness and efficiency of the innovator's sales and marketing process." As an entrepreneurial venture grows, so does its need for professional managers with an expertise in taking the

---

[12] Labor market institutions largely determine whether they do so as employees or as independent consultants. Held et al. (2018b) show that while employees and founder team members are complements, external expertise can substitute for in-house employees.

business to a mature stage and mitigating the internal knowledge problem (Sautet 2000) so that misuse and conflict do not impede the discovery, exploitation, and sharing of local knowledge (Ghoshal et al. 1995).

4. *Early-stage financiers*: The founder's equity (possibly complemented by (soft) loans from family and friends) often finances a firm's early phase, but external equity financing is usually necessary if a new entrepreneurial firm is to grow into a significant industry player. Debt finance plays a minor role at this stage of the firm life cycle because of the high risk and typically negative cash flow. Nonetheless, start-ups sometimes do obtain business loans early on, and founders frequently pledge personal assets and wealth as collateral to obtain loans to finance their ventures (Held et al. 2018a). Research shows that such business loans positively affect survival and growth (Cumming and Groh 2018; Cole and Sokolyk 2018). Similarly, Landström and Mason (2016) show that early-stage external equity finance matters for nonfinancial reasons. Business angels, and also banks, play an instrumental role in providing tight screening and close monitoring of the firm's progress, markedly reducing moral hazard problems. Hence, the early involvement of an external, disciplining entity in the firm is as important as the financial resources per se. VC investors, who usually come in later in the life cycle, would have far fewer potentially successful candidates to choose from, were it not for these earlier contributions.

Individuals with extensive experience in the industry in which they invest often perform the business angel and VC function (Busenitz et al. 2014). When circumstances are appropriate, they can combine several high-risk opportunities to achieve a more acceptable overall risk level through portfolio diversification; they identify entrepreneurs and their projects, determine whether and how much to invest, and decide how the investment should be valued. Importantly, they also contribute critical skills to the entrepreneurial venture, such as management expertise, market knowledge, and access to their business networks. If need be, they can also enforce change and appoint new management better equipped to lead the company. Thus, a varied and competent VC industry can provide a crucial component of the early-stage selection machinery of the collaborative innovation bloc. Provided such a sector exists and is sufficiently developed, diversification across VC funds makes it possible even for actors with low risk tolerance, such as institutional investors and banks, to invest in start-ups and innovative ventures. That said, the VC business model is labor intensive and has proven hard to scale up (Polzin et al. 2018a). This may help explain the recent emergence of platform-based alternatives to "traditional" business angel and VC markets, such as equity (Estrin et al.

2018) and debt crowdfunding (Hornuf and Schwienbacher 2018; Signori and Vismara 2018). While still marginal in size, these new sources of finance currently grow at double or even triple digit rates, and they are particularly open to the relatively modest amounts commonly demanded in entrepreneurial venturing (Polzin et al. 2017).

5. *Later-stage financiers*: Well-functioning exit markets are crucial to (a) incentivize VC firms by enabling them to unload their investments when their operations have run their course (Eliasson 2000) and (b) provide entrepreneurs with the large equity infusions typically required to turn a nascent venture into a sizable firm. In the case of sustained inferior performance, later-stage financiers also assess whether there are potential profits from assuming control and replacing the entrepreneur and the firm's top management.

    The most common exit strategy is through a trade sale, in which the entrepreneur/founder hands over full control to the buyer (usually another firm in the same industry). A trade sale is likely an indication that the firm currently lacks some crucial skill or resource (e.g., distribution networks and marketing expertise), making an independent scaling up of its operations unfeasible or too risky (Lerner and Tåg 2013). Another important exit market actor is the buyout firm, which operates much like a VC firm, albeit dealing with much larger sums. Evidence suggests that buyouts lead to a reallocation of firm resources to more productive uses (Tåg 2012; Olsson and Tåg 2017), partly by bringing in better knowledge of management practices (Bloom et al. 2009) and access to resources, infrastructure, and networks that are particularly relevant when scaling up (Duruflé et al. 2017). Wealthy industrial families and owner activists are also important actors in the secondary market; whether any of them will be able to act in a forceful manner depends, in no small measure, on the extent to which they can expect capital infusions from passive investors (such as pension funds and open-ended stock market funds) if the firm develops well. Of course, the functioning of exit markets depends on the prevailing institutions that shape incentives and payoffs for venture owners and acquirers alike.

6. *Competent customers*: Consumers are the ultimate arbiters of an innovation's success, yet they hardly appear in the cast in most accounts of innovation. The omission is regrettable; Bhidé (2008) defines "venturesome consumption" as the willingness and ability of intermediate producers and individual consumers to take a chance on and effectively use new know-how and products and argues that it may be as crucial to a country as its capacity to undertake high-level research. Even in an entrepreneurial venture's early stages, demanding collaborators can function as particularly

important sources of information on consumer needs and preferences. Sometimes, they even act as strategic partners, taking an active part in the development and commercialization of products (Bhidé 2008; von Hippel et al. 2011). In the extreme, when qualified venture capitalists are absent, large enterprises rich in capital often step in to play this role. However, this substitution is unlikely to yield radical innovations because it restricts such financing to technologies close and complementary to those of the partnering industry (Eliasson 2000).

The outline above should give an idea of the interconnectedness of the agents and resources in a collaborative innovation bloc. Certainly, the details of the commercialization process vary, and actors typically work alongside each other or overlap during different phases. Frequently, however, the process begins when an entrepreneur identifies a potential opportunity through her interactions with demanding customers, which she then strives to develop together with an inventor into a successfully commercialized innovation. Generally, the early commercialization phase mainly involves entrepreneurs and, to a lesser extent, key personnel (Held et al. 2018b). In this experimental stage, uncertainty is high and equity financing is critical, but debt financing can also play an important role. A study covering the USA, the UK, Germany, and Italy found that up to 10% of start-ups acquired loans in their first or second round of funding (Held et al. 2018b), and debt-financed ventures also tend to do well in terms of innovation and growth, as long as the debt is not the personal debt of the founder (Cole and Sokolyk 2018).

Early-stage financiers usually propel the project into a scale-up phase, during which the conjectured entrepreneurial profits can be realized (assuming the project reaches this point). At this stage, the entrepreneur requires more key personnel, often with highly specialized skills. Later-stage financiers assume responsibility for financing, which (depending on the sector) may be substantial. In parallel, competitors begin to imitate the innovation if they perceive it to be promising, and the market grows through the operational scaling-up of activities resulting from differential growth and selection (Metcalfe 1998). Eventually, the process stabilizes (Witt 1996), with the market taking the form of a monopoly, an oligopoly, or a competitive situation involving multiple actors. By this point, organizational behavior, strategy, and business models will have become relatively uniform and standardized. While entrepreneurial profits are often exhausted at this point (Dopfer and Potts 2009), the scope for innovation is by no means exhausted: firms can, for example, introduce more efficient production and distribution methods or change the attributes of a good or a service to enhance its value.

Part of what it means to be an entrepreneur is having the ability to gather actors with different skills and resources in a collaborative innovation bloc and productively combine them into a collaborative team. From the above, we can broadly distinguish knowledge, finance, and labor as the key resources an entrepreneur needs to acquire, with the emphasis shifting between them in different stages of the venture process. This suggests that entrepreneurs indeed must be "jacks-of-all-trades" (Lazear 2004) and possess a broad and balanced skill mix. Even then, the task may be arcane for any individual if the bloc in question is not of sufficient breadth and depth. Moreover, the institutional context in which teams compete determines the supply of these scarce resources and the conditions under which teams compete for them. It is in this context that economic policy and the institutional framework underpinning the innovation bloc come into play.

## 1.3   No One-Size-Fits-All Strategy

Scholars began to examine the link between institutions and entrepreneurship in earnest following William Baumol's (1990) landmark paper establishing that the way a society's institutions structure economic payoffs influences the nature of entrepreneurial efforts and activities (Baumol 1990; see also North 1990; Murphy et al. 1991; Sobel 2008; Acs et al. 2008; Stenholm et al. 2013; Calcagno and Sobel 2014; Urbano and Alvarez 2014). The current literature suggests that entrepreneurship takes different forms between countries or regions because of institutional differences (see, e.g., Case and Harris 2012; WEF 2013; Stam 2014), and the (formal) institutions thought to be particularly important in this respect include the protection of private property, the rule of law, intellectual property rights, tax codes, social insurance systems, employment protection legislation, and competition policy (Hall and Jones 1999; Henrekson and Johansson 2009; Bjørnskov and Foss 2013).[13] Reform directed towards more entrepreneurship-friendly institutions in these areas should, the reasoning goes, improve the environment for entrepreneurial venturing in Europe.

This reasoning is correct, subject to some caveats. For one thing, as Samuel Bowles (2016) has argued in his thoughtful book *The Moral Economy*, incen-

---

[13] Informal institutions influencing entrepreneurship include social capital, trust, inclusiveness, individualism, power distance, and uncertainty avoidance (Hechavarria and Reynolds 2009; Taylor and Wilson 2012). Policymakers should take them into account when they fit reform proposals to local contexts, but as these institutions are much less amenable to reform and policy interventions, they are beyond the scope of this book. The interested reader is referred to a longer discussion in Elert et al. (2017, pp. 71–74).

tives are a double-edged sword: incentivizing policies can erode individuals' intrinsic social motivations unless policymakers combine them with a convincing moral message. In our context, this means that institutional reforms directed towards an entrepreneurial society will likely only be effective if accompanied by recognition of the importance of entrepreneurship. According to McCloskey (2016), such a cultural shift goes a long way towards explaining the innovative miracle that created the modern world during the industrial revolution. Bowles (2016) also notes that monetary incentives should never be divorced from the policy process that introduced or allowed for them; reforms risk backfiring if they are imposed without public consultation and buy-in. Here, of course, the national and local contexts are crucial.

While the EU has seen top-down and bottom-up convergence over the years, even member states with similar levels of per capita income continue to differ substantially in their institutional organization. The diversity is not surprising given the documented importance of historical values and norms, lock-in effects, and path dependency in institutional evolution (Arthur 1989; Reher 1998; Acemoglu et al. 2001; Nunn 2009; Alesina et al. 2015). Indeed, these cross-country differences are a starting point in the various incarnations of the varieties of capitalism (VoC) literature, which is closely associated with the seminal work of Hall and Soskice (2001). Research in this tradition sees the existence of institutional complementarities as the main driver of the persistence of institutional differences across VoC, with institutions being complementary "if the presence (or efficiency) of one [institution] increases the returns from (or efficiency of) the other" (Hall and Soskice 2001, p. 17).[14] Specifically, it makes little sense for European member states to try and emulate US-style alumni donations to universities or Chinese-style infrastructure investments when the supporting cultural and deeply embedded, historically evolved complementary institutions are absent. It is better to look at the best of your closest peers and adopt, e.g., German-style apprenticeships or Finnish educational policies.

The VoC literature illustrates how a distinct set of institutions governs the exchange between companies and their national labor markets, financial markets, and research and development infrastructure. The particulars of this syn-

---

[14] One salient example is the sizeable cross-country variation in corporate governance models of large listed firms: It ranges from the archetypical Anglo-American model based on management control and dispersed ownership, to various models of concentrated family control by means of dual-class shares, pyramiding, and cross-ownership, common in Europe and Asia (Bebchuk and Roe 2004). The complementarity of elements in these specific corporate governance models is crucial. Reforms limited to a particular element risk giving rise to inconsistencies that make the overall model less efficient (Schmidt and Spindler 2002).

ergy translate into different innovation, technology, and production outcomes across economies—varieties of capitalism that are thought to be particularly stable because of the complementarities between their underpinning institutions. The perspective helps explain the nonrandom interconnectedness of various institutions, the persistence of institutional forms that are (seemingly) not conducive to entrepreneurship and growth, and thus the prospects for amending these institutions.

To date, however, the VoC literature has largely neglected entrepreneurial venturing, evolving instead through studies of incumbent firms and the institutions channeling their behavior. Dilli et al. (2018) filled this research gap by illustrating how distinct institutional constellations relate to specific types of entrepreneurship in a study focusing on the USA and 20 European economies: countries fall into four distinct families or clusters with a similar set of institutions governing finance, labor markets, education and training, and inter-firm relationships. According to Dilli et al. (2018), these constellations facilitate the development of different types of entrepreneurship, ranging from risk-loving, growth-aspiring ventures based on radical innovations to risk-avoiding, growth-averse ventures based on imitation.

These findings are both discouraging and revealing. If distinct institutional constellations govern the emergence of distinct forms of entrepreneurship, then merely pushing a regulatory button in isolation is unlikely to yield the desired results. Such an action might even make matters worse if it removes or weakens an institution whose presence is essential for the working of other institutions in the complex web that comprises the entrepreneurial ecosystem. For example, implementing some isolated fiscal reform to strengthen incentives for VC providers would hardly be effective in facilitating more Schumpeterian entrepreneurship in Continental, Southern, and Eastern Europe. To achieve this goal, policymakers more likely need to deregulate both labor and financial markets in a sensible manner so that VC-funded ventures can also hire and fire employees more freely, implement strong incentive contracts for founders, and a viable exit market is allowed to emerge. Only under those conditions the classical VC model can actually function. Reform failure is likely if policymakers do not take these important institutional complementarities into account.

However, the steps necessary in an appropriate and effective reform strategy are similar across VoC at a sufficiently high level of abstraction. In all regions and countries, one must begin by assessing the most salient features of the institutional framework in place and tracing its historical roots. This makes it possible to assess strengths and weaknesses and identify bottlenecks in the entrepreneurial ecosystem using the structured analysis of primary and secondary data. These insights should then be applied to a menu of evidence-based policy interventions, allowing appropriate interventions to be selected and tailored to fit the specific country or region by heeding the relevant local, regional, and national institutional complexities. In this book, we present such a menu of evidence-based policy interventions for six institutional areas that we identify as particularly critical to the creation of flourishing collaborative innovation blocs and, ultimately, an entrepreneurial society.[15] Looking across the proposals developed in this book, we identified a set of common core principles that we believe can inform and guide reform proposals in any specific context.

## 1.4 Principles

The common principles underlying all proposals in this book are: *neutrality, transparency, moderation, contestability, legality, and justifiability.* These words can take on different meanings depending on the context in which they appear, meaning that we must take care when explaining how we employ them when formulating our reform agenda. Below, we briefly discuss each of these six principles.

Frequently, *neutrality* is described as the state of not supporting or helping either side in a conflict or disagreement. It may seem odd for a book arguing in favor of entrepreneurship to adopt this principle. In actuality, however, we rarely argue that policymakers should bestow favors upon entrepreneurs because they do not need to be pampered. Instead, we wish to level the playing field between entrepreneurs and those they challenge—a playing field that at present is all too often tilted against entrepreneurs. Adhering to the neutrality principle, which implies that a level playing field is restored and maintained, will often already go a long way towards supporting entrepreneurs in their efforts.

*Transparency*, as commonly used, means operating in such a way that it is easy for others to see what actions are performed and what consequences they will entail. As such, transparency implies openness, communication, and accountability. This principle guides many proposals because it is essential for

---

[15] The evidence base is not equally extensive for all proposed interventions; the policymaking world is not a laboratory, meaning that data on the impact of the proposed interventions are often absent. If we restricted our menu to evidence-based policies only, we could only include policies that policymakers have already implemented somewhere. More radical ideas and suggestions would not qualify. In such cases, we present the arguments and propose that policymakers implement the reforms with caution. The implementation of such policy suggestions will aid in building an evidence base, provided that they are carefully designed and evaluated.

(potential) challengers to know the criteria upon which their venture will be evaluated. Ensuring more transparency about the criteria that determine how labor, knowledge, and financial resources are made available to new ventures would, we believe, reduce this source of uncertainty in entrepreneurial venturing.

*Moderation* is commonly defined as the avoidance of excess or extremes or the process of eliminating or lessening extremes. This principle underlies many of our proposals in the realms of taxation and subsidization, as excessive interventions are particularly damaging in these areas. Furthermore, uncertainty is all around us, including when making policy and implementing institutional reforms. The future is unknowable; therefore, policymakers should be modest in extracting and allocating resources lest such measures become costly to reverse.

*Contestability* is a key for entrepreneurial venturing and also for policymaking. When followed, this principle entails that all vested positions, opinions, and truths should be open to challenge and debate. Such openness lends legitimacy to the status quo and ensures that institutions support those ventures that represent the best of our knowledge to date. If institutions, policies, and markets cease to be contestable, they risk becoming outdated and obsolete in an ever-changing environment. Contestability is thus the cure for sclerosis and rigidity.

*Legality* refers to the idea that de jure and de facto institutions need to coincide, such that legality ensures the rule of law is both upheld and aligned with the institutional framework. This principle is a fundamental precondition in all modern economies and underpins any liberal democratic political order—to the point that it is occasionally taken for granted in much of the EU. Nevertheless, it is important to realize that formally enacting the appropriate laws does not automatically ensure the legality of institutions that support an entrepreneurial society.

*Justifiability* refers to the appropriate balancing of public and private interests that is needed to justify policy interventions beyond a simple laissez-faire attitude. Moreover, not only active policies and institutions need to be justified but also passive institutions, such as (intellectual) property rights, if they are to be effectively implemented and respected. If institutions are perceived to benefit entrepreneurs at the expense of their consumers, employees, inventors, financiers, or society at large, these institutions cannot be justified and should be reformed to ensure a long-run stable license to operate for entrepreneurs that seek to challenge the status quo.

In our more concrete proposals for institutional reform discussed below, most proposals can be related to one or more of these underlying principles. We also believe that with these principles in hand, many more potentially effective reforms can be conceptualized for specific contexts. We present them here, individually and together, as essential guidelines for drafting an effective reform strategy that supports innovative, inclusive, and sustainable growth at any level of aggregation and policymaking.

## 1.5    Book Outline

The principles outlined above safeguard the coherence of our overall reform strategy by making it easier to structure the discussion and weigh proposals against one another. For the sake of concreteness, we also identify the governance level that has the power and/or competence to implement the proposed reforms. As our book seeks to be useful for policymakers, we have chosen to structure our proposals along six broad policy areas. The six reform areas we discuss in separate chapters in the remainder of this book are as follows:

1. *The rule of law and protection of property rights*: These institutions are fundamental to any market economy and crucial to any attempt to build an entrepreneurial society. To understand how they can be strengthened in an entrepreneurship-friendly manner across the EU, we first emphasize the principle of *legality*, i.e., considering de facto rather than de jure institutions. Moreover, the protection of property rights cannot be absolute; in particular, the realm of intellectual property requires a careful balancing of public and private interests to ensure *justifiability*. Given the European Commission's competencies in international negotiations on these issues, a clear and actionable reform agenda presents itself.
2. *Taxation*: In this chapter, we systematically cover all areas of taxation that we deem relevant to an entrepreneurial society. Such an exercise is important because taxes shape and bias the incentives for corporations, individuals, and organizations. The principles of *moderation, neutrality*, and *transparency* guide us when we propose reforms in this area. Biases in favor of entrepreneurship can sometimes be justified in the case of strong positive external effects, but more often, we argue for leveling the playing field and moderate taxation to restore or maintain market incentives. Since the EU typically has limited capabilities in terms of taxation, we primarily address such reforms at the level of the member states, carefully discussing the direction in which they could reform their tax systems in support of a more entrepreneurial society.
3. *Savings, finance, and capital*: Here, we cover the institutions that govern the intermediation of savings across Europe while adhering to the princi-

ples of *neutrality, transparency,* and *justifiability*. History and evolution have created a largely bank-based and highly regulated system of financial markets in which wealth and savings are predominantly "locked-up" in professionally managed funds and assets. In such a system, investees without collateral, strong balance sheets and long track records are fighting an uphill battle to gain access to credit and financial resources, whereas important public interests (e.g., in a secure payment system and stable pension funds) require careful balancing against the needs of the entrepreneurial society. The principles help us offer proposals aimed at leveling the playing field and mobilizing more of Europe's ample financial resources for entrepreneurial ventures. Given the shared competencies in this area, most proposals in this chapter are addressed towards both the EU level and the member states.

4. *Labor markets and social security*: To a large extent, these institutions determine the allocation of human resources, notably skilled labor, to entrepreneurial ventures. Again, these culturally deeply embedded systems typically favor large, stable incumbent firms, meaning that experimental, innovative ventures struggle to obtain human resources. Our proposed reforms do not follow the naïve neoliberal logic of all-out liberalization but rather aim to improve the situation for entrepreneurs and employees in Europe by making rights more portable and social security more universal and unconditional. The principles of *moderation, neutrality, contestability,* and *justifiability* all play important roles in this area. As in the case of taxes, our proposals in this chapter are addressed to the member states primarily, as they retain most legal competencies in this area.

5. *Contestable markets for entry and exit*: This is an area of strong and extensive EU competencies by virtue of the single market, but Europe can do more to promote contestable markets for entry and exit. Here, we draw on the principles of *contestability, transparency,* and *justifiability* to better understand how reforms ensuring a vibrant entrepreneurial society can come about. Lower entry barriers and functionally specified quality standards are key to this reform area, especially for services, where in the (semi-)public domain (e.g., health care and education), there is room for productive venturing under appropriate constraints. To facilitate entry in many sectors, exit must also be well arranged, leading us to proposals in the area of bankruptcy law and the smooth liquidation of outdated and failed ventures.

6. *Mobilizing human capital for entrepreneurship*: Since the Treaty of Lisbon, innovation policy is part of the European Commission's competencies, but we have yet to see institutional reform actions to promote the building of a European knowledge space where useful knowledge flows freely to the

benefit of both incumbents and challengers. When formulating proposals in this direction, we draw on the principles of *justifiability* and *contestability* to ensure that the positive externalities of knowledge creation and diffusion through commercialization are balanced with private interests of privacy and competitive advantage.

After discussing no less than 50 proposals in these six policy areas, we conclude this volume with a chapter that sketches the agenda for future research and, more importantly, policy reform. We would also like to alert interested readers to the (forthcoming) companion volume *The Entrepreneurial Society Part II: Implementing the Reform Strategy for Italy, Germany and the UK* (Marx et al. 2019), which complements this volume by illustrating how the menu of reforms presented here can be prioritized and adjusted to specific Varieties of Capitalism in member states across Europe.

# 2

# Entrepreneurship, the Rule of Law, and Protection of Property Rights

## 2.1 General Principles

Today, almost 250 years after Thomas Paine stated that "in free countries the law ought to be king," the legal principle that a polity should not be governed by arbitrary decisions made by autocratic rulers or government officials is considered a central building block of a free society and essential for any country striving for prosperity (Bingham 2011). Possibly, the only competitor to the rule of law for the title of most fundamental economic institution is the protection of private property rights—the existence of legal titles to hold property and the protection thereof (North and Weingast 1989; Libecap 1993; Acemoglu et al. 2001, 2005; Rodrik et al. 2004; North et al. 2009; Besley and Ghatak 2010). In practice, these fundamental rules of the game strengthen and complement each other; when of sufficiently high quality, they prevent undue uncertainty and ensure that entrepreneurs can engage in productive activities. By contrast, weak rule of law and property rights protection within a country discourage entrepreneurs from making entrepreneurial discoveries and from (re)investing (retained) earnings in their ventures (Johnson et al. 2002). The division and specialization of labor are also hampered in such instances, to the detriment of collaborative innovation blocs and their actors, whether financiers, personnel, or customers.

That said, the rule of law is not enshrined in any particular legal rule; what happens in practice matters more than what the law says. Likewise, formal property rights that do not offer control rights in practice are useless, while the absence of formal property rights need not be prohibitive if control rights are sufficiently strong (Rodrik 2007). When assessing the current state of the

© The Author(s) 2019
N. Elert et al., *The Entrepreneurial Society*, International Studies in Entrepreneurship 98,
https://doi.org/10.1007/978-3-662-59586-2_2

rule of law and protection of property rights in Europe, therefore, a first guiding principle is *legality*, i.e., to consider de facto rather than de jure institutions (Feld and Voigt 2003; Acemoglu et al. 2005; Woodruff 2006). The distinction is crucial: while the *acquis communautaire* (the accumulated legislation, legal acts, and court decisions that constitute the body of EU law) ensure that a candidate member state's formal legal framework is more or less aligned before it is allowed to join the EU, differences among members in terms of the effective enforcement of the rule of law and property rights protection remain substantial.

Table 2.1 shows that the countries with the best judicial systems and the highest quality of government are the Nordic, Anglo-Saxon, and Benelux countries, followed by Germany and France. The Eastern bloc scores especially low on most survey items, but this is also true for Greece and Italy and, to a lesser extent, for Spain and Portugal.[1] Table 2.1 also includes measures of government effectiveness and regulatory quality; as can be seen, countries rank similarly along these dimensions. Most importantly, however, the table highlights the distinction between de facto and de jure institutions, especially considering that the EU member states all share the same formal legal environment. The discrepancies have implications not only for the rule of law and the protection of property rights but also for a member state's overall ability to get things done (Hulten 1996; Aschauer 2000; WEF 2015).

Economic actors can (and do) compensate to some extent for weaknesses in the rule of law and property rights protection by undertaking more activity off-the-books; as a result, member countries that perform poorly in these respects have larger underground economies (Schneider 2015a; see Appendix Fig. A.1). In Bulgaria and Romania, the shadow economy is estimated to be approximately 30% of official GDP, while in Northern European countries, the proportion is less than half of that. However, shadow economy activity is generally a poor substitute for formal sector activity, partly because it creates unfair competition for firms that adhere to rules and regulations. More importantly, firms in the shadow economy do not benefit from the division of labor and specialization of collaborative innovation blocs to the same extent as formal firms and are therefore unlikely to grow large.

---

[1] Suse and Hachez (2017, p. 79) point out that the concept of the rule of law represented by indicators such as these is thinner than the concept espoused by most international organizations. Specifically, the EU defines the rule of law as "a wider view of the legal system" that provides a stable framework protecting citizen's expectations and captures the populations' values and aspirations, ushering in a society free of violence and oppression.

**Table 2.1** The rule of law and the quality of government: four indicators for the EU member countries and the USA

| Country | Rule of law | Security of property rights | Government effectiveness | Regulatory quality |
|---|---|---|---|---|
| Finland | 100.00 | 9.29 | 98.08 | 96.63 |
| Sweden | 99.04 | 8.27 | 96.15 | 95.67 |
| Denmark | 97.60 | 8.18 | 95.67 | 92.31 |
| Netherlands | 97.12 | 8.68 | 96.63 | 98.56 |
| Austria | 96.15 | 8.09 | 91.83 | 90.87 |
| Luxembourg | 95.19 | 8.86 | 93.75 | 93.75 |
| UK | 92.79 | 8.83 | 90.87 | 94.23 |
| USA | 91.83 | 7.86 | 92.79 | 92.79 |
| Germany | 91.35 | 7.60 | 94.23 | 95.19 |
| France | 89.42 | 7.29 | 87.98 | 83.65 |
| Ireland | 88.94 | 8.29 | 87.02 | 91.83 |
| Belgium | 87.50 | 7.91 | 85.10 | 86.54 |
| Estonia | 86.54 | 7.34 | 83.65 | 93.27 |
| Malta | 85.10 | 6.88 | 80.77 | 87.98 |
| Portugal | 84.13 | 6.15 | 87.50 | 79.33 |
| Czech Rep. | 83.65 | 6.05 | 81.25 | 86.06 |
| Slovenia | 82.69 | 5.63 | 84.62 | 72.12 |
| Spain | 81.25 | 6.08 | 81.73 | 79.81 |
| Lithuania | 80.77 | 5.57 | 80.29 | 83.17 |
| Latvia | 80.29 | 5.06 | 78.85 | 82.69 |
| Cyprus | 79.81 | 5.87 | 79.81 | 81.25 |
| Slovakia | 71.63 | 5.23 | 75.00 | 76.44 |
| Hungary | 70.19 | 3.84 | 70.19 | 73.08 |
| Poland | 68.27 | 5.11 | 74.04 | 78.85 |
| Romania | 63.94 | 5.64 | 46.15 | 70.19 |
| Croatia | 63.46 | 4.38 | 72.60 | 68.75 |
| Italy | 62.50 | 5.04 | 69.71 | 75.00 |
| Greece | 56.73 | 4.81 | 66.35 | 62.98 |
| Bulgaria | 51.92 | 4.18 | 63.94 | 72.60 |

Note: *Rule of law* captures perceptions of the extent to which agents have confidence in and abide by the rules of society, in particular the quality of contract enforcement, property rights, the police, and the courts, as well as the likelihood of crime and violence. *Security of property rights* captures the extent to which individuals have secure rights to property, including the fruits of their labor. *Government effectiveness* captures perceptions of the quality of public and civil services and the degree of their independence from political pressures, the quality of policy formulation and implementation, and the credibility of the government's commitment to such policies. *Regulatory quality* captures perceptions of the ability of the government to formulate and implement sound policies and regulations that permit and promote private-sector development. All scores except for the security of property rights are standardized from 0 to 100, where the value 100 is assigned to the leading country. Singapore is the leading country for the third and Hong Kong is the leading country for the fourth measure

Source: World Bank, *World Governance Indicators 2018* (based on the data for 2017), and Fraser Institute, *Economic Freedom of the World 2018 Annual Report* for security of property rights (based on the data for 2016)

The second guiding principle we identify in this area is *justifiability*. It has been said that civilizations only flourish when attaining a balance between protecting expectations and allowing adaptation to new conditions (Kuran 1988, p. 145): on one hand, we want to protect private property to incentivize productive investment through the accumulation of private wealth; on the other hand, it is necessary to maintain an open and contestable market for new entrants to keep unproductive rent seeking (e.g., lobbying for closed and complex standards) and destructive entrepreneurship (e.g., ventures that disregard public health, exploit natural resources, or appropriate other non-market goods) at bay. This balancing act is particularly important when applied to intellectual property rights (IPR), where one must weigh the interests of inventors against the positive spillover effects of knowledge diffusion. The rules of the game need to reward value creation but discourage pure rent seeking.

Because of their encompassing characteristics, safeguarding the rule of law and the protection of property rights requires (concerted) policy action at the local, regional, and national levels. As to the issues we shall discuss that relate to IPR, these mainly fall under the domain of national governments and the competencies of the EU in negotiating international treaties and regulations referring to IPR.

## 2.2    Proposals

Regarding the rule of law, the protection of property rights, and the effectiveness of government, laggard countries should do their utmost to converge towards the level of the best-performing countries. Such improvements are in the long-term best interest of all citizens in these countries, although powerful elites and interest groups may well have a short-term interest in blocking the process. The reality is that deficiencies in these factors negatively impact all agents in collaborative innovation blocs and induce people to conduct activities and hide their capital in the shadow economy. The poorest EU member states are high-medium-income countries, and even in the VoC literature, there is no support for the view that they can compensate for deficiencies in the most fundamental rules of the game through other institutional measures.

Proposal 1: Strengthen monitoring and enforcement mechanisms to improve and safeguard the performance of all member states on rule of law, protection of property rights, and government effectiveness.

This proposal acknowledges the first guiding principle of focusing on legality. Unfortunately, even though the effective enforcement of the rule of law and property rights is the foundation of virtually all economic activity, this is not self-evident in all European member states. For example, the time it takes to settle civil court cases in Italy is prohibitively long (Sanders et al. 2018a), and institutional backsliding among new members once they have been admitted has been highlighted as a real concern (Suse and Hachez 2017). Imperfections in these institutions hurt all actors in the economy, but especially cash-constrained small and young ventures. Addressing such fundamental issues would go a long way towards supporting a more entrepreneurial and innovative economy.

These facts notwithstanding, the potential for the EU's formal admission process to promote the rule of law in candidate countries has been called into question; backsliding among admitted members such as Hungary and Poland is a case in point. One must, therefore, be "wary of expecting too much from rule of law promotion and should certainly not hope that full integration into a defined 'rule of law-compliant' model of legal system is possible" (Suse and Hachez 2017, p. 80). Hence, while the EU should urgently strive to find new methods to improve the legal frameworks in laggard countries, the fact remains that member states themselves control most matters pertaining to the de facto rule of law and the legal protection of property rights (Suse and Hachez 2017). As such, the efficiency of a country's government is an issue of paramount importance.

That said, the protection of private property rights can never be absolute. Such rights are continually renegotiated and need to be justified. For example, landowner property rights, which extended from hell below to heaven above in Roman times, were curtailed when the development of the airline industry required free airspace. Furthermore, many governments around the world have nationalized the ownership rights to minerals below a certain depth (the USA is a notable exception). Zoning laws, environmental regulations, and heritage protection restrict private property rights and prevent entrepreneurship from becoming a destructive force. In regard to preventing unproductive rent seeking and even destructive entrepreneurship (Baumol 1990; Desai et al. 2013; Sanders and Weitzel 2013), such restrictions are justified, provided a legitimate authority can set the rules transparently and enforce them neutrally: as long as the rules apply equally to all under the law, productive entrepreneurs can play by these rules and contribute to well-being.

It is particularly relevant to justify the IPR framework by balancing private incentives and public benefits. Knowledge is unique in the sense that it is often tedious and expensive to create. However, once discovered, it is nonrival in use and can be shared freely without being diminished. On one hand, if IPR protection is too weak or too easily circumvented, creators will need alternative ways to recover the costs of knowledge generation and early diffusion (Merrill et al. 2004; Acs and Szerb 2007; Baumol et al. 2007; Kauffman Foundation 2007). On the other hand, if protection is overly strong, the inventor or his delegate will extract excessive rents from entrepreneurs *ex post*. Such rents come about if the IPR time frame is too long or if it is too easy to obtain protection even for bits and pieces of potentially useful knowledge and inventions that have yet to be developed into useful innovations. Such features of IPR protection inhibit the free flow of knowledge and reduce incentives to commercialize, leaving the economy less competitive and less innovative as a consequence (Jaffe and Lerner 2004; Acs and Sanders 2012). Strong(er) IPR protection then becomes the problem rather than the solution, making it necessary to consider more fundamental reforms to the system itself to promote the diffusion and use of knowledge. In line with the principle of justifiability, we therefore propose the following:

> Proposal 2: Limit the breadth, width, and span of patent protection to cover working prototypes and market-ready innovations only for a short period of time, and permit economic actors to infringe upon patents that have not been commercialized.

This proposal is quite fundamental and requires careful planning to ensure a smooth transition to the new situation. If implemented, it would limit the extent of IPR protection to strike a better balance between public and private interests following our guiding principle of justifiability. However, this is a big "if": the EU, after all, is party to international treaties that set minimum requirements for IPR, such as the WTO TRIPS Agreement. Of course, the EU should not violate or disregard these treaties. Instead, the Union should use its influence in the governing bodies to enable reforms in the desired direction. The limitations to patent rights would still fall well within the institutional structure in place but would significantly reduce the risk that entrepreneurs are being sued for infringements on patents they did not even know existed (Jaffe and Lerner 2004).

Moreover, in line with Schumpeter (1934), we believe that a substantial European bottleneck to innovation is found in commercial application of knowledge. As the knowledge spillover theory of entrepreneurship (Acs et al. 2009; Braunerhjelm et al. 2010) argues, commercial application is essential for knowledge spillover and diffusion. Thus, rebalancing IPR in favor of entrepreneurs to promote the diffusion of knowledge would be a move in the right direction.

Proposal 3: Require patent applicants to set the price for the license before the commercial application is known instead of allowing them to negotiate the terms of a license contract afterwards.

If this proposal became reality, it would clarify the division of labor within collaborative innovation blocs by making the entrepreneur the residual claimant to all the rents of commercialization, while the inventor would retain the right to claim the costs she incurred in knowledge generation. To the extent that commercialization is an innovation bottleneck, such reforms would increase the rate of innovation and growth (Acs and Sanders 2012).

Of course, patent protection works differently in different sectors and different stages of the industry life cycle. Some parts of the economy can achieve similar protection with trade secrets (e.g., software), whereas mandatory and highly uncertain certification procedures make it difficult to conceive of efficient alternatives to patents in other sectors (e.g., pharmaceuticals). It could perhaps be that the functions of patenting can be fulfilled more efficiently in other ways, and it certainly does not require allowing inventors to monopolize and thereby limit the profitable use of the knowledge they have generated. Nevertheless, given legal complexities and institutional complementarities, a cautious, experimental approach that retains the system's benefits while increasing the free flow of knowledge is advisable. Here, a promising venue is the introduction of the so-called "open source" patents, which would retain the functions of knowledge repository and verification while improving access to knowledge for commercial use (Boettiger and Burk 2004).

Proposal 4: Introduce and support existing experiments with open source patent registration.

This proposal is justified, as it restores the balance between the public interest in free knowledge disclosure and dissemination and the private interest in obtaining fair and just rewards for creating new knowledge. A public register and repository can help inventors claim fair (monetary and non-monetary) rewards while guaranteeing open and free access to non-rivalrous knowledge to ensure dynamic efficiency.

As for the implementation of proposals 2–4, treaties and case law in the EU already underline the importance of balancing the public interest and private property rights. Suse and Hachez (2017, p. 86) note that "[r]ecently, the

[European Court of Justice] was faced with the question of a potential conflict between intellectual property rights and other rights relevant to entrepreneurship, such as the right to conduct a business (Article 16 Charter)." The conclusion of the case saw the Court insisting on imposing limits on the protection of intellectual property in the face of other (public) interests, in perfect alignment with the principle of justifiability.

The EU has strong competencies in (re)negotiating the treaties that govern IPR at the international level. It is hard, if not impossible, for individual member states, let alone the regions or localities within them, to deviate from such international arrangements. The Union must therefore first negotiate for the space to experiment before member states and lower polities can engage in such experimentation. And while Brexit means that the UK will leave the EU, Germany is also a major patenting nation whose role in international treaty negotiations should not be underestimated (see Sanders et al. 2018b, c for a more detailed analysis of these issues).

## 2.3   Summary

Table 2.2 summarizes the principles presented in this chapter together with the proposals derived from them and the level(s) at which political action should take place to make them a reality. Because the rule of law and protection of property are encompassing characteristics of the institutional environment for entrepreneurs, the first proposal will require (concerted) policy action at the local, regional, and national levels. Put differently, effective enforcement at the national level is likely to be ineffective if regional and local authorities can still introduce uncertainty by discretionary decisions that favor vested interests and protect rents. By contrast, proposals 2–4 emphasize IPR protection and can only be taken up by national or even supranational bodies with the power to (re)negotiate the international treaties that currently bind local and regional policymakers.

**Table 2.2** Summary of proposals regarding rule of law and property rights protection, specifying the level in the governance hierarchy where the necessary decisions should be made

| No. | Principle(s) | Policy area | Proposal | Policy level[a] |
|---|---|---|---|---|
| 1 | Legality | The rule of law | Strengthen monitoring and enforcement mechanisms to improve and safeguard the performance of all member states on rule of law, protection of property rights, and government effectiveness. | EU, MS, REG, LOC |
| 2 | Justifiability | Patents and intellectual property | Limit the breadth, width, and span of patent protection to cover working prototypes and market-ready innovations only for a short period of time, and permit economic actors to infringe upon patents that have not been commercialized. | EU, MS |
| 3 | Justifiability | Patents and intellectual property | Require patent applicants to set the price for the license before the commercial application is known instead of allowing them to negotiate the terms of a license contract afterwards. | EU, MS |
| 4 | Justifiability | Patents and intellectual property | Introduce and support existing experiments with open source patent registration. | EU, MS, REG |

[a]*EU* federal level, *MS* member state level, *REG* regional government level, *LOC* local/municipal level

# 3

# Taxation and Entrepreneurship

## 3.1 General Principles

With a scope seven times that of Fyodor Dostoyevsky's *War and Peace*, the US tax code should leave nothing to chance. However, as shown by Sull and Eisenhardt (2015), authors of *Simple Rules: How to Thrive in a Complex World*, when 45 tax professionals took up the task of calculating one fictional family's tax bill, they came up with 45 different estimates, with differences ranging in the tens of thousands of dollars. No wonder that "to navigate this (tax) labyrinth, U.S. citizens employ 1.2 million [tax professionals], more than all the police and firefighters in the country combined" (Sull and Eisenhardt 2015, p. 23). The example reveals how complexity can spiral out of control; in our context, it highlights William Baumol's (1990) fundamental insight that society's rules of the game give rise to a "social structure of payoffs" determining whether individuals devote their time and energy to productive, unproductive, or destructive purposes. The European situation regarding corporate and personal income taxation appears to be comparable in that respect (PwC 2019). Complex rules, especially in an area of such immense importance for entrepreneurial venturing as taxes, will likely limit the scope of productive entrepreneurial activity and the workings of collaborative innovation blocs.

Any analysis of the effects of taxes on entrepreneurship is further complicated by the fact that no specific tax on income from entrepreneurial efforts exists in practice in the USA, Europe, or anywhere else. Governments tax entrepreneurial value creation in several ways, notably as labor income, business income, current capital income (dividends and interest), or capital gains. The complex interactions among these taxes shape incentives. To disentangle

© The Author(s) 2019
N. Elert et al., *The Entrepreneurial Society*, International Studies in Entrepreneurship 98,
https://doi.org/10.1007/978-3-662-59586-2_3

these effects, we begin by focusing on the three main theoretical ways in which the tax system affects entrepreneurial activity (Henrekson and Sanandaji 2016).

First, an *absolute effect* influences the supply of potential entrepreneurs and the effort they exert in the economy, as an increase in the taxation of entrepreneurial incomes lowers their (expected) after-tax reward, adversely affecting entry, growth, and liquidity. Second, there is a *relative effect* influencing the relative returns for different activities; for example, a tax system favoring certain forms of savings and investments over others can have considerable indirect consequences for entrepreneurship. Likewise, a higher relative tax on formal employment may encourage income shifting and push more people into self-employment; whether it is the "right" people and whether they are choosing self-employment for the right reasons are different matters altogether. Lastly, the tax system (and regulation in general) can be so opaque and complex that it puts potential productive entrepreneurs at a disadvantage relative to individuals able and willing to game the system to their advantage. As such, the *complexity effect* benefits rent seekers, lobbyists, and tax arbitrageurs to the disadvantage of new entrants and productive ventures.

Bearing these effects in mind, we choose moderation as a first guiding principle: tax rates should be low to promote an entrepreneurial society. Perhaps more important still is to espouse the second principle of neutrality and aim for as small a bias as possible with regard to taxes across different owner categories, sources of finance, and economic activities (Elert et al. 2017). Finally, adherence to the principle of transparency is vital to make the tax system less opaque and exception-ridden.

Tax systems tend to grow increasingly complex and opaque over time because politicians, often prompted by vocal interest groups in society, continually tinker with the system at the margins. This corrosion highlights the need for an occasional overhaul of the tax code to do away with the exceptions and loopholes typically introduced to fix imbalances caused by changes elsewhere in the tax code. Because such a tax code reform requires a strong political mandate and momentum, the optimal moment of implementation is hard to predict; but when an opportunity presents itself, policymakers should embrace it.

The EU's tax competencies are quite limited, meaning that most of the proposals presented below are directed to member states individually. That said, the EU can play a role by "nudging" national governments in the right direction and has several policy instruments at its disposal to do so. Such instruments include recommendations, policy statements developed by the Council, and nonbinding agreements between member states, which could be coupled with regular assessments, peer pressure, and the exchange of best practices between member states. The EU is entitled to take such supporting and coordinating actions whenever tax reforms touch upon the proper functioning of the internal market. This is arguably the case for taxes with a bearing on the efficient allocation of capital in the EU, such as corporate income taxation, dividend and capital gains taxation, and the fiscal treatment of debt, equity, and stock options (Suse and Hachez 2017).

## 3.2    Proposals

Given the complexities inherent in the relationship between taxes and entrepreneurship, we present reform proposals for the major tax categories in EU member states one at a time: labor, corporate, dividend, and capital gains, wealth, and stock options taxation. These proposals should primarily be considered at the member state level, either in isolation or, preferably, as part of a comprehensive tax reform.

### 3.2.1    Labor Taxation

While some entrepreneurs (such as owner-managers in incorporated businesses) are employees in their own companies, they seldom pay themselves a high salary, especially in early phases when liquidity tends to be constrained. Nevertheless, the emphasis on key personnel in the collaborative innovation bloc underscores the central role of labor taxation for successful entrepreneurial venturing. EU member states differ substantially in this respect.

While the top marginal tax rates on labor income range from 15% in Hungary to 60% in Sweden, the total marginal tax wedge is in many ways a more informative measure, with more relevant effects on entrepreneurial venturing. Defined as the share of total labor cost at the margin, it consists of the sum of mandatory social security contributions paid by the employer and/or the employee and the marginal income tax rate. In a country such as Belgium, as much as two-thirds of total labor cost consists of income taxes and social security contributions, while the share in Poland is only about half as large (see Table 3.1). In part, the differences reflect the diversity in political preferences and cultures across Europe. Generally, labor taxation is high, both on average and at the margin, in the old member states and the Nordic welfare states. Rates are much lower in the East, where tax codes are more recent, and in the Anglo-Saxon countries, with their less extensive welfare states.

**Table 3.1** Top marginal tax rate on labor income, and marginal rate of income tax plus employee and employer contributions less cash benefits (tax wedge), 2017

| Country | Top marginal tax rate on labor income | Tax wedges | | |
| --- | --- | --- | --- | --- |
| | | Single no child, 100% AW | Single, no child, 167% AW | Married, 2 children, 100 and 67% AW |
| Austria | 48.0 | 59.7 | 42.2 | 59.7 |
| Belgium | 46.0 | 66.4 | 68.5 | 65.6 |
| Czech Rep. | 20.1 | 48.6 | 48.6 | 48.6 |
| Denmark | 55.8 | 42.0 | 55.8 | 42.0 |
| Estonia | 19.7 | 41.2 | 41.2 | 41.2 |
| Finland | 49.0 | 55.6 | 58.3 | 56.4 |
| France | 53.9 | 58.5 | 59.9 | 60.4 |
| Germany | 47.5 | 60.4 | 44.3 | 57.9 |
| Greece | 55.0 | 49.1 | 61.6 | 49.1 |
| Hungary | 15.0 | 46.2 | 49.0 | 46.2 |
| Ireland | 48.0 | 54.0 | 55.8 | 35.9 |
| Italy | 42.3 | 54.7 | 63.3 | 55.3 |
| Luxembourg | 41.4 | 55.5 | 55.5 | 52.1 |
| Netherlands | 49.7 | 51.6 | 52.7 | 51.6 |
| Poland | 22.1 | 37.0 | 37.2 | 37.0 |
| Portugal | 50.0 | 51.1 | 60.8 | 51.1 |
| Slovakia | 21.7 | 46.4 | 46.5 | 46.4 |
| Slovenia | 39.0 | 51.0 | 60.4 | 43.6 |
| Spain | 43.5 | 48.3 | 37.0 | 48.3 |
| Sweden | 60.1 | 48.3 | 67.3 | 48.4 |
| UK | 45.0 | 40.2 | 49.0 | 40.3 |
| USA | 46.3 | 43.6 | 43.6 | 34.3 |

Note: The marginal tax wedge refers to the principal earner with an income of 100% of average wage (AW) and the secondary earner with an income of 67% of AW in the rightmost column
Source: OECD, *Taxing Wages 2016–2017*

To offset the negative impacts of high marginal and average labor taxation on labor supply, policymakers have tied many of the valuable transfers and welfare state services that these taxes finance (e.g., child care and pension rights) to employment. Moreover, taxation and social security have often been individualized to stimulate female labor participation (Lindbeck 1982). Such individualized conditionality explains why a country such as Sweden has the EU's highest employment rate despite high marginal and average taxes on labor. However, if systems are poorly designed, they push people away from small, risky, and innovative ventures into secure, salaried employment in the public sector or in incumbent firms. More often than not, these high-taxation–high-conditionality systems violate our principles of moderation, neutrality, and transparency.

For Sweden, it has been argued that a reform to lower the marginal tax in the top bracket would probably more than finance itself (Sørensen 2010; Holmlund and Söderström 2011). The situation is different in the new eastern member states: despite low labor income tax rates, they exhibit little improvement-driven opportunity entrepreneurship and couple low employment with large underground economies. These circumstances suggest that factors other than high labor taxes are binding constraints for this cluster of countries and that lowering such taxes more would merely result in a harmful loss of tax income and the deterioration of public sector effectiveness. In contrast, labor taxation seems to be a clear impediment to venture creation and growth in the Mediterranean countries, as well as in Belgium and France. There, high taxes and the employment-related obligations of employers penalize both the employment of people and attempts to realize growth. Reforms in these countries should aim to combine lower labor taxes with more universal access to public services and social security, such as childcare and pension rights. We return to these issues when discussing the organization of labor markets and social security systems in Chap. 5.

Regarding labor taxation, we contend that countries with high marginal labor tax rates should refrain from following the Swedish model. Instead, they should reduce their marginal labor tax rates where possible because conditionality always benefits well-defined, existing forms of employment. Policymakers should not try to offset imbalances caused by high taxation by introducing additional layers of complexity. Instead we propose:

> Proposal 5: Reduce high tax burdens on labor instead of making subsidies, pension rights, and social benefits more conditional on employment status.

The proposal would ensure tax neutrality between different types of labor market engagement, reducing the disproportionately high penalty small employers face when hiring workers. Moreover, the proposal serves the principle of transparency by reducing the roundabout method of taxing labor income to finance transfers and to provide subsidized services to those that paid the tax.

## 3.2.2 Corporate Taxation

Corporate taxation has significant ramifications for the interplay between entrepreneurs and financiers in the collaborative innovation bloc; specifically, a high tax rate on business profits discourages equity financing and encourages

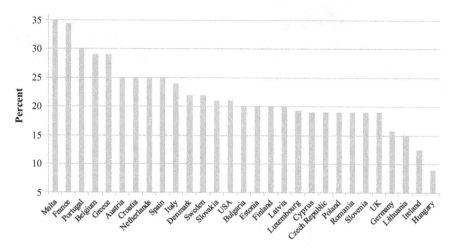

**Fig. 3.1** The statutory corporate tax rate in EU countries and the USA, 2018. Source: OECD and Eurostat

debt financing if interest payments are tax-deductible (Desai et al. 2003; Huizinga et al. 2008). Because debt financing is less costly and more readily available to larger firms, high corporate tax rates coupled with tax-deductible interest payments put smaller firms and potential entrepreneurs at a disadvantage (Davis and Henrekson 1999) while also reducing the retained earnings that can be used to expand ventures after start-up. Consequently, taxing profits can be expected to affect growth negatively, especially in small firms (Michaelas et al. 1999).

In the EU, the statutory corporate tax rate ranges from 35% in Malta to 9% in Hungary (Fig. 3.1). While healthy institutional competition among member states along this margin keeps rates down, the EU has a central role to play to prevent a race to the bottom, and it must act as a watchdog against opaque sweetheart deals negotiated between national governments and large multinational corporations or national champions. Although they reduce effective tax rates, such exceptions violate the principles of neutrality and transparency; the Union should therefore encourage member states to remove discrepancies between statutory and effective corporate income tax rates stemming from these deals.[1]

---

[1] Discrepancies can be due to accelerated depreciation rules, inventory valuation rules, and ad hoc country- or industry-specific tax reductions. They are usually the result of effective lobbying by vested interest; at best, they do little harm, but typically they distort the behavior of various agents in the business sector, e.g., by favoring specific industries, ownership forms, and sources of finance (King and Fullerton 1984).

Proposal 6: Eliminate discrepancies between statutory and effective corporate income tax rates.

It is imperative that these discrepancies be addressed, as it becomes more difficult to realize the behavioral effects that policymakers envision if economic actors can obtain an effective tax rate lower than the statutory one (Chetty et al. 2009). Moreover, all firms should be treated equally under corporate income tax law.

There is, however, one (transparent but decidedly non-neutral) exception to the equal treatment rule that we would consider appropriate: that start-ups be allowed to retain their profits for reinvestment. The fact that new firms create useful knowledge about new technologies and business models (even if they ultimately fail) justifies this departure from the neutrality principle. This does not mean that personal incomes earned from start-ups should be tax exempt, as this could trigger unproductive tax arbitrage and promote solo self-employment (Liebregts 2016). This reform would make it easier and more attractive to make and reinvest profits while simultaneously creating a tough selection environment for firms without creating a need to develop (transparent, democratic, and accountable) criteria for public support. In addition, this supports new ventures without siphoning off resources from successful firms and avoids the risk that direct government support is channeled to the wrong firms. The latter risk is far from negligible; it could induce entrepreneurs to spend less time and effort on catering to consumer demands, and more on developing expertise in getting such public support (Gustafsson et al. 2018). In the extreme case, entrepreneurial profits could be made fully tax exempt. However, such a policy would only be effective when statutory corporate tax rates are also effective corporate tax rates, as proposed above.

Generally, a corporate income tax is not a potent way to tax the income of firms, especially incumbents, since they respond to such measures by increasing their prices and/or lowering the returns to their production factors. Corporate income taxation may have made sense in times when collecting taxes on personal income and consumption was cumbersome and complicated, but digitalization has made these indirect methods of taxation redundant. Ultimately, they only distort incentives and give rise to fiscal arbitrage. The principle of transparency justifies making all corporate profits tax exempt (not only those of young firms) while taxing primary incomes and consumption directly.

Proposal 7: Grant full corporate income tax exemption to genuinely new, innovative start-ups through their 3rd year, with the long-term goal of abolishing
corporate income taxation altogether.

Clearly, the short-term goal of this proposal violates one of the principles
we hold dear: neutrality. Moreover, it may give rise to undesirable tax-induced
arrangements and does not distinguish between innovation-based new ventures producing knowledge spillovers and low-tech replicative ventures.
However, because it is difficult for bureaucrats to distinguish deserving from
non-deserving ventures, it is probably best to refrain from fine-tuning this
further. Regardless, start-ups rarely make big profits in their first years, meaning that the proposal will not be costly in terms of foregone tax revenue.
Fulfilling its long-term goal could, furthermore, make it a vital step towards a
tax system in line with the desired principles of transparency, neutrality, and
moderation.

### 3.2.3   Taxation of Dividends and Capital Gains

The returns to entrepreneurship mainly accrue to investors and entrepreneurs
in the form of dividends and capital gains on their firm ownership stake. A
high dividend tax rate encourages entrepreneurs to rely on retained earnings
to finance expansion but can also trap capital in incumbent firms, thereby
obstructing the flow of capital to the most promising projects in a collaborative innovation bloc (Chetty and Saez 2005). This imbalance is probably part
of the reason why owners receive most of their economic return from successful entrepreneurship in the form of increased share values. Consequently, the
taxation of capital gains on stock holdings typically has a substantial effect on
the financial incentives of potential high-impact entrepreneurs and their
(equity) financiers (Cumming 2005; Da Rin et al. 2006).

As shown in Table 3.2, standard tax rates on dividends and capital gains
differ substantially among EU countries. Moreover, there are many ways in
which effective rates can and do diverge from standard rates (Grant Thornton
2016).[2] For example, the Swedish dividend and capital gains tax rates vary
between 20 and 60% for physical persons; in Ireland, meanwhile, the divi-

---

[2] These divergences depend on factors such as the holding period, firm size, whether the firm is private or
traded on a stock exchange, and whether ownership is passive or active. Other decisive factors are whether
the firm and/or the investor qualifies for inclusion in a tax-favored scheme (e.g., a scheme geared towards
encouraging innovative start-up activity), and the tax status of the body (a natural or a juridical person,
etc.) receiving the capital income.

**Table 3.2** The standard dividend and capital gains tax rates (short-term/long-term) in EU member countries and the USA, 2018

| Country | Dividends | Capital gains | Country | Dividends | Capital gains |
|---|---|---|---|---|---|
| Austria | 27.5 | 27.5 | Latvia | 0.0 | 20.0 |
| Belgium | 30.0 | 0.0 | Lithuania | 15.0 | 15.0 |
| Bulgaria | 5.0 | 41.0 | Luxembourg | 21.0 | 42.0 |
| Croatia | 12.0 | 12.0 | Malta | 0.0 | 35.0 |
| Cyprus | 17.0 | 0.0 | Netherlands | 25.0 | n/aª |
| Czech Republic | 15.0 | 15/0 | Poland | 19.0 | 19.0 |
| Denmark | 42.0 | 42.0 | Portugal | 28.0 | 28.0 |
| Estonia | 0.0 | 21.0 | Romania | 5.0 | 10.0 |
| Finland | 28.9 | 34.0 | Slovakia | 7.0 | 25/0 |
| France | 30.0 | 30.0 | Slovenia | 25.0 | 25/0 |
| Germany | 26.4 | 26.4/0 | Spain | 23.0 | 23.0 |
| Greece | 15.0 | 15.0 | Sweden | 30.0 | 30.0 |
| Hungary | 15.0 | 15.0 | UK | 38.1 | 28.0 |
| Ireland | 51.0 | 33.0 | USA | 29.2 | 39.6/20 |
| Italy | 26.0 | 26.0 | | | |

Source: OECD Statistics, Table II.4 Overall Statutory Tax Rates on Dividend Income, and the websites of the respective national tax agencies
ªThe Dutch tax rate on capital gains does not depend on the realized return. It is a flat tax of 30% on an assumed nominal rate of return

dend tax rate is 51%, whereas the capital gains tax rate can be reduced from 33% to zero under certain conditions. Levels are low, and variation is smaller in the Netherlands, Poland, and Estonia.

What most European member states have in common, however, is that their tax schemes for dividends and capital gains are complex, thereby feeding a thriving but macro-economically unproductive tax advice business. Countries should thus aim for dividend and capital gains tax rates with few exceptions and few (opaque) concessionary schemes. Here, Eastern European countries, such as Poland and Estonia, offer exemplary models: tax rates are at reasonable levels, and the effective tax rate is largely independent of any particular circumstances. Arguably, the simplicity is due to the relatively recent transition of these former communist countries to liberal market-based democracies. These economies essentially had to start from scratch in the early 1990s and were exempt from the burden of decades of lobbying and the type of political compromises obfuscating the tax system in most Western European countries.

Proposal 8: Countries should aim for low dividend and capital gains tax rates with few exceptions and few (opaque) concessionary schemes.

Dividend taxation also creates an undesirable differential in the risk-adjusted returns on debt and equity that possibly biases the supply of financial capital away from small, uncertain, experimental entrepreneurial venturing. We would, therefore, propose dividend taxation be kept low and at a par with the fiscal treatment of interest income on debt to avoid such biases. A similar argument holds for capital gains taxation to the extent that retained profits drive capital gains. To promote a more entrepreneurial society, the tax system should not be biased against the most relevant sources of finance for entrepreneurial venturing.

### 3.2.4 Taxation of Private Wealth

"Triple-F" finance plays an important role in the early stages of many ventures in a collaborative innovation bloc. When entrepreneurs exhaust their own resources, friends, family, and "fools" typically step in (Mitter and Kraus 2011). The last category includes informal investors, who, perhaps contrary to the general perception, contribute resources neither blindly nor foolishly. Entrepreneurs distribute ownership rights to informal investors early in the start-up process, putting the lie to the idea that triple-F financiers act out of charity (Kotha and George 2012; Ford and Nelsen 2014). In fact, the supply of such finance typically follows demand closely, and the amounts invested are of the same order of magnitude as amounts committed by angel investors in later stages of development (Burke et al. 2014). In other words, entrepreneurs mobilize significant funds from their personal and informal networks that aid in the development of their nascent ventures. It is possible, therefore, that more private wealth would increase the supply of informal finance, ultimately enabling more entrepreneurial venturing.

> Proposal 9: Harmonize and reduce taxes on private wealth, private wealth transfers, and inheritance if productively invested.

Because the incomes used to build up private wealth have typically already been taxed, some would argue that any form of private wealth taxation is double taxation (Boadway et al. 2010). A country may choose to tax the wealth of its citizens for equity reasons, but the fact that this gives rise to unproductive tax arbitrage (Harrington 2016; Zucman 2014, 2015; Montes 2018) is probably why most European countries have lowered wealth taxation. However, as shown in Table A.1 in the Appendix, countries such as France and Spain still tax wealth at steep rates even if the exempted amounts are sizable. The real effective tax rate on wealth income can become extremely high in the current low interest regime: For instance, a wealth tax of 2% is a real tax that is levied in addition to any tax on the nominal return of the asset. Invariably, this problem forces the government to introduce distortionary safety valves (e.g., Du Rietz and Henrekson 2015).

Equity considerations, while relevant, should take a backseat to ensuring that accumulated private wealth is mobilized and productively invested (Krippner 2005; Hudson and Bezemer 2012; Piketty et al. 2013; Bezemer 2014; Bezemer and Hudson 2016). The entrepreneurial society loses out when its wealthy families become rentier dynasties, i.e., passive portfolio investors in large incumbent firms and real estate. Preferably, their accumulated wealth should be used to create opportunities for the next generation of entrepreneurs (Acs and Phillips 2002; Acs 2006; Auerswald and Acs 2009). Acs and Phillips (2002) argue that in the USA, wealthy entrepreneurs perform this function in part through philanthropy. Historically, European nations have relied more on the taxation of accumulated wealth, wealth income, and inheritance, redistributing the proceeds through publicly funded investments in, e.g., education and health.

To ensure that Europe's wealthy families reinvest their fortunes in promising ventures on their own accord, a preferential treatment of equity investments in young SMEs could be considered. Alternatively, leaving private wealth invested unproductively could carry a penalty (Shakow and Shuldiner 1999).[3] Whichever route is chosen to mobilize more private wealth for entrepreneurial venturing, a strong case can be made for a harmonization of wealth taxation at the Union level. Appropriately implemented, such a measure would prevent a legislative race to the bottom and minimize the scope for unproductive tax evasion. Such considerations would benefit the current debate on European wealth taxation, which appears to be dominated by concerns of tax revenue and equity (Astarita 2014; Krenek and Schratzenstaller 2018).

Regarding inheritance taxation, another delicate balance must be struck—this time between preventing the build-up and entrenchment of passively invested dynastic fortunes on one hand and incentivizing the accumulation of wealth through productive investment on the other hand. Table A.2 in the Appendix reveals that inheritance taxes differ widely across member states, being zero or close to zero in 14 of the 28 member states but very high in some of the larger states, such as the UK, Germany, France, and Spain, as well

---

[3] This need not be complicated. For example, the Dutch system for taxation of private wealth assumes a 4% return on assets (above a threshold of 30.360 euros per person) which is taxed at 30%, implying a tax on the value of wealth above the threshold of 1.2%. Since 2017 the percentage increases with the size of the wealth. By assuming the return instead of measuring it, the wealth owner has an incentive to invest her wealth with higher risk and earn a higher return.

as in Finland and Belgium. As private wealth is most often invested productively in ventures when investors are knowledgeable about local conditions, fiscally motivated movement of capital to avoid inheritance taxation is unproductive. The EU should aim for harmonization in this area to prevent such wasteful actions.

> Proposal 10: Harmonize inheritance taxes across member states and introduce a moderate flat tax rate and exempt the majority of inheritances from taxation.

Most Western European countries have reduced their inheritance taxation significantly since the 1960s. Interestingly, the tax is least popular among the lower income brackets. Following the work of Piketty (2015), however, the issue of preventing the accumulation of "dead" wealth has resurfaced in the policy debate (e.g., The Economist 2017). While there are strong arguments for taxing inheritances, the devil is, as always, in the details. The primary purpose of this tax should not be to raise revenue but to incentivize the productive investment of wealth. People should be discouraged from rolling over large fortunes into risk-free portfolios of government bonds, and the liquidation of productive ventures to avoid inheritance taxation would be especially damaging. A moderate and harmonized inheritance tax would broaden the tax base while limiting the incentives and opportunities for tax avoidance. Furthermore, in member states where family-owned businesses are engines of innovation and growth, policymakers should consider additional means to strengthen the entrepreneurial society, for example, by introducing exemptions for wealth that remains productively invested in family firms.

Reducing and simplifying the taxation of private wealth are the first steps towards freeing up more savings for productive investment in entrepreneurial ventures. Those steps are not enough, however, if the interests and skills of private wealth owners do not meet the entrepreneurial sector's needs. Here, a well-developed financial sector, to which we return below, has an important role as a matchmaker and intermediary.

### 3.2.5   Tax Neutral Treatment of Equity and Debt

Innovative entrepreneurs have limited access to bank credit and tradable debt obligations. They may borrow from friends, family, and fools or through crowdlending, but these types of lending are often exposed to the same risks as equity and given in anticipation of the same return profiles (with no formal governance rights). The reason is that innovative start-ups face large disadvantages in attracting more formal forms of debt finance due to high uncertainty and the lack of a robust track record and readily collateralizable assets. Therefore, tax structures that favor debt over equity investments will, often unintentionally, bias the flow of financial resources away from innovative entrepreneurial venturing and impede the workings of the collaborative innovation bloc. Moreover, the tax-deductibility of interest payments has provided large firms with ample room for artificially shifting profits to low or zero-tax locations (OECD 2017).

Currently, national tax systems in Europe favor debt finance. Debt becomes (too) cheap relative to equity because interest payments are deductible as operating costs, while dividends are subject to corporate income taxation before they can be paid out to shareholders. Moreover, strong legal creditor protection reduces risks for creditors that would otherwise justify a higher risk premium on debt finance. Together, these fiscal and institutional arrangements bias the supply of finance towards debt, and entrepreneurs are at a disadvantage when competing for debt relative to homeowners, large multinationals, and other actors. As such, debt finance channels society's available savings into the reproduction and growth of the existing capital stock, and a case can be made that only equity type investments finance innovation and progress beyond the status quo (Polzin et al. 2018a).

Neutrality between debt and equity can be achieved in two principal ways: by reducing the tax advantages of debt finance or by giving similar advantages to equity (e.g., De Mooij and Devereux 2016). The EU's efforts in this regard have mainly been to reduce interest deductibility. In 2016, the European Council (2016) adopted the Anti-Tax Avoidance Directive (ATAD), which lays down rules against tax avoidance practices that directly affect the functioning of the internal market. Article 4 in the Directive stipulates a limit to interest deductions: net interest payments cannot exceed a certain percentage of company earnings, typically defined as 30% of earnings before interest, taxes, depreciation, and amortization (EBITDA), allowing for a minimum deductible amount independent of earnings. Table A.3 in the Appendix shows that almost all member states have instituted such rules, with most of them settling for a minimum deductible amount of EUR 3 million.

Unfortunately, the Council has prioritized its concern regarding tax base erosion over the need to even out the imbalance between debt and equity as sources of finance. It is unclear to what extent the EBITDA rules will be binding for incumbent firms, and if the rules are not binding, they will do nothing to reduce the difference in effective taxation of debt and equity.

A better route to follow to achieve neutrality would be to introduce a so-called *comprehensive business income tax*. This measure would eliminate the fiscal favoring of debt-financed investment by disallowing any deduction for

interest payments while compensating the business sector with a commensu-
rate lowering of the corporate tax rate. If implemented, this proposal would
promote an entrepreneurial society by lowering the taxation of high profits,
thereby incentivizing the pursuit of ventures with high risk and high expected
returns. Moreover, although firms are allowed to deduct interest payments
from corporate taxes, the creditors appropriate most of that benefit, as competition in debt markets is much higher on the demand side than on the supply side. Nevertheless, resistance against such a reform will likely be extensive;
it is in the best interest of creditors (notably banks) to lobby against it, and
many firms also (believe that they) benefit from the favorable tax treatment of
debt finance. In practice, therefore, policymakers may need to opt for an
*allowance for corporate equity* scheme instead. Such a scheme would replace
the deductibility of actual interest payments by allowing the deduction of an
amount corresponding to the normal return applied to the book value of the
firm's total assets. While this scheme eliminates the bias towards debt finance,
such a reform would, in fact, tax profits at a higher rate than before. It would
thus reduce the bias, and also reduce firms' ability to retain funds. In the short
run, however, it may be the best we can hope for.

> Proposal 11: Initiate a balanced program aiming to achieve tax neutrality
> between debt and equity finance.

In an entrepreneurial society, it is (primarily) equity investments that enable
innovative entrepreneurial venturing and thereby generate useful knowledge
about the products, services, and business models that work or fail. This
knowledge constitutes a positive externality, which may even justify the preferential tax treatment of equity investments over debt.[4] At the very least, the
long-term ambition should be to eliminate any fiscal advantages held by debt
finance over equity.

### 3.2.6   Taxation of Stock Options

The fiscal treatment of stock options deserves special mention, harking back
to the role played by key personnel in the collaborative innovation bloc. As a

---

[4] The same logic suggests that banks and other investors should be encouraged to disclose information on
loan applications they accept or turn down. Of course, the traditional banking business model relies in
part on exclusive access to financial information on clients, but as European banks have largely aban-
doned the traditional relationship-based banking model, it is difficult to justify exclusive access. Presently,
alternative platform finance is exploring practical ways to collect and disseminate such information. We
return to this issue in Chap. 4.

promise of a future ownership stake, employee stock options are used to encourage and reward individuals who supply key competencies to a young firm that is typically short on cash. However, their value—and effectiveness as an incentive mechanism—greatly depends on the option tax code, notably on whether employees can defer the tax liability until they sell the stocks (and whether they are taxed at a low capital gains tax rate at this point) (Gilson and Schizer 2003).

The effective tax treatment of option contracts is a major determinant of the size of the VC-funded entrepreneurial sector (Henrekson and Sanandaji 2018a). In a cross-country perspective, the tax rates on stock options vary considerably. For instance, the tax rate is as low as 7% in Ireland, while it typically exceeds 70% in Italy, and the tax rules tend to be highly complex (see Table A.4 in the Appendix). The VC sector remains small in most countries where the tax rate on stock options is high, while low-tax countries such as Hong Kong and the USA have large and highly dynamic VC sectors (Armour and Cumming 2006).

Proposal 12: Taxes on capital gains on stock options and the underlying stock in start-ups should be low and only be taxed when exercised and/or sold, i.e., when gains are realized.

In many EU countries, the lower taxation of gains on employee stock options in the start-up sector is necessary, both as a means to lure talented people away from traditional careers in incumbent firms and to channel institutional capital into the entrepreneurial sector, which should be mediated by a professional VC sector. A tax break that targets human capital in this segment would promote innovative entrepreneurship without the high fiscal cost of broad capital gains tax cuts (Henrekson and Sanandaji 2018c).

## 3.3   Summary

Taxation is essential to any government's ability to finance essential public infrastructure and collective goods. Therefore, where we argue in favor of moderation, healthy government finances are assumed. Inevitably, this implies that countries in the Union will end up with different tax levels and rates. However, given the aggregate level of tax income required to ensure a long-term stable government budget, we maintain that *moderate, neutral,* and *transparent* taxation are key to boosting entrepreneurial venturing across Europe. Adhering to these three principles requires an ongoing effort to keep

**Table 3.3** Summary of proposals regarding taxation, specifying the level in the governance hierarchy where the necessary decisions should be made

| No. | Principle(s) | Policy area | Proposal | Policy level[a] |
|---|---|---|---|---|
| 5 | Neutrality and transparency | Labor taxation | Reduce high tax burdens on labor instead of making subsidies, pension rights, and social benefits more conditional on employment status. | MS |
| 6 | Transparency | Corporate income taxation | Eliminate discrepancies between statutory and effective corporate income tax rates. | EU, MS |
| 7 | Moderation and transparency | Corporate income taxation | Grant full corporate income tax exemption to genuinely new, innovative start-ups through their third year, with the long-term goal of abolishing corporate income taxation altogether. | EU, MS |
| 8 | Moderation and transparency | Dividend and capital gains taxation | Countries should aim for low dividend and capital gains tax rates with few exceptions and few (opaque) concessionary schemes. | EU, MS |
| 9 | Moderation and neutrality | Wealth taxation | Harmonize and reduce taxes on private wealth, private wealth transfers, and inheritance if productively invested. | MS |
| 10 | Moderation and neutrality | Inheritance taxation | Harmonize inheritance taxes across member states and introduce a moderate flat tax rate and exempt the majority of inheritances from taxation. | EU, MS |
| 11 | Neutrality | Debt and equity taxation | Initiate a balanced program aiming to achieve tax neutrality between debt and equity finance. | EU, MS |
| 12 | Moderation | Stock options taxation | Taxes on capital gains on stock options and the underlying stock in start-ups should be low and only be taxed when exercised and/or sold, i.e., when gains are realized. | EU, MS |

[a]*EU* federal level, *MS* member state level

the tax system simple, clear, and effective in the face of interest groups lobbying for exemptions and exceptions. The alternative is less transparency, impaired neutrality, and increased complexity, which will distort behavior.

Table 3.3 provides a summary of our proposals regarding taxation and the level(s) of the governance hierarchy at which political action should take place to make them a reality. In contrast to the previous chapter, the proposals in this chapter require little policy coordination across policymaking levels: the legislative powers in tax policy are almost exclusively reserved for the member states. However, as Suse and Hachez (2017) note, the EU can and should use a number of nonbinding instruments and approaches to influence the tax policies of its member states.

# 4

# Savings, Finance, and Capital for Entrepreneurial Ventures

## 4.1 General Principles

The nature and estimated cost of innovations foregone as a result of institutional obstacles will always be shrouded in uncertainty because we can only speculate about what is "not seen," in the words of Frédéric Bastiat (1850). In a given institutional setting, we see only those market transactions and those entrepreneurial activities that the institutional setting allows and supports; innovations that do not conform to the existing economic order will not attract the required skills and resources and therefore not materialize. Thinking in terms of what is seen and unseen is valuable when pondering how existing rules governing savings, finance, and capital in Europe affect entrepreneurial activity and how they should change.

Europe certainly has no shortage of savings (OECD 2019a). However, as we have already mentioned, the nature of entrepreneurial venturing makes some forms of finance more suitable than others. In other words, the problem is not quantitative but qualitative: the allocation, rather than the volume, of European savings is what matters for entrepreneurial activity. Though plentiful, financial resources in the EU are mainly intermediated through universal banks and institutional investors who prefer large, low-risk, debt-based assets and blue-chip stock over small, risky equity-based investments (Westerhuis 2016). This systemic problem has considerable ramifications for collaborative innovation blocs; one can only speculate as to the number of fundamentally sound entrepreneurial projects that never got off the ground because the financial playing field was tilted against them.

© The Author(s) 2019
N. Elert et al., *The Entrepreneurial Society*, International Studies in Entrepreneurship 98,
https://doi.org/10.1007/978-3-662-59586-2_4

In this chapter, we present reform proposals intended to increase the flow of financial resources to small and new firms with high potential for entrepreneurial venturing. Our proposals aim to ensure that more of the existing resources become available to new ventures at the right time and in the appropriate form and quantities. For these goals to materialize, policymakers should reform existing institutions governing the allocation of capital in Europe. While proven recipes from outside Europe can be adopted, digital platform technology allows entirely new ones to be tried. As such, the reform proposals will enable vested institutions, promote proven alternatives, and experiment with new technologies to allocate more of the available capital to innovative entrepreneurs.

Again, a few basic principles underlie our proposals. First, because the framework surrounding savings and finance often puts entrepreneurs at a disadvantage, we adhere to the principle of neutrality by creating a level playing field for entrepreneurial ventures in the competition for financial resources. When followed, the principle guarantees that entrepreneurs are given a fair shot without being pampered. Second, we aim for increased transparency to reduce asymmetric information problems for investors. Adhering to this principle ensures that entrepreneurs know the criteria upon which the success of their venture will be evaluated, reducing a substantial source of uncertainty in entrepreneurial venturing. Finally, the principle of justifiability enters the discussion when we consider enabling reforms in the banking sector and pension funds. Given the seemingly conflicting aims of providing financial stability and financing productive venturing, the justifiability principle helps balance important functions, thus increasing the probability that reforms are effectively implemented and respected.

As stated, financial resources are not in short supply in Europe; the problem is the way in which they are intermediated. Therefore, we first discuss reforms that prevent some savings from ending up with institutionalized intermediaries, as this would free up resources for start-ups in the form of private and informal investments. Then, we consider whether and how Europe might emulate the successful American model of business angels and VC before addressing reforms that would enable Europe's historically dominant banking sector and more recently built up pension funds to invest parts of their vast portfolios in growing entrepreneurial firms. Because some of the proposals touch upon the so-called FinTech innovations, we conclude the chapter with a discussion of business models for alternative finance on digital platforms.

Proposals referring to private wealth accumulation and pension funds are primarily addressed to the member state level, as the European treaties do not give strong and effective competencies to European policymakers in these areas (Suse and Hachez 2017, pp. 40–41).[1] However, it does seem that the European policy level has ample competencies and instruments to implement reforms for the banking sector and FinTech innovation, while lower levels of policymaking are better suited to promote small-scale, arm's length financing for early-stage start-ups and the development of vibrant local and regional VC sectors.

## 4.2  Proposals

### 4.2.1  Financing Early-Stage Venturing

A large share of savings in European economies currently goes into banks and pension funds (OECD 2018a). This share can be expected to grow in the future, as funded systems increasingly substitute for pay-as-you-go systems and an increasing number of European workers opt for voluntary or collectively agreed upon supplementary pension plans (PensionsEurope 2017). These institutions primarily invest the funds of their clients and beneficiaries in liquid debt-based assets or tradable equities. This preference is unsurprising given the inability of such investors to take an active role in firm management.[2] The large economies of scale in managing loan portfolios (e.g., Philpot et al. 1998; Hughes and Mester 1998; Piketty 2014; Fagereng et al. 2016) also cause a bias towards "big ticket" investments and tradable securities. As a result, the resources managed by banks and pension funds can typically not be used for the type of smaller, long-run, equity-based investments that are so central to small and young ventures in collaborative innovation blocs (Kramer-Eis et al. 2017).

The lack of equity capital in smaller ticket sizes constrains (potential) high-growth firms more than others because such firms require regular infusions of

---

[1] Still, the EU has some coordination tools available, and the Commission has substantial powers whenever proposals relate to the internal market for financial services. For example, in 2013, the Commission adopted a proposal establishing uniform rules to enable venture capital funds to "market their funds and raise capital on a pan-European basis across the Single Market." Moreover, since the financial crisis, European coordinating, supervisory, and legislative powers have been expanded through the establishment of the Banking Union in 2012 and the Capital Markets Union. The aim of the latter is "to *deepen and further integrate the capital markets* of the 28 EU member states" and its gradual buildup is projected to be completed in 2019 (https://www.consilium.europa.eu/en/policies/capital-markets-union/).

[2] The 23 associations in 21 European countries that are members of PensionsEurope (2017, p. 12) hold some 30% of assets in equity, but these holdings are typically passive. When pension funds actively engage with the firms in which they invest, it is usually to promote corporate social responsibility (e.g., O'Rourke 2003).

external equity to sustain growth (Baumol et al. 2007, p. 205). This reliance increases (relative to debt) with the degree of risk and opacity, both of which are greater among younger and more innovative firms. Therefore, entrepreneurial start-ups usually struggle to raise funds in general and funds from large financial institutions in particular (Tilburg 2009). Part of the problem is that wealth-constrained would-be entrepreneurs do not have a track record, cannot put up collateral or make sizable equity infusions of their own to credibly signal their project's worth to outside investors. Higher levels of private wealth accumulation could remedy this problem of asymmetric information (Nykvist 2008; Parker 2018) or even enable the entrepreneur to make equity infusions that are large enough to capitalize the firm at inception. Such capitalization is essential for later venture success and performance (Henrekson and Sanandaji 2016).

Moreover, greater private or family-based savings could increase the pool of potential business angels and other informal investors who can help entrepreneurs overcome liquidity constraints in the early stages of venture creation (Ho and Wong 2007). The entrepreneur's family can be crucial in this respect, especially in regions where family ties are strong (Dilli and Westerhuis 2018). Conversely, a lack of private wealth impedes entrepreneurial venturing; any arrangement channeling savings and asset control away from large institutional investors and back to private individuals is, therefore, likely to increase the supply of equity capital and "soft" loans in smaller ticket sizes with early-stage entrepreneurs, even if much of it will end up in lower mortgages and savings deposits at banks.

A first best option for institutional reform is to reduce the share of institutionalized savings: the flow of finance into entrepreneurial venturing would potentially increase if less European wealth were tied up in compartmentalized institutional investment funds. The best way to ensure entrepreneurial financing is the pursuit of policies that encourage private wealth accumulation and the free flow of that wealth into entrepreneurial ventures (Pelikan 1988).

> Proposal 13: Allow more wealth to accumulate and remain in private hands and make it possible, easy, and attractive to invest such wealth in entrepreneurial ventures.

This proposal complements Proposal 9, which argues for the moderate taxation of private wealth holdings and transfers. While fiscal incentives matter, soft measures can be instrumental in developing a vibrant investment climate, especially when they take the form of information campaigns, matchmaking events, and the development of an effective support and information infrastructure for informal investors. To the extent that private investors allocate their capital towards small equity ticket deals, this corrects for the bias in Europe's financial system, returning it to neutrality by increasing transparency.

Unfortunately, financial markets show a growing tendency towards institutionalization with funds managed on behalf of individual investors (e.g., Pilbeam 2018). And even if policymakers adopted Proposal 13, it would take time for private wealth to accumulate in significant amounts. Therefore, we should consider other initiatives to make more savings available to early-stage start-ups. Indeed, with increasing shares of savings going into pension funds and in light of demographic trends, most member states of the EU are contemplating reforms.[3] A crucial ingredient of such reforms should be to give participants more discretion over their pension savings, enabling them to buy unlisted stock, and invest part of their pension savings in start-ups if they want to.[4]

Proposal 14: Allow people to individually choose how and where to invest part of their pension savings.

Not everyone has the inclination and skill to manage a portfolio of early-stage equity investments. Moreover, financial literacy remains low, and people are generally susceptible to behavioral biases and have a hard time selecting the products and services that best fit their preferences and risk attitudes (Rooij et al. 2011; Madrian et al. 2017). This justifies significant regulation on how different options should be presented and those who prefer that their pension savings be invested in low-risk assets should, consequently, always have a secure alternative. But while policymakers must strike a balance between public and private interests to justify the reforms, allowing people to invest some of their pension savings in entrepreneurial ventures can democratize capitalism, especially when combined with, e.g., crowd investing platforms (Shiller 2013; Mollick and Robb 2016; Stevenson et al. 2019). This facilitation could help jumpstart Europe's embryonic professional angel and VC sector, to which we turn next.

---

[3] See Ebbinghaus (2011, 2015), Hinrichs (2016), Carone et al. (2016), and PensionsEurope (2017) regarding the trend away from pay-as-you-go and towards the privatization of pension systems in Europe and reforms proposed to introduce risk-sharing by participants through defined contribution schemes.

[4] This goes against the grain of, for example, the Pan-European Pension Product initiative of the European Council that aims to develop a European market for pension products, which will increase the level of savings tied up in professionally managed funds. See, for example, European Commission (2017a) and European Council (2018).

## 4.2.2    Financing Scale Ups

Beyond the early stage, business angels and VC can play a crucial role for high-performing entrepreneurial firms with growth ambitions (Cumming 2012). Their funding is considered superior to bank finance because it comes with expertise and access to crucial networks (Keuschnigg and Nielsen 2004a; Ho and Wong 2007). As Table 4.1 shows, substantial differences exist in the size of VC investments across Europe, with Eastern European and Mediterranean countries at the bottom, while the UK, Sweden, Finland, and France are clearly in the lead. Nevertheless, these differences pale in comparison to the huge gap with the USA—arguably a major reason why US firms grow faster than their European counterparts (Bottazzi and Da Rin 2002; Scarpetta et al. 2002; Da Rin et al. 2006; Henrekson and Sanandaji 2018b).

Table 4.1 Venture capital investments as a share of GDP, and the ease of getting credit in EU member countries and the USA, 2017

| Country | VC investment, % of GDP | Ease of getting credit score (0–100) | Country | VC investment, % of GDP | Ease of getting credit score (0–100) |
|---|---|---|---|---|---|
| USA | 0.400 | 95 | Belgium | 0.033 | 65 |
| Denmark | 0.032 | 70 | Spain | 0.043 | 60 |
| Luxembourg | 0.030 | 15 | Austria | 0.026 | 55 |
| Finland | 0.055 | 65 | Poland | 0.011 | 75 |
| Ireland | 0.040 | 70 | Bulgaria | 0.010 | 65 |
| Portugal | 0.010 | 45 | Czech Rep. | 0.002 | 70 |
| France | 0.055 | 50 | Italy | 0.005 | 45 |
| Sweden | 0.060 | 55 | Romania | 0.003 | 80 |
| Netherlands | 0.044 | 45 | Greece | 0.000 | 50 |
| UK | 0.076 | 75 | Croatia | n/a | 55 |
| Germany | 0.035 | 70 | Cyprus | n/a | 60 |
| Estonia | 0.006[a] | 70 | Malta | n/a | 35 |
| Latvia | 0.006[a] | 85 | Slovakia | n/a | 70 |
| Lithuania | 0.006[a] | 70 | Slovenia | n/a | 45 |
| Hungary | 0.021 | 75 | | | |

Note: The ranking of economies on the ease of getting credit is determined by their distance to the leading country for getting credit. These scores are the distance to frontier score for the sum of the strength of legal rights index (range 0–10); and the depth of credit information index (range 0–8). New Zealand is the leading country
Sources: Invest Europe (2018, p. 47) for venture capital and World Bank, *Doing Business 2018* for ease of getting credit. Data for venture capital for the USA is from OECD, *Entrepreneurship at a Glance: Highlights 2018*
[a]For VC-investments, values for Estonia, Latvia, and Lithuania are a Baltic average

More private wealth is but a first step towards developing a VC industry. Here, policymakers ought to learn from the US experience of the 1970s and 1980s and adopt a broad-based policy approach: an encouraging legal framework allowing pension funds to invest in high-risk securities issued by small and new firms as well as VC funds (Gompers and Lerner 1999; cf. Keuschnigg and Nielsen 2004a, b). Because the current trend of a progressively larger share of savings going into pension funds is unlikely to reverse anytime soon (OECD 2018a), a wise policy measure would allow at least part of these assets to be invested in entrepreneurial firms and not just in real estate, public stocks, and high-rated bonds. Moreover, since large financial institutions do not have the competence to invest directly in small and new firms, such a measure would create a demand for a professional VC sector.

Proposal 15: Pension funds and other institutional investors should, on an experimental basis, be allowed to invest more in equity in general and in venture capital specifically.

In implementing a reform of this kind, policymakers should judiciously consider the balance between public and private interests. Crucially, such a scheme should be combined with cuts in capital gains taxes and the effective tax treatment of stock options in young entrepreneurial firms, as discussed in Chap. 3. Only a broad-based policy effort would enable VC firms and other actors in the entrepreneurial ecosystem to supply their services profitably and design the appropriate incentive contracts needed to build innovative firms (Henrekson and Rosenberg 2001; Kaplan and Strömberg 2003; Lerner and Tåg 2013; Udell 2015). A sizable and efficient VC sector cannot evolve without significant demand and a favorable fiscal climate.

By contrast, promoting VC in Europe by directing more public funds to VC investors will likely not result in more productive entrepreneurial venturing. Granted, European VC firms are at best moderately successful in picking the winners among high-risk projects (Gompers and Lerner 2004; Birch 2006; Svensson 2008; Gompers et al. 2009), but there is little to suggest that subsidized organizations are better placed in this respect (Baumol et al. 2007, p. 220). Such organizations may—directly or indirectly, openly or furtively, partly or completely—base their decisions on political rather than commercial considerations and therefore underperform. It may be possible to channel some additional funding into VC by matching private investment, but it is of key importance that decision makers in the VC industry retain a substantial personal stake in their decisions (Grilli and Murtinu 2014a, b; Cumming et al. 2017). Instead of throwing public money at the sector, we believe these resources are best spent developing the skills and competencies to allocate venture capital. The business model of carefully selecting and coaching ventures resists efficient scaling. For the VC sector to grow, therefore, we need more people who can do the job. The absence of VC expertise currently biases the flow of capital against high-growth firms; promoting its formation in Europe would return financial markets to neutrality. We therefore propose:

> Proposal 16: Develop competencies for private equity and venture capital investment in the field and avoid promoting VC capital with funding directly.

At the same time, this proposal calls into question the approach suggested under, e.g., the Investment Plan for Europe, the so-called Juncker Plan (European Commission 2015a), which provides sizable additional public funding. The plan's target now stands at 500 billion euros by 2020, some 32% of which was allocated to small firms up to 2019 (European Commission 2019b). Unfortunately, the requisite competence to channel these funds to young, high-growth firms is lacking (Schneider 2015b). The problem with VC is not a lack of money or skills per se. Rather, a substantial degree of "skin in the game" needs to be retained to avoid moral hazard as returns and the risk of failure are likely to depend on entrepreneurial effort and investors' commitment to the venture. Too much "easy" public funding may actually reduce the chances of success. Even professional fund managers will make expensive mistakes and invest in projects with high risks and low returns if allowed to play with "other people's money" (Kay 2015). Therefore, reforms should aim at strengthening the demand and supply of private VC funds and ensure that incentives to invest are strong while the potential to offload losses onto taxpayers is kept to a minimum.[5]

After all, a VC fund is involved in a venture's lifespan for a relatively short but crucial period, after which it strives to find a quick and profitable exit opportunity. Strengthening such opportunities would be a valuable complement to the aforementioned tax reforms.

---

[5] Germany, for example, does not seem to suffer from a direct lack of VC funds and its geographical distribution nicely matches the entrepreneurial ecosystem (Klagge et al. 2017). However, the German market remains small, arguably because of low demand. Direct subsidies under these circumstances will only cause too much cheap money to chase too few projects. Moreover, as public funds necessarily come with rules and regulations to ensure accountability, they would introduce a bias against the radically innovative start-ups that need this type of investment.

Proposal 17: Reduce barriers to the sale, acquisition, and IPO of VC-funded start-ups to facilitate profitable exits.

It may seem, with mostly large incumbent firms currently buying up small ventures for strategic reasons, that this proposal would strengthen their position. However, what we intend here is that improved access to exit markets will intensify competition among potential buyers, which will then increase the value of innovative entrepreneurial ventures. If policymakers help build the skills, enhance the incentives, and create the demand for VC, the European VC sector is likely to flourish to the benefit of all venture creation. This sector is urgently needed to restore a level playing field in the competition for available financial resources, but we warn against propping up VC with (more) public funds.

## 4.2.3   The Role of Banks

Although Europe's financial system remains predominantly bank-based, significant deleveraging in all euro countries since 2008 caused the average share of banks in total financial market assets to drop from 57% to approximately 45% in 2016 (ECB 2017, p. 7). As can be seen in Fig. 4.1, the Eurozone average hides considerable variety across national jurisdictions. The banks' total assets as share of GDP ranges from 2500% in 2008 for Luxemburg down to approximately 75% for Lithuania in 2016. Overall, the banking sector has deleveraged and contracted between 2008 and 2016 in all euro countries. Nevertheless, banking in Europe (especially Germany and France) continues to dominate in finance and is large relative to GDP. The share of bank assets in the top countries is high by international standards, and recent research (Hassan et al. 2011; Arcand et al. 2012) has shown that shares well above 100% of GDP tend to become a drag on growth. More important than the size of the banking sector relative to GDP, however, is its share in the total intermediation of national savings. Financial development typically increases with GDP, whereas banking's share in the financial mix first rises (capturing market share from informal finance) and then declines (losing market share to bond and stock markets) as financial markets develop (Levine 1997; Dufey 1998). The share of banking in total financial market assets also varies substantially across euro countries, with approximately 10% in Luxemburg and over 90% in Greece (ECB 2017, p. 9), but it lies well above 50% in most Eurozone countries. Moreover, when controlling for the size of the corporate

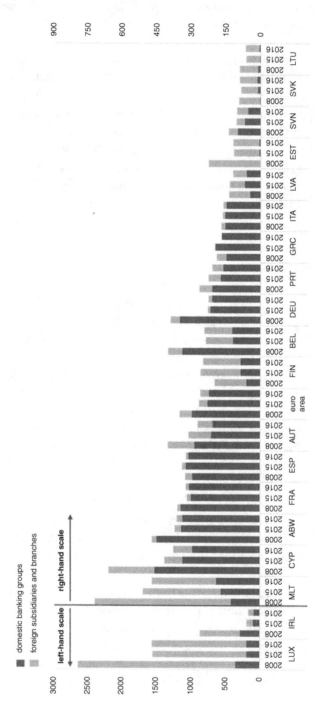

**Fig. 4.1** Total assets of domestic banking groups and foreign-controlled subsidiaries and branches in relation to GDP in euro area countries in 2008, 2015, and 2016. Note: Data for domestic banking groups and foreign subsidiaries are consolidated, and hence include branches and subsidiaries that can be classified as other financial institutions (OFIs), except insurance companies. Source: ECB (2017)

loan book, most European countries still rely heavily on banking as a channel for intermediation (Kraemer-Eis et al. 2017, e.g., Fig. 40).

As a result, more than 50% of European SMEs report bank loans and over-drafts as relevant sources of finance (Lee et al. 2015; Udell 2015; Kraemer-Eis et al. 2017). While the absolute size of the banking system is not problematic from the perspective of an entrepreneurial society, how banks allocate their credit is (Hernández-Cánovas and Martínez-Solano 2010). Here, Europe's banking system exhibits some worrying trends with respect to regulation, consolidation, leveraging, and lending practices. While the roots of these developments can be traced back decades (Westerhuis 2016), they are far from irreversible; the EU has already used its significant competencies to implement reforms in the banking sector. For example, under the Banking Union and Capital Markets Union programs, European banks can offer their services across the Union when they obtain a "passport."[6] The recent financial crisis can be used as a cautionary tale to motivate the implementation of more initiatives.

It is well established that Europe's universal bank-based system mixes inherently public with private functions (Liikanen et al. 2012; Vickers Commission 2013; Bordo and Levin 2017). The system combines the public function of providing access to a payment system based on secure assets free of default risk with the for-profit allocation of capital to viable projects. The combination implies that regulations to secure the first objective may limit banks' ability to achieve the second. While (implicit or explicit) public guarantees to (large) banks serve a public function, they also mean that banks can finance their assets at a significant discount in the market (Davis and Tracey 2014; Schich and Aydin 2014; Toader 2015). In a competitive market, this would be good news for customers because competition would force banks to pass on their lowered funding costs by providing cheaper credit to all. Public guarantees without such competitive pressures give banks a strong incentive to take on high risks and play a "heads I win, tails you lose" strategy (Gropp et al. 2013).

Unfortunately, the European banking sector is far from competitive (Apergis et al. 2016). Due to economies of scale and scope, aggregate market shares of 80% or more for the five largest banks in a country are not uncommon (ECB 2017, p. 32). The result is not cheap credit but monopoly rents for bank employees and shareholders (Molyneux et al. 1994; Carbó et al. 2009).

---

[6] The Capital Requirements Directive and Regulation (CRD IV and CRR IV respectively) regulate these bank passports. Their investment banking is generally covered under the Markets in Financial Instruments Directive (MiFID II), which was updated and came into effect in January 2018. Non-banks can obtain similar passport rights under the Alternative Investment Fund Managers Directive (AIFMD) and Undertakings for Collective Investment in Transferable Securities Directive (UCITS).

Moreover, because public guarantees mean that taxpayers are ultimately liable for any losses beyond a small equity buffer, regulators must strictly supervise the lending practices of banks, especially those deemed "systemically important." Following the financial crisis of 2008, European regulators tightened their supervision and now enforce a harmonized set of stricter European rules (e.g., European Banking Authority 2019). The regulation aims to reduce the risk of a single bank collapsing by imposing risk-weighted reserve requirements and subjecting banks to stress tests (Focarelli and Pozzolo 2016).[7] However, the unintended consequences of such tightened regulation are further bank concentration and even less credit flowing to ventures that cannot offer high-quality collateral, strong and long track records, or reliable cash flow predictions.

As previously mentioned, Europe's fiscal and social security systems are also strongly biased towards large portfolios of professionally managed assets and debt-based finance (Kay 2015). The imbalance makes financial markets in Europe highly concentrated, largely debt- and bank-based, and biased against small- and medium-sized firms in general and young, innovative ventures in particular (Liikanen et al. 2012; Pohl and Tortella 2017; Miklaszewska 2017). Ironically, regulation to limit the micro risk for individual banks, funds, and portfolios thus creates systemic and macro risks by eliminating diversity and shifting investment away from small-scale experimental ventures. To maintain a competitive return on equity, the system as a whole is highly leveraged, and citizens end up investing their savings in liquid, marketable assets. These assets have a low real return because they do not finance innovative and productive ventures (Bezemer and Hudson 2016) but instead go to large incumbent firms with strong balance sheets, further entrenching the status quo.

Policymakers can take many steps to address this bias and make some of Europe's abundant savings available to entrepreneurs, also through bank credit. One option would be to set up a system of loan guarantees for entrepreneurs and SMEs; such schemes are already in place in several member states and work reasonably well in channeling financial resources into small- and medium-sized firms.[8] Second, the Union has already established a legal

---

[7] Under the auspices of the Banking Union (BU), for example, the Commission has prioritized safety. The key pillars of the BU are stronger prudential regulation, improved depositor protection, and the single resolution mechanism aimed at preventing the need for taxpayer bailouts. No doubt unintentionally, these measures make bank finance even less accessible for entrepreneurial ventures.

[8] The evidence on SME loan guarantee schemes is mixed (Udell 2015). While schemes seem to have been successful in channeling additional resources to SMEs in Italy (Zecchini and Ventura 2009) and Korea (Oh et al. 2009), a similar scheme in Japan seems to have caused firm performance to deteriorate (Uesugi et al. 2010). Also, UK evidence shows that the impacts may differ substantially across regions (Craig et al. 2007).

right to feedback from credit institutions on their credit decision under Article 431 in the EU Capital Requirements Regulation (European Parliament and Council of the European Union 2013). This initiative is laudable because it helps entrepreneurs and individuals understand their financial position and improve their chances of obtaining financing in the future (European Commission 2018a; cf. European Banking Federation 2017). This information is valuable to third parties as well, but it is presently not common practice to demand such disclosure: Irish banks, for example, currently do not disclose information about any publicly guaranteed credit they grant or turn down under the credit guarantee scheme (see, e.g., Strategic Banking Corporation of Ireland 2019). In line with the principle of transparency, we propose the following:

> Proposal 18: Maintain the systems of bank loan guarantees for start-ups and ensure that (appropriately anonymized) credit decision information becomes publicly available.

Strictly speaking, this proposal violates the neutrality principle, but given the existing biases against start-ups in banking, the risk is small that it would tilt the playing field far in their favor. The proposal would gain further traction if policymakers linked it to provisions enhancing transparency for other types of investors.

Nevertheless, it would be preferable to address the issue at a more fundamental level, notably by increasing banks' mandatory equity ratios, i.e., the minimum proportion of a bank's lending and other investments that has to be financed by its own equity (equity/total assets). Under the new Basel IV agreement, ratios stand at 3% of unweighted assets. These levels of equity are thought to be sufficient to absorb the risks on current bank balance sheets, but they severely limit the risk banks can responsibly assume in their lending.[9] Therefore, these balance sheets are currently dominated by mortgages, government bonds, and corporate loans with low credit risk. If European banks are to take on more micro risk by increasing their lending to innovation-based entrepreneurial firms, they will (first) need larger buffers to avoid putting their clients' deposits at risk.

---

[9] The Basel IV agreement also details risk weights and sets reserve requirements for risk-weighted assets. As weights cannot be objectively determined or immediately translated into profits and returns, they are subject to intense lobbying. Banks frequently underestimate risks and have even been known to manipulate weights (Mariathasan and Merrouche 2014). This matter is beyond the scope of this book, but as risk weights tend to disadvantage SME lending, we would prefer a simple unweighted equity ratio in line with the principles of transparency and neutrality.

Proposal 19: Increase the mandatory equity ratio in banking gradually to 10–15% to allow them to responsibly take on more risk in their lending portfolios.

We do not expect this measure to cause banks to start lending massively to early-stage, high-risk ventures. That is the province of venture capitalists. However, this proposed change will make it easier for entrepreneurial ventures to acquire additional funding and grow in the later, less risky stages of their life cycle. With more "skin in the game," banks will be able to enter earlier in a firm's life cycle, responsibly assuming slightly more risk (Admati et al. 2010). Mandatory higher equity ratios also give them the incentive to do so. Lower leverage implies lower returns on equity, which should lead banks' shareholders to push for higher returns on the bank's portfolio and shift credit towards riskier, but more rewarding ventures that can on average afford higher interest rates and risk premia.[10] Of course, the rates for mortgages, large corporations, and governments would also rise—but credit to these sectors of the economy is currently too cheap, arguably fueling unproductive speculative bubbles rather than productive investment (Bezemer and Hudson 2016). The gradual phasing-in of the proposal would enable banks to use retained profits to increase equity, and portfolio impacts should be closely monitored during the transition. As such, the proposal is justifiable as it serves both private and public interests, while its simplicity satisfies the principles of transparency and neutrality.

Nevertheless, a higher equity ratio across the board is a second-best solution, as it is unable to yield the more diverse banking system we need to cater to the diverse demand for financing in the entrepreneurial society. Traces of diversity in banking are still found in Europe: in Germany, for example, a few very large and highly leveraged banks (e.g., Deutsche Bank and Commerzbank) coexist with many small, often locally operating banks (*Sparkassen*) that operate in different niches. A multitude of small, locally embedded banks survive in Italy as well.[11]

In such situations, there is a risk that minimum equity ratios cause a reduction in diversity that makes the entire system more vulnerable (Haldane and

---

[10] Of course, it is also true that banks' shareholders would like the bank to take on very high risks when leverage is high, especially once the little equity remaining is wiped out but the bank remains liquid (Fox 2010). However, this type of speculation at the expense of depositors is not the kind of productive risk taking we refer to here.

[11] Verdier (2002) gives an excellent historical account of the development of diversity in banking systems across Europe. These historical processes explain how diversity in banking has emerged and hold important lessons on how it can be retained or fostered.

May 2011). A first best approach would, therefore, allow some banks to operate in a low-risk low-return niche with high leverage, while others could opt for a smaller, riskier, and high-yielding portfolio with more equity on their balance sheet. The market, rather than the regulator, would then determine each bank's required equity ratio. This end state is desirable but would require that banks cease the essential public good functions that currently justify and motivate their strong regulation and supervision. Only when the public interest is firmly secured can banks be set free to intermediate the savings they attract as they see fit based on their customers' and financiers' risk-return preferences, with contestability and competition leading to the best business models in a variety of niche markets.

The more diverse and entrepreneurial banking sector envisioned above sits uncomfortably with banks' legally sanctioned ability to attract deposits in current accounts. Due to public guarantees and technological development, these deposits have largely replaced the publicly issued alternative—cash—as the preferred medium of exchange and store of value. Thus, commercial banks finance a substantial part of their balance sheet with the type of monetized debt that has come to circulate in the economy as money.[12] In the wake of the financial crisis, many have questioned banks' prerogative to create money by giving credit, and monetary reform has been proposed for a variety of reasons (e.g., Benes and Kumhof 2012; Vickers Commission 2013; Wolf 2014; Dyson et al. 2016). Our point here is that freeing up the balance sheets of Europe's banking industry just a little would help channel a small share of total savings to young and innovative ventures—a change that could have a huge impact on promoting an entrepreneurial society.

When considering ways to secure public functions while freeing up resources in the banking sector, we believe the introduction of central bank digital currency (CBDC) is the most suitable candidate for exploration.[13] CBDC is a digital form of fiat money that is a currency established as money by government regulation or law; its introduction would provide consumers and firms with a risk-free alternative to bank deposits for transactions and as a store of value (Barrdear and Kumhof 2016; Kumhof and Noone 2018;

---

[12] The share of cash in circulation has been falling in the monetary aggregates of all European countries for decades and has now reached less than 15% of M1 in the Eurozone in 2017 (ECB 2019). The share of cash in transactions, especially among young people, has also fallen below 20% in countries like the Netherlands and Sweden (DNB 2018).

[13] This subject is a matter of debate among central bankers. For example, the IMF's Christine Lagarde (2018) has argued that experiments with CBDC be explored globally. European central banks (e.g., the Bank of England and the Dutch Central Bank) are looking into the issue, and the Swedish Central Bank (Riksbanken 2018) is working towards a field experiment with a digital Krona.

Bordo and Levin 2019). Gradually abandoning the deposit insurance scheme would cause money held for transaction and store-of-value purposes to flow from commercial banks' balance sheets to central banks' balance sheets and force commercial banks to return to a pure intermediation role: borrowing to lend and paying and charging appropriate risk premia. Once the security of citizens' wealth is no longer tied to the survival of their bank, regulators can reduce the strict supervision and regulation of banks' asset side, ushering in increased differentiation and diversity. When available, CDBC provides everybody with a secure alternative for storing wealth and settling transactions, and the need to justify public guarantees for commercial bank deposits disappears. In the absence of such guarantees, commercial banks can revert to investing for their own risk and return. They can therefore be deregulated so that they can take on the important role Schumpeter (1934 [1911]) foresaw for them in the entrepreneurial society: that of selecting viable ventures for investment.

> Proposal 20: Introduce central bank digital currency to replace deposits at commercial banks as the dominant risk-free store of value and medium of exchange.

The implementation of such a fundamental reform close to the heart of the European economy should not be rushed. The operation can be compared in scope and complexity with the introduction of the euro two decades ago and will require a comparable amount of planning and a broad public discussion before it can be implemented. Some technical issues will need to be addressed to realize this proposal, but bitcoin and other cryptocurrencies show that the technology is there for central banks to use. The advantage of CDBC over private cryptocurrencies should be obvious, as central banks are the only party that can guarantee and stabilize the value of a digital currency, eliminating the kind of volatile and speculative trading plaguing private cryptocurrencies. That being said, an implementation of the proposal would be nothing short of a monetary paradigm shift, and such shifts are not to be implemented lightly. However, once completed the reform would also make monetary policy more effective, by (re)establishing a more direct link between the money supply (M1) and the monetary base (M0) (Bordo and Levin 2017). It is therefore encouraging that central banks inside and outside the EU are currently discussing and researching this issue, with several experiments being planned or under way. Such developments will help achieve a more diverse banking sector that can cater to the diverse financial needs of small and large, young, and old firms in Europe to the benefit of entrepreneurial society.[14]

---

[14] With its Capital Markets Union (CMU), the Commission shows a keen awareness of the unintended consequences for entrepreneurial finance stemming from tight regulation (see, e.g., European Commission

Overall, the focus of the discussion in this section has been on creating a situation in which banks and institutional investors can responsibly intermediate funds, directing more of Europe's savings to deserving new ventures without jeopardizing the stability of the system. If banks are to play a role in the financing of tomorrow's firms, they should perhaps (be forced to) withdraw from also providing our medium of exchange, as the two activities seem incompatible. Modern technology offers the opportunity to rebalance public and private interests in the banking sector and correct this apparent flaw in our current financial system. But new technology also allows for alternatives to banking altogether. We now turn to a discussion of such "alternative finance."

### 4.2.4 Experimenting with New Technology to Finance Venturing in All Stages

Alternative modes of financing are on the rise as sources of entrepreneurial funding (Bruton et al. 2015; Vulkan et al. 2016; Block et al. 2018). Notably, today's small firms can access large pools of financial resources through crowdfunding and peer-to-business platforms, which are characterized by many small investments adding up to a large and growing total. Modern platform technology can even decentralize informal finance and help entrepreneurs, especially in business-to-consumer markets, to combine finance, marketing, and sales. Evidence from London's equity crowdfunding scene suggests that (regulated and well-managed) alternative finance helps to address the entrepreneurial equity gap and bridge the infamous "valley of death" in venture finance (Estrin et al. 2018; cf. Frank et al. 1996; Auerswald and Branscomb 2003), especially in new sectors (Polzin 2017). For these benefits to materialize, it is essential that regulators and supervisors resist their instinct to protect small-scale investors. One cannot regulate equity crowdfunding with the goal of eliminating all risks involved. Taking on risk is an essential part of such activities.

> Proposal 21: Implement a light-touch regulatory regime for equity crowdfunding and peer-to-business lending.

Vigilance on this matter is well founded: German regulation (the *Kleinanlegergesetz*) recently threatened to limit crowdfunding for real estate

---

2017b). The CMU pushes for a European venture capital market and considers passporting for FinTech firms, which could help yield a level playing field between entrants and incumbents.

investments and was averted only at the last moment (Crowdfunding Insider 2017). While its proponents typically cite stability, investor protection, and other seemingly compelling reasons, restrictive regulation risks preventing valuable services from emerging in the first place. In our view, a regime of tight supervision but loose regulation, akin to the one implemented in the UK, would better encourage experimentation with this new form of finance. Peer-to-business lending warrants a similar approach, especially considering that it proved to be an important buffer against the impact of the financial crisis in countries where it existed (Mills and McCarthy 2014).

Moreover, these systems of alternative finance benefit entrepreneurial start-ups more than they do large, incumbent firms and corporate groups. Crowdfunding platforms are better than traditional finance channels at handling smaller ticket investments (Polzin et al. 2017). They also reduce opacity and information asymmetry because their open character generates access to valuable information in addition to handling financial resources (Polzin et al. 2018b; Toxopeus 2019).

The principle of neutrality warns against using public funding for entrepreneurial finance: administrative procedures to allocate funding risk being gamed or biased against exactly the type of players that such programs intend to support. That said, the decentralized decision characteristics of crowd financing can be a useful tool for improving access to public funding for small, innovative ventures (Hervé and Schwienbacher 2018). Such financing could, for example, be beneficial for the Juncker Fund, a high-profile public funding scheme that has been criticized for emphasizing "shovel-ready" projects over smaller, more risky, innovative ventures (Schneider 2015b).

> Proposal 22: As part of its efforts to allocate the Juncker Fund, the European Investment Bank could experiment with a euro-denominated European crowdfunding platform and match successful campaigns with public funds.

Member states and local authorities running similar national and local support schemes could adopt this proposal's logic as well. It fits well under the neutrality principle, given that projects in the platforms compete on a level playing field that is not biased against small, risky, and radically innovative projects.

## 4.3   Summary

The financial system plays a central role in any modern economy; its primary functions include the efficient allocation of available savings and the provision of a secure payment system. In Europe, this system is bank-dominated and

**Table 4.2** Summary of proposals regarding savings, capital, and finance, specifying the level in the governance hierarchy where the necessary decisions should be made

| No. | Principle(s) | Policy area | Proposal | Policy level[a] |
|---|---|---|---|---|
| 13 | Neutrality and transparency | Private wealth | Allow for more wealth to accumulate and remain in private hands and make it possible, easy, and attractive to invest such wealth in entrepreneurial ventures. | MS, REG, LOC |
| 14 | Neutrality and justifiability | Pension funds | Allow people to choose how and where to invest part of their pension savings individually. | EU, MS |
| 15 | Neutrality and justifiability | Pension funds | Pension funds and other institutional investors should, on an experimental basis, be allowed to invest more in equity in general and in venture capital specifically. | EU, MS |
| 16 | Neutrality and justifiability | VC | Develop competencies for private equity and venture capital investment in the field and avoid promoting VC capital with public funding directly. | MS, REG, LOC |
| 17 | Neutrality | VC | Reduce barriers to the sale, acquisition, and IPO of VC-funded start-ups to facilitate profitable exits. | EU, MS |
| 18 | Neutrality and transparency | Banks | Ensure that (appropriately anonymized) credit decision information becomes publicly available in the system of bank loan guarantees for start-ups. | MS, REG |
| 19 | Neutrality and justifiability | Banks | Increase the mandatory equity ratio in banking gradually to 10–15% to allow them to take on more risk responsibly in their lending portfolios. | EU |
| 20 | Neutrality and justifiability | Banks | Introduce central bank digital currency to replace deposits at commercial banks as the dominant medium of exchange. | EU, MS |
| 21 | Neutrality | FinTech | Implement a light-touch regulatory regime for equity crowdfunding and peer-to-business lending. | EU, MS |
| 22 | Neutrality and transparency | FinTech | As part of its efforts to allocate the Juncker Fund, the European Investment Bank could experiment with a euro-denominated European crowdfunding platform and match successful campaigns with public funds. | EU |

[a]*EU* federal level, *MS* member state level, *REG* regional government level, *LOC* local/municipal level

heavily institutionalized, with tight regulation and economies of scale conspiring to bias access to financial resources against small, young, and rapidly growing businesses. Since adequate capitalization in the early stages of development is a major driver of venture survival and success, the proposals in this section attempt to rebalance the financial sector. They do so, on one hand, by preventing resources from being "institutionalized" in the first place and freeing them up once they are; on the other hand, the proposals develop and facilitate the evolution of alternative channels that have proven effective in the USA and hold promise for Europe as well. Table 4.2 provides a summary of our proposals and the level(s) of the governance hierarchy at which political action should take place to make them a reality.

# 5

# Labor Markets and Social Security in the Entrepreneurial Society

## 5.1 General Principles

A necessary condition for the long-term success of a new venture is that the entrepreneur can recruit key personnel at the opportune time to scale up the business to a full-grown firm (Eliasson 1996; Elert and Henrekson 2019). While new ventures are free to offer jobs and recruit workers as they see fit, they do not compete for the talent they need on a level playing field. Unlike other inputs in the production process, employing labor typically comes with responsibilities that go beyond paying a competitive wage—responsibilities that may be particularly hard for new ventures to shoulder. Such issues make access to key personnel more constrained than it need be, to the detriment of the workings of collaborative innovation blocs.

Because labor is a critical input in all economic activities, we propose neutrality as a first principle to guide reforms in this area. In this context, the neutrality principle refers to equal access, i.e., that employers can compete for workers and employees can compete for jobs based on the relevant characteristics of the job and the potential recruits. Moreover, employees should be free to move from one job to the next, just as employers should be free to adjust the labor force to the needs of their venture (subject to rules guaranteeing that any dismissal of redundant or allegedly underperforming workers follows a fair and transparent procedure). Only when both sides have this flexibility can the matching in labor markets promote an entrepreneurial society.

As labor constitutes the primary source of income in a market-based economy, it is not surprising that employees greatly value security, stability, and equitable distribution. While these values are valid, they also imply that an

© The Author(s) 2019
N. Elert et al., *The Entrepreneurial Society*, International Studies in Entrepreneurship 98,
https://doi.org/10.1007/978-3-662-59586-2_5

efficient labor market matching of the kind just envisioned is far from the most important criterion used by Europeans to assess labor markets and social security institutions. When proposing reforms to labor and social security arrangements, we must carefully weigh and balance these values so that our proposals conform to the principle of justifiability.

Carefully separating individual and collective responsibilities is the best way to achieve this balance. Basic social security is a collective responsibility best organized through moderate universal arrangements that do not unduly reduce flexibility for employers or mobility for employees. Individual employers will then reward merit, and employees will invest in talent, ensuring a reasonably efficient wage structure that is also fair.[1] If enacted, the proposed reforms would increase the mobility of workers and flexibility for employers by removing onerous labor market regulations while providing the social security system with much needed risk pooling for the risks all individuals face but cannot manage individually.

The incentives that encourage activation, mobility, and risk-taking are best served by universal insurance systems that disregard labor market status, history, or attachment. These institutions should, therefore, ensure portability of tenure rights and pension plans as well as a full decoupling of health insurance from current employers. Such measures would avoid punishing individuals who leave secure, tenured employment positions and pursue entrepreneurial projects, whether as entrepreneurs or as employees in entrepreneurial start-ups. Finally, the extent to which these risks are collectively insured should be moderate, and systems should be kept simple to achieve the salience necessary for people to act rationally and avoid costs from spiraling out of control.

The EU has limited competencies for implementing reforms pertaining to labor markets and social security systems, which is logical given that the same reforms can be expected to work out quite differently in different contexts.[2] Thus, we primarily address the following proposals to the member states (cf. Suse and Hachez 2017, p. 49).

---

[1] To be sure, what is considered fair is highly context dependent and remains an open question (e.g., Binmore 2005). We propose here that a fair income distribution enables everyone to have a universal social minimum living standard while rewarding people for effort and merit. Ultimately, these outcomes result from ongoing political and bargaining processes, which, in turn, depend on productivity differences emerging across the labor market. In this chapter, we focus on ways to make portable those claims, benefits, and services that are best provided universally, such that these considerations do not drive and bias the allocation of labor.

[2] Here, the only legislative competencies in the treaties are those intended to ensure mobility of worker rights across member states (e.g., Article 153(2)(b) TFEU). In practice, this may give the Union some legislative power because rights that are not portable across employers are often also not portable across national borders.

## 5.2   Proposals

We begin this section by presenting our analysis and proposals relating to employment protection regulations. This is followed by our analysis and proposals with respect to social security.

### 5.2.1   Employment Protection Legislation

Figure 5.1 shows the stringency of employment protection legislation (EPL) in the EU countries and the USA for temporary and permanent contracts. While the Anglo-Saxon countries have the least stringent employment protection by far within the EU, most other countries have liberalized their legislation for temporary employment considerably in recent decades (Skedinger 2010; Martin and Scarpetta 2012). Sweden and Germany stand out for their substantial liberalization of temporary contracts over the past 20 years; notably, these are two of the top-performing EU countries in terms of employment. Arguably, this has to do with their high shares of temporary employment

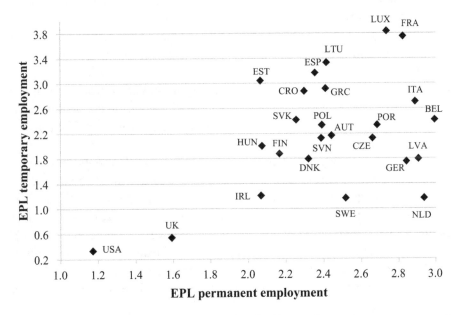

**Fig. 5.1**  Stringency of employment protection legislation for workers on permanent and temporary contracts in EU countries and the USA, 2013. Note: The scale of the index is 0–6, where 6 represents the most stringent regulation. 2013 is the latest available year. The index for permanent employment is the index for individual and collective dismissals. Source: OECD/IAB Employment Protection Database, 2013

(OECD 2016a). In 2017, employment through temporary contracts constituted 22.2 and 13.8% of total employment in Germany and Sweden, respectively (OECD 2019b).[3]

Figure 5.1 also reveals considerable gaps between temporary and permanent employment; for example, the Netherlands ranks 2nd for permanent and 26th for temporary contract protection out of 33 OECD countries (OECD 2013). Such discrepancies may have some logic to them: policymakers may see tight labor protection for permanent employees as necessary to maintain high levels of firm-specific human capital (Adnett et al. 2004) yet prefer temporary work over unemployment when it serves as a stepping stone to permanent contracts (Scherer 2004; Gash 2008). Nonetheless, the widening gap has caused concern about the emergence of dual labor markets (Gebel 2010; Hirsch 2016a; Dolado 2016). While it is true that this constellation allows employers to retain a fixed core of competencies while adjusting the size of their labor force to demand fluctuations at low costs, the productivity of the jobs created remains low (Kleinknecht et al. 2006). Moreover, the disparity implies that government-enforced regulation tilts the playing field against entrepreneurial ventures: the greater the disparity between temporary and permanent contracts, the greater the opportunity cost for an employee on a permanent contract of accepting a job in a high-risk firm.

Interestingly, all Eastern European countries have increased the stringency of their legislation related to temporary contracts. Without implying direct and strong causality here, we take note of their generally weak employment performance, especially among the more populous Eastern European member states Poland and Romania (see Fig. 1.1). Overall, legislation concerning both types of contracts remains strict in most Mediterranean and Continental European countries.

To mitigate the adverse effects of overly stringent EPL, policymakers in many European countries have instituted firm-size thresholds below which regulations are more relaxed. In practice, however, the threshold is the equivalent of a tax on firm growth and has been shown to incentivize firms to remain small in, e.g., Germany (Autio et al. 2007), France (Garicano et al. 2016), Portugal (Braguinsky et al. 2011), and Italy (Schivardi and Torrini 2008). Discouraged by such thresholds, many entrepreneurs never discover whether they could have become high-impact entrepreneurs. More generally, there is a

---

[3] In the absence of controlled experiments it is hard to firmly establish causality from such correlations and some have suggested alternative explanations for the data (e.g., Kahn 2009). Germany also allowed for wider wage dispersion and Sweden implemented several other reforms as well. These changes may have contributed to employment growth in these countries.

negative relationship between the overall strictness of EPL and the rate of high-growth expectation early-stage entrepreneurship (the percentage of individuals engaged in entrepreneurial activity who expect their firms to grow to employ at least five employees within 5 years), as seen in Fig. 5.2.

If the EU is to become more inclusive, innovative, and entrepreneurial, its most regulated countries should reduce the stringency of their EPL for permanent contracts. Competently implemented liberalization would reduce job security but increase employment security for workers because it would increase labor demand and result in the creation of more labor market opportunities.

Proposal 23: Relax the stringency of employment protection legislation for permanent contracts.

That said, the impact and strictness of EPL depend on a complex combination of components, such as grounds for individual dismissal, redundancy procedures, mandated periods of advanced notice, severance payments, special

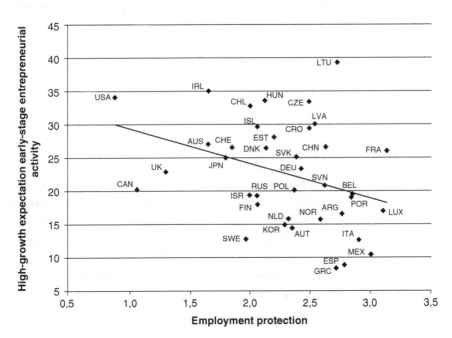

**Fig. 5.2** The strictness of employment protection, 2013, and high-growth expectation early-stage entrepreneurial activity, 2015–2018. Note: High-growth expectation early-stage entrepreneurial activity is averaged over the 4 years 2015–2018. Permanent EPL is given a weight of 2/3 and temporary EPL a weight of 1/3. Sources: Global Entrepreneurship Monitor and OECD/IAB Employment Protection Database, 2013 update

requirements for collective dismissals, and rules favoring disadvantaged groups. For liberalization to produce the desired results, countries must consider and possibly emulate the paths already explored in similar countries. As we shall argue below, such a strategy also presupposes the implementation of complementary social insurance institutions.

A relatively simple way for policymakers to make the labor supply more flexible and responsive to the needs of entrepreneurs would be to give workers and employers more freedom to contract on working hours. Such freedom should apply to weekly and daily hours, holiday, overtime, and irregular hours, for which the EU and its member states have implemented detailed and stringent minimum standards (e.g., European Union 2018b; Messenger et al. 2007).

> Proposal 24: Allow for more flexibility in working hours by reconsidering overly stringent minimum requirements for daily and weekly working hours, holidays, irregular hours, and overtime.

Policymakers should also strive to promote worker mobility across jobs, industries, and regions. Notably, confidentiality agreements and non-compete clauses often prevent knowledge from flowing freely between firms and sectors. The fact that non-compete clauses are not allowed in California (as opposed to, say, Texas) is seen as an important element in the development of the golden state's highly successful entrepreneurial ecosystem (Gilson 1999).[4]

> Proposal 25: Lift the legal enforceability of confidentiality agreements between employers and their employees.

Finally, it would be beneficial to reduce job tenure-related wage scales and severance pay; these insider benefits tend to lock people into their current job and shift bargaining power in the labor market to large, incumbent employers (Lindbeck and Snower 2001; Eichhorst et al. 2017). However, before employment protection and job security can be reformed, it is wise to put in place a social security system that empowers (all) workers vis-à-vis their employers by creating a robust fallback option.

---

[4] Marx et al. (2009) further highlight the importance of non-compete clauses: Examining Michigan's 1985 reversal of its non-compete enforcement policy, they find that this weakened worker mobility, especially for inventors with firm-specific skills and specialists in narrow technical fields.

## 5.2.2   Social Insurance Systems

In principle, providing insurance for the usual social risks (loss of income due to unemployment, illness, disability or old age, and high medical, child care, or educational expenses) enables individuals to consider and pursue entrepreneurial endeavors by mitigating the burden of uncertainty. Social security systems still vary a great deal across Europe,[5] but the design features of these systems are more relevant than their overall levels and generosity. As Sinn (1996) argues, when insurance is closely linked to tenure in a specific job, it does not promote an entrepreneurial spirit. What matters for the individual is the opportunity cost, i.e., how much an employee who transfers to self-employment or a risky job in an entrepreneurial firm has to sacrifice in terms of income and security. If there are no public or collective insurance schemes, these costs can be prohibitive. Company-specific health insurance plans, as are common in the USA, are an obvious example; another is accumulated pension assets that are difficult to transfer when switching employers, industries, or countries of residence. If policymakers decoupled these and other benefits from the current employer–employee relationship, they would increase labor mobility and eliminate the competitive advantage held by large mature companies in attracting and retaining talent.

> Proposal 26: Guarantee equal access to welfare state arrangements for all, regardless of tenure in a specific job or labor market status.

An important role model in this respect can be Denmark's flexicurity system, which combines generous welfare protection and opportunities for retraining with weak job security mandates (Andersen 2005). Danish employees lose little when they switch employers or labor market status, making Danish talent available on equal terms for entrepreneurial firms (Bredgaard 2013). By contrast, a Swedish employee who voluntarily gives up a tenured position for self-employment typically has no more security than what is provided by (means-tested) social welfare. Thus, the opportunity cost of giving up a tenured position in Denmark is substantially lower than in Sweden.

EU member states should embrace the general principles of flexicurity, which can be summarized as flexible and reliable contractual arrangements, comprehensive lifelong learning strategies, effective active labor market

---

[5] As shown in Fig. A.2 in the Appendix, replacement rates for unemployment insurance, for example, vary a great deal among European countries. It should also be noted that irrespective of duration and family constellations the USA is invariably found at or close to the bottom of the ranking.

policies, and modern social security systems providing adequate income support during transitions (European Commission 2007). However, while the general principles of flexicurity are almost invariably met with approval by policymakers at the EU level, the devil is in the details: member states should carefully consider the impact of flexicurity reforms on young SMEs. We stress this last point as it is politically convenient and often tempting for policymakers to shift the burden of administration and risks in lifelong learning strategies onto employers, whether through sectoral training funds or by giving employers the responsibility to invest in the employability of their workers (Vermeylen 2008; Verdier 2009). Unions will push for such measures on behalf of their members, while large firms will typically not resist them. However, such responsibilities are more burdensome for small employers and it is better to leave such responsibilities with the employee when this is possible and collectivize them at the sectoral or national level where necessary. As small and especially not-yet-existing employers have a harder time lobbying for their joint interests, politicians must resist the tendency to make individual employers responsible for the employability of their workers. Flexicurity reforms should decouple the protection of employees from their employer so as not to tilt the playing field more against entrepreneurial ventures.

Proposal 27: Carefully consider the impact of flexicurity reforms on young firms and do not force them to take on excessive risks and burdens.

Behavioral biases are known to cause adverse selection and the underinsurance of risks. Basic risks in the labor market are therefore best covered by collective and mandatory insurance, ensuring that employees do not compete on social insurance coverage in a race to the bottom. That said, employers should be allowed to offer complementary pension plans as long as the accumulated assets are fully portable when employees switch employers or become self-employed.

Proposal 28: Introduce mandatory universal insurance to cover healthcare costs, old age, and disability.

Making such insurance mandatory prevents adverse selection problems; making them universal prevents unproductive compartmentalization in the labor market and ensures full portability of entitlements. The Dutch system for health care costs may be a role model here: though mandatory, it allows insurance companies to compete for patients (Maarse et al. 2016). Crucially, the design of such systems should ensure that competition focuses on price and avoids causing a race to the bottom in quality or coverage. In the Dutch case, detailed product specifications are set by law, and insurers must accept all patients. However, they can and do compete on brand loyalty; although 4–7% of consumers indicate that they intend to switch providers every year, fewer turn this intention into reality (Schut et al. 2013). As a result, insurers can extract significant rents from the human tendency to prefer the status quo. Employers collectively bargaining on behalf of their employees have even created a closer link between current employment and health benefits than existed previously.[6] Possibly, allowing insurance companies to bid for collective blocks of insurance policies would lessen the need to advertise, whereas adequately designed closed-bid auctions may keep prices and costs at a reasonably low level.

A core aim in this reform area should be to make the individual's social benefits independent of tenure at an employer—regardless of whether the insurance is public, paid by the individual herself, or paid by the employer based on individual or collective agreement. Tenure often plays a role in unemployment benefit entitlements and disability insurance. Unemployment benefits insure against the involuntary loss of income, but when someone switches into or out of self-employment or between jobs, the counter is often reset, reducing both the duration and the benefit level in the case of a new unemployment spell. With disability, benefits are often made dependent on the level of income and tenure in the job held at the time the disability occurs; the risk of losing these entitlements prevents beneficiaries from moving into other occupations or sectors.

One example of how to achieve full portability is the Austrian reform of 2003, which converted uncertain firing costs for employers into a system of individual savings accounts funded by a payroll tax (Hofer 2007). The system guarantees the employer who hires someone certainty about the cost of any future dismissal, while workers do not lose their entitlement to severance pay should they decide to quit and take a new job. Similar measures could also make unemployment benefit entitlements and disability insurance portable.

Proposal 29: Ensure full portability of social security entitlements by making them independent of tenure at a specific employer.

This proposal is highly relevant for a country such as Germany, where labor market mobility is low, geographically (Niebuhr et al. 2012; Bentivogli and Pagano 1999), occupationally (Korpi and Mertens 2003; König and Müller

---

[6] These collective policies on average are between 3 and 10% cheaper and there are some 56,000 of which 60% are by employers, also SMEs. See, e.g., Commissie Evaluatie Risicoverevening ZVW (2012).

1986), within firms (Fitzenberger et al. 2015), and across industries (Gangl 2003; Bachmann and Burda 2010). In part, the low mobility may be a result of Germany's "orderly" educational system, which sets people on a highly predictable career path. Linking social security entitlements to job tenure is then perhaps a consequence of, as much as a cause for, immobility. Under such circumstances, any portability reform would have to be accompanied by reforms in the educational system to be effective.

Furthermore, it should be evident that complexity and opacity in social security systems make both beneficiaries and employees risk averse, reducing the attractiveness of any nonstandard labor market offerings. Such corrosion is perhaps inevitable over time, but as with the tax system, an occasional redesign of the social security system from the ground up could enhance transparency and neutrality. One form that such a reboot could take in European welfare states would be the introduction of a universal negative income tax system. Such a reform provides the system with an unconditional floor on which policymakers can build more detailed and complicated structures.

Proposal 30: Investigate the possibility of establishing a modest but unconditional floor in the social security system through a negative income tax system.

The main benefit of a negative income tax scheme would be to reduce the need to reform current welfare state arrangements to create access for self-employed and freelance workers who, though hard to classify, will make up a growing share of the labor force in an entrepreneurial society (Noorderhaven et al. 2004; Hatfield 2015). Once more, this reform would constitute a fundamental paradigm shift in providing social security benefits and will involve careful long-term planning, small scale experimentation, and step-by-step implementation to ensure success. But once a basic level for a decent living is provided collectively, other features of the system—unemployment benefits, disability and sickness insurance, child care, educational allowances, and pension schemes—go from being peoples' only source of income and support to being add-ons that can arguably be left (more) to private or collective initiatives and self-insurance. With the universal basic level to fall back on, entrepreneurs and self-employed individuals will not need expensive insurance for temporary involuntary unemployment or illness. As such, the guarantee enables them to compete on quality and not on their ability to self-insure such risks. This may be helpful both for R&D workers wishing to start innovative high-tech ventures and for the growing army of everyday entrepreneurs that are important in an entrepreneurial society (Welter et al. 2017).

That said, the results from the Finnish basic income experiment have been mixed. While the experiment seems to have made participants happier and less stressed, it did not achieve the intended effect of giving people more incentives to find work than the traditional system (Meyer 2019). More generally, there is a risk that a negative income tax may encourage activity in the informal economy, which, as mentioned, is already a major concern in Southern and Eastern Europe. Maintaining a low floor will also become increasingly difficult as time goes by and politicians are tempted to try to buy votes. Overall, such a system is probably only viable in countries with low corruption and high tax compliance; only then will the institutional environment be robust against the corrosive effects and the inevitable incentives to game the system.

Investing in the ability of people to rejoin the labor market soon after losing a job is better than income insurance in case of joblessness. To prepare people for the new labor market, an efficient flexicurity model must encourage the retraining of redundant workers, preferably in the dual sense that training should be a right and a mandatory responsibility.

Proposal 31: Establish or strengthen retraining programs to prepare workers for new occupations.

The proposal falls under the broader heading of active labor market policies commonly advocated for and implemented throughout the EU (European Commission 2018b). Job creation and destruction are relatively high in a country such as the UK, and small firms are disproportionately responsible for this. The implication is that employees in a more entrepreneurial society need to be equipped with the skills necessary to switch jobs and employers (Hijzen et al. 2010). As neither government agencies nor private providers have proven effective in retraining workers, local and regional governments should think carefully about how to organize these programs. Because training works best when people are motivated (Fouarge et al. 2013), the impact of such programs is probably the greatest if trainers can motivate, convince, and help people to help themselves.

## 5.3   Summary

The labor market allocates scarce labor resources in the economy while providing most people with their main source of income. Because the administrative burden and the insurance of social risks by employers fall disproportionately on small and young firms, reforms should aim for moderate universal social insurance and transparent and straightforward systems. The full portability of entitlements and flexible employment contracts would create a more level playing field in the competition for labor, given that young, innovative firms can seldom offer long and secure tenure. Flexibility measures would also be justifiable when they balance the collective interests of social security and fair income distribution with the private interest of fair compensation for merit and the efficient matching of people to jobs.

Table 5.1 provides a summary of our proposals regarding labor markets and social security, specifying the level in the governance hierarchy that should make the necessary decisions. The institutions in this area are typically highly country-specific, path-dependent, and complementary, meaning that policymakers must carefully fit them to local contexts when implementing reforms. The competencies for doing so are limited at the EU level, but this is probably not to be lamented; the diverse varieties of capitalism in Europe mean that the same reforms can be expected to work out quite differently in different contexts, and reforms are more urgent in some member states than in others.

Although the articles in the various treaties are not intended to give the Union a say over the level, shape, or form of member states' labor market institutions, the EU has many soft instruments available to coordinate and inform. As the institutional arrangements in the labor market and social security operate at the national level, there is also little scope for regional and local policymaking in this area, even if some member states have at times decentralized the execution of the programs. For these reasons, we address most of the proposals primarily at the member state level, where reforms following our general principles need careful fitting to the specific national context to achieve their aims.

Proposals on social security and labor market regulation all aim to mobilize Europe's most knowledgeable and valuable employees. The portability of social security entitlements across jobs, sectors, and labor market statuses will eliminate the lock-in of skilled labor in gilded jobs and reduce the barriers for employers. As such, they would create a level playing field for start-ups on the demand side and for marginalized groups in the labor market on the supply side. Creating a level playing field will also entail forcing the self-employed to join collective social insurance, e.g., for pension and health costs. This will make growth in Europe more inclusive, equitable, and innovation driven.

**Table 5.1** Summary of proposals regarding labor markets and social security, specifying the level in the governance hierarchy where the necessary decisions should be made

| No. | Principle(s) | Policy area | Proposal | Policy level[a] |
|---|---|---|---|---|
| 23 | Neutrality and transparency | Employment protection | Relax the stringency of employment protection legislation for permanent contracts. | MS |
| 24 | Neutrality | Employment protection | Allow for more flexibility in working hours by reconsidering overly stringent minimum requirements for daily and weekly working hours, holidays, irregular hours, and overtime. | EU |
| 25 | Neutrality and transparency | Employment protection | Lift the legal enforceability of confidentiality agreements between employers and their employees. | EU, MS |
| 26 | Neutrality | Social security | Guarantee equal access to welfare state arrangements for all, regardless of tenure in a specific job or labor market status. | EU, MS |
| 27 | Neutrality and transparency | Social security | Carefully consider the impact of flexicurity reforms on young firms and do not force them to take on excessive risks and burdens. | MS |
| 28 | Transparency and justifiability | Social security | Introduce mandatory universal insurance to cover healthcare costs, old age, and disability. | MS |
| 29 | Neutrality | Social security | Ensure full portability of social security entitlements by making them independent of tenure at a specific employer. | EU, MS |
| 30 | Neutrality and moderation | Social security | Investigate the possibility of establishing a modest but unconditional floor in the social security system through a negative income tax system. | EU, MS |
| 31 | Neutrality | Active labor market policy | Establish or strengthen training programs to prepare workers for new occupations. | EU, MS, REG, LOC |

[a]*EU* federal level, *MS* member state level, *REG* regional government level, *LOC* local/municipal level

# 6

# Contestable Markets for Entry and Exit

## 6.1 General Principles

In his 2011 book, *Adapt: Why Success Always Starts with Failure*, economist Tim Harford highlights three core tenets central to individuals or societies striving to "learn from failure." The first is the importance of *variability*. In the market, this occurs when firms are heterogeneous and dispersed throughout the economy and differ with respect to size, age, technology, and so forth. As no one can know a priori which business models will be successful, there is a need for a large number of different experiments (Audretsch and Fritsch 2002; Metcalfe 2010). Second, as numerous experiments will inevitably fail, they should be conducted on a sufficiently small scale so that the system as a whole will survive such failure. This *survival* emerges in the market because all entrepreneurs select the strategy, technology, behavior, and organizational structure they believe could help them outcompete their rivals (Eliasson 1996; Dosi and Nelson 2010; Vivarelli 2013). Finally, Harford (2011) stresses the importance of *selection*, i.e., that successful experiments be pursued and copied, while unsuccessful ones are identified and quickly terminated. The profit and loss signals conveyed through prices and driven by market competition combine to form an imperfect but crucial selection mechanism. Prices encourage agents to devote resources to their most highly valued use (Hayek 1945), enabling successful firms to survive and grow, while unsuccessful firms exit (Dosi and Nelson 2010). Progress in an entrepreneurial society is not the aim but the result of this evolutionary process, which can only be expected to work if the institutions underpinning the market indeed ensure variability, survival, and selection.

© The Author(s) 2019
N. Elert et al., *The Entrepreneurial Society*, International Studies in Entrepreneurship 98,
https://doi.org/10.1007/978-3-662-59586-2_6

In this chapter, we address the related policy areas of market regulation, competition policy, and bankruptcy policy. The principles guiding reforms are threefold: contestability, transparency, and justifiability. Contestability here refers to openness to innovation and challengers, which is crucial to markets but also relevant to the soundness of individual firms, bureaucratic organizations, and a host of other contexts; put simply, the system will progress only if it allows better ideas to drive out inferior ones. Furthermore, contestability is most effective when the rules of the game are well defined and guided by transparency: only under this principle can we ensure that potential challengers know what to expect—and what not to expect—when entering a competitive situation.

To safeguard contestability, policymakers must keep incumbent lobbyists at arm's length and refuse their attempts to coauthor the standards, rules, and regulations of their industry. That said, policymakers also have a responsibility to ensure that the challengers' interests are balanced against those of their financiers, employees, customers, and other stakeholders, ensuring that a competitive edge is justifiable and does not come at the cost of the public interest. When they govern markets, these principles help limit the resources that are wasted on losing and flawed projects (Type 1 error) while also avoiding the imposition of undue constraints on winners and successful projects (Type 2 error).

The EU enjoys far-reaching competencies for market regulation, competition policy, and bankruptcy policy.[1] In addition to opening up markets by enforcing Treaty provisions on the free movement of goods and services and the freedom of establishment, the Commission may order member states to remove legislative and regulatory restrictions on the movement of goods and services and the right of establishment. That said, member states do retain significant regulatory power (Suse and Hachez 2017, p. 63).[2] Both cooperation in civil matters and the regulation of the internal market are shared competencies, meaning that the EU and its member states jointly shape national bankruptcy and insolvency laws. Furthermore, member states have some room to maneuver where aspects of EU law are subject to minimum standards

---

[1] While the power to regulate the internal market is a shared competence (Article 4(2)(a) TFEU), competition policy is an exclusive Union competence (Article 3(1)(b) TFEU)—to the extent that the anticompetitive conduct has cross-border effects (Articles 101, 102, and 107 TFEU).

[2] First, there is room for deviating from the Treaty rules for purposes of advancing overriding public policy objectives. Second, the power to regulate the internal market is a shared competence: member states retain the power to regulate particular aspects of their markets to the extent that EU law does not already apply. Third, national competition laws apply whenever anti-competitive conduct lacks cross-border effects.

established by a directive (Suse and Hachez 2017, p. 66).[3] For these reasons, we address all proposals in this chapter to the EU and its member states.

## 6.2   Proposals

### 6.2.1   Regulations of Goods and Service Markets

While environmental, health, safety, and quality regulations are often well motivated and well intended, they can be abused by incumbents to limit entry and competition. It is therefore vital that such regulation is clear, transparent, and neutrally formulated to ensure that new, alternative ways of doing old and new things are permitted. Excessive reliance on rules and procedures discourages potential entrepreneurs and hampers the process of creative destruction, but uncertainty and the absence of clear regulation can be equally damaging.

As a principle, contestability entails preventing market-leading incumbents from building and exploiting a dominant market position by unduly restricting market entry. To this end, low entry barriers are crucial, as is the opening of industries and markets that have thus far barred outside challengers. Within a system characterized by goal-oriented rules, regulations, and public financing, there should be ample room for commercial and cooperative initiatives that challenge the status quo. As a first precondition for contestability, it should be easy and cheap to formally start a venture.[4]

> Proposal 32: Excessive barriers to new business formation and new entry should be lifted where possible.

This proposal may have different implications in different countries: in Italy, for example, "excessive" is the operative word, as Italian firm founders report a wide variety of bureaucratic and administrative barriers to starting up a venture. Italy ranks 51st in the World Bank's ease of doing business ranking, scoring particularly poorly in terms of ease of paying taxes, obtaining credit,

---

[3] The EU has no explicit legal basis in the Treaties to adopt bankruptcy and insolvency legislation. However, the provisions of Article 81 of the TFEU, on judicial cooperation in civil matters, and the harmonization clauses in Articles 114 and 115, may serve as legal bases for enacting EU law in this area.

[4] Figure A.3 in the Appendix shows how the EU countries compare with respect to the ease of starting a business relative to the USA and New Zealand, which are the leading countries. Countries such as Germany, Austria, and Malta show considerable room for improvement, while the western EU countries have high overall scores on this measure. Apart from Poland and the Czech Republic, this is also the case for the Eastern European countries.

and enforcing contracts (World Bank 2018). There is also room for improvement in Germany, which ranks on par with Georgia in the ease of starting a business, with founders perceiving bureaucracy and regulation as barriers to business formation (Sanders et al. 2018b). Austria, Poland, and the Czech and Slovak Republics find themselves in similarly dire positions (World Bank 2018).

An entry barrier warranting special attention is occupational licensing, which was originally intended to ensure the quality of services that consumers are unable to determine themselves. In theory, the license indicates that the provider is capable and abides by the rules, ensuring a minimum quality level of the service. In practice, however, occupational licensing often results in unjustified profit opportunities for license holders and abuse of market power, rather than consumer protection. Today, Europe's regulated professions involve more than 50 million people or 22% of total employment (European Commission 2015a; Koumenta and Pagliero 2017). Evidence from the USA and the EU shows that such regulation has a significant impact on prices and labor mobility, while little to no evidence supports the claim that quality is higher (Kleiner 2000; Kleiner and Krueger 2010, 2013; Johnson and Kleiner 2017; Koumenta and Pagliero 2017; Bowblis and Smith 2018; Barrios 2018). It seems that such protection no longer serves its original purpose: according to the European Commission (2015a, p. 7), "many of these regulations are now disproportionate and create unnecessary regulatory obstacles to the mobility of professionals, lowering productivity" (cf. Erixon and Weigel 2016).

The Services Directive and the Professional Qualifications Directive[5] give the Commission extensive competencies concerning occupational licensing, and a rigorous process of evaluation of regulated professions has been put in place as part of the European Semester. Member states have implemented reforms and opened up such professions, ushering in more jobs and lower prices while maintaining service quality (Koumenta and Humphris 2015; Pagliero 2015; Athanassiou et al. 2015). Thus far, the Commission has devoted its liberalization attempts to occupations such as civil engineers, architects, accountants, lawyers, real estate agents, tourist guides, and patent agents (European Commission 2015a), but a list of some 6468 regulated occupations is under systematic review (European Commission 2019a).

---

[5] Directive 2005/36/EC, recently amended by Directive 2013/55/EC.

Occupational licenses imply that contestability is curtailed.[6] They keep challengers out and lock incumbents in, thereby reducing allocative efficiency and innovation. These consequences directly affect the flow of labor into and out of new ventures. Recognizing that occupational licensing is already on the EU policy agenda, we propose, in line with all three principles above:

> Proposal 33: Create transparent and open systems of occupational certification, such that people can easily move across occupations and in and out of new ventures.

Product market reform is the second ingredient in the European integration effort; European policymakers consider similar product market regulations in all EU countries to be necessary to transform the EU into a single market. Despite several rounds of deregulation, however, member states still exhibit substantial differences in the extent of their product market regulations. Differences in service sector regulations are still larger. As Fig. 6.1 shows, the two measures are strongly correlated; countries with highly regulated product markets tend to have strictly regulated service markets as well. Arguably, reducing this complexity and opacity is easier said than done because policymakers typically allow lobbyists and incumbents to influence the process. Granted, one should not ignore the genuine interests of incumbents offhand; they often provide valuable technical know-how and facilitate the adoption of new standards and regulation. Nonetheless, a more detailed and complex system should be avoided because it works in incumbents' favor vis-à-vis potential challengers, running counter to the principles of contestability and justifiability.

> Proposal 34: Continue to harmonize and liberalize product and service markets in the Union by setting functional and transparent minimum requirements and limiting the influence of lobbyists.

We should note that there is little correspondence between the indices of product and service market regulations and the World Bank's (2018) ease of starting a business index. For example, Austria and Germany score poorly in terms of the ease of starting a business despite their lenient product and service market regulations. The discrepancy is probably observed because a great

---

[6] For example, Koumenta and Pagliero (2017) find that foreign-born practitioners are underrepresented by about one-third in licensed occupations, but no similar discrepancy in unregulated or certified occupations. Moreover, certified workers invest more in training than licensed workers, but the latter earn a wage premium of about 4% on average.

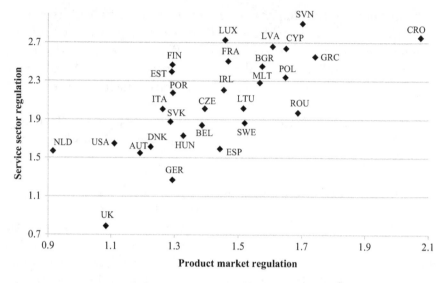

**Fig. 6.1** Strictness of product and service market regulations in EU countries and the USA, 2013. Note: The scale of the index is 0–6, where a larger number means a more stringent regulation. 2013 is the latest available year. The product market regulation index is OECD's aggregate indicator; the service sector index is the arithmetic average of the OECD indices for professional services, retail trade, and the network sectors (transportation, energy, telecom, and mail). The indices are based on responses of national governments to the OECD Regulatory Indicator Questionnaires. Source: OECD, *Product Market Regulation Database*

deal more is involved in setting up a firm than just product market regulations; excessive taxes, red tape, and poor conditions for financing matter a great deal as well. Removing such obstacles is part and parcel of the EU policy agenda already, and we encourage these efforts, with the caveat that well-justified barriers to entry can be useful to keep unproductive and destructive ventures out (Stenholm et al. 2013; Darnihamedani et al. 2018). While it should be easy for challengers to enter (and exit) markets, these challengers should be serious and professional. Regulation that sets reasonable and functional restrictions on new ventures helps prescreen challengers on quality.

This seems particularly relevant in the regulation of publicly provided services. With "publicly provided services," we here refer to collectively financed services provided by a government to people within its jurisdiction, whether directly (through the public sector) or by financing service provision. These services are relevant for the future of Europe's entrepreneurial ecosystem for multiple reasons. First, demand in these sectors is growing: the share of health and education in total GDP is rising in all advanced countries due to demographic and technological trends. Arguably, another driver is Baumol's cost disease: the rise of salaries in jobs that have experienced no or a low increase in labor productivity in response to rising salaries in other jobs that have experienced higher labor productivity growth.[7] In the long run, the rising demand for public services is unlikely to be satisfied, barring significant efficiency improvements and entrepreneurship-driven innovation. If onerous regulation limits access for challengers in these domains, the long-run consequences can be detrimental for the economy as a whole. However, reforms to open up these areas for private initiatives should not take the form of naïve wholesale privatization and laissez-faire. Evidence from the USA suggests that privatized healthcare and education are not necessarily cheaper or better; again, much depends on the institutional framework that makes these special markets work (Reinhardt et al. 2004; Squires 2012).

That said, although there are ways to introduce contestability in public sector organizations, it is easier to do so in a market context. The challenge for policymakers is to ensure quality and access to health care and other social services without resorting to full bureaucratic regulation and public production. Doing so likely involves the clever combining of partially open markets with strict legal and institutional frameworks while drawing a clear line between the market domain and the bureaucratic domain. A case in point could be the Dutch system of universal private health insurance: introduced in 2006, it requires private suppliers to offer a standardized policy at a (competitive) price while obliging all citizens to buy such a policy (Schäfer et al. 2010). Competition on coverage is prohibited, and private insurance providers must accept all applicants, leaving price and quality as the sole dimensions on which to compete.

The deregulation of some health and public services promises to open entirely new arenas for private innovation and entrepreneurial venturing, even if direct public financing is likely to remain the default option in most EU countries. Of course, confounding factors, such as strong asymmetries in information and market power or economies of scale and scope, can effectively preclude market systems as a viable option. When this happens, the public sector can still organize contestability in bureaucratic organizations by giving users a "right to challenge" public sector provision[8] and by holding

---

[7] Liu and Chollet (2006) find income and price elasticities of demand of about 0.1–0.2 for healthcare services in the short run. The evidence suggests that in the short run people have no choice but to demand the services regardless of income and price, whereas, in the long run, the demand for these services rises faster than GDP. The long-run income elasticity for health care and education, however, is probably closer to 1.6 (Fogel 1999). In relation to Baumol's (2012) cost disease, this fact implies that a rapidly rising share of income and employment in the total economy will be absorbed in these sectors.

[8] In the UK, for example, the right to challenge is instituted as a right for local communities to challenge public sector provision of rescue and firefighting services. There are also examples of community-based challengers in care and social service provision. See, e.g., My Community (2019).

competitions on relevant dimensions among smaller organizational units. In line with the principle of contestability, we therefore propose the following:

Proposal 35: Undertake the responsible deregulation of publicly provided services to introduce contestability into these growing areas of the economy.

One challenge to the implementation of the proposals is the fact that consumers can rarely assess the quality of the service provided or discipline producers directly. If countries are to tap the potential and handle the challenge of this combination of semi-public financing and semi-private production, they must create novel institutional arrangements and dare to experiment. When the state acts as an intermediary for an absent third party (the taxpayers) and removes market discipline on producers, no level of competition or freedom of choice will eliminate the scope for manipulation and rent seeking.[9] Moreover, producers typically have limited options to offer and charge for extra quality beyond what a bureaucratically organized and tax-financed system prescribes. When equal access is considered more important than maximum efficiency, such as in basic health care, such constraints can be justifiable; in other instances, policymakers could achieve welfare improvements by allowing for more private for-profit and nonprofit initiatives in the social domain.

Proposal 36: Allow experiments with private actors providing public services in carefully designed markets and learn from these experiments.

The regulatory framework discussed here governs activities characterized by a mixture of private production and public financing. Unless they experiment with this framework, countries cannot reap the full benefits of innovation and entrepreneurial initiatives. Allowing private initiatives in these areas would also create investment opportunities for Europe's institutionalized savings through VC firms, thereby spurring innovation in the social domain.

Hovering over the issue of market contestability is the current trend in the EU towards digitalization—a development that, like most developments, presents both opportunities and challenges. The digital revolution is beginning to change the way we organize society across the board, touching on the very institutions that allocate capital, labor, and knowledge in society (deGryse 2016; Ferrari 2016; Mackenzie 2015; Lin et al. 2009). Currently, the Nordic countries, the Netherlands, and the UK rank high in terms of networked

---

[9] Welfare services are supplied and consumed in the so-called quasi-markets that are characterized by a series of problems that must be addressed, see Le Grand and Bartlett (1993).

readiness (WEF 2016). Laggard countries such as Germany can improve their ranking, providing fertile ground for new firm formation and promoting a more dynamic and innovative entrepreneurial ecosystem without jeopardizing their existing routine-based, incremental innovation paradigms (Sanders et al. 2018b). If policymakers proactively embraced the digitalization trend, they would allow entrepreneurs to act on the new opportunities that technology offers while protecting European citizens from the risks.

Digitalization also brings with it strong positive network externalities, which offer a compelling argument for collective action: A no-regret policy would be to provide an excellent, publicly financed, Information and Communications Technology (ICT) infrastructure in Europe that allows entrepreneurs to scale up their innovative ideas to the EU level and beyond in a rapid fashion. Such an effort would integrate more European citizens in the common market for digital services and facilitate information exchange, essentially enabling them to act as venturesome consumers (Bhidé 2008). In essence, building an open platform for European entrepreneurs would promote contestability by increasing transparency.

Proposal 37: Invest in excellent, open access digital infrastructure for European citizens and businesses.

In addition to providing European entrepreneurs and consumers with a springboard to the global marketplace, a high-quality ICT infrastructure is also essential in the urgently needed transition to a circular economy; that is, an economic system aimed at minimizing waste and making the most out of resources (Ellen MacArthur Foundation 2013; European Commission 2012). Currently, our economic model is geared towards a linear model of production from virgin resources to waste (Haas et al. 2015), where prices are believed to convey the most relevant information regarding production and opportunity costs throughout the value chain. However, price alone no longer conveys the most relevant information, and information flows are increasingly becoming both multidimensional (concerning quality, origin, ecological impact, etc.) and multidirectional (running, for example, from users to intermediate producers and back). Circular business models are better placed to address these complexities but also require much more intense cooperation and communication throughout the value chain (Subramanian and Gunasekaran 2015). The same holds for the more intense use of peer-to-peer lending and equity crowdfunding, proposed in Chap. 4: Lin et al. (2013) show that even the social media contacts of borrowers convey valuable information to lenders. A reliable and secure ICT infrastructure managing more complicated information flows could be a prerequisite for the transition to a more sustainable economy. This justifies public investment and interventions to create a transparent and open digital infrastructure.

> Proposal 38: Develop open but responsible standards and open regulation for the many digital platforms that emerge to facilitate peer-to-peer and business-to-business trade, services and finance.

That said, carefully considering the position of workers and customers on these platforms is essential. Frenken et al. (2017), for example, voice concern about the quality of work and the possibility that digital platforms may undermine social security. Additionally, privacy issues, digital rights, and consumer protection remain important areas of EU policy. Technological developments necessitate the careful modernization of labor market protection and social security systems (in line with proposals in Chap. 5) and adequate investment in human capital (in line with proposals in Chap. 7) to ensure that digitalization contributes to inclusive growth.

The EU could be instrumental in establishing standards that would boost European entrepreneurship on digital platforms.[10] Given its leading position in terms of platform-based financial innovation, the UK was in an excellent position to set such standards before Brexit (Sanders et al. 2018c). Now, the torch will have to pass to the Netherlands and the Nordic countries, as they also have a high degree of network readiness (WEF 2016).

### 6.2.2 Bankruptcy Law and Insolvency Regulation

The entrepreneurial ecosystem is experimental at its core, which makes frequent failure inevitable and, to some extent, desirable. Failed projects should not be considered a waste of resources, and bankruptcies are neither unproductive nor destructive; instead, firm failure provides valuable information to economic agents about whether a business model is viable. Failed ventures must end so that their resources can be turned to more productive uses, but "fear of failure" should not prevent new entrants from challenging the status quo. Learning by failure is of paramount importance for both the entrepreneur and society. Moreover, a restructured venture with new management or

---

[10] The proposals in this subsection are well aligned with the Commission's Digital Single Market initiative, it's Circular Economy Package (European Commission 2017c), and the Digital Agenda (European Commission 2014). The European Commission has substantial legal competencies and supportive measures available to act in this domain.

a different firm can often recycle and improve upon the knowledge and ideas from failed projects, making past failure the foundation for future success. Of course, failure also implies that people suffer, psychologically and financially, and such damage should be minimized. Thus, it is reasonable to institute relatively generous bankruptcy laws and insolvency regulations, with provision for discharge clauses, the postponement of debt service and repayment, and the possibility of restructuring.

Efficient handling of ailing firms calls for bankruptcy and insolvency regulation that minimizes the time and costs to society in phasing out unprofitable and inefficient firms while limiting the damages for creditors, customers, suppliers, employees, and the government. Importantly, a distinction must be made between insolvent firms, which should be closed down, and illiquid ones, which should be allowed to remain operative. A firm is insolvent when the value of its assets is less than its debt and its equity is negative. However, a firm could be unable to honor its obligations simply because it is experiencing temporary financial difficulties. If so, the best solution for both the firm and its creditors is debt restructuring and possibly reduction (a "haircut") through negotiations with the firm's creditors to avoid a "fire sale" of valuable firm assets.

As Fig. 6.2 shows, Finland and Germany have the best regulatory framework for insolvency among the EU countries—Finland even scores better

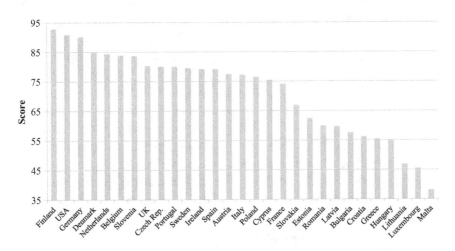

**Fig. 6.2** Ease of resolving insolvency in EU member countries and the USA, 2018. Note: The ranking of economies on the ease of resolving insolvency is determined based on their distance to frontier scores for resolving insolvency. These scores are the simple average of the distance to frontier scores for the recovery rate and the strength of insolvency framework index. Finland is also the most highly ranked country in the world. Source: World Bank, *Doing Business 2018*

than the USA (World Bank 2018)—and the rest of Western Europe also scores high (with the notable exception of Luxembourg). Meanwhile, the Eastern European and Mediterranean countries rank low, with Portugal, Slovenia, and Cyprus being interesting exceptions (World Bank 2018). Overall, the picture suggests substantial room for improvement.

Reform efforts should strive for insolvency regulation that protects inherently healthy and promising ventures while smoothly putting bad ventures to rest once the verdict is clear. If they are too hastily shut down, with their remaining assets shifted out to creditors, the result could be excessive value destruction. Not all insolvent operations should be considered a failure: it is often sufficient that the current owners lose their equity, that the debt is restructured, and that the consortium of debtors finds a new controlling owner after restructuring (Becker and Josephson 2016). Reforms taking these concerns into account would be in line with the principle of justifiability, as they balance the interests of the entrepreneur and other stakeholders in the venture.

> Proposal 39: Insolvency regulation should protect ventures that are inherently healthy and promising and allow for a quick and ex ante transparent liquidation of those that are not.

The European Commission adopted a recast of the Insolvency Regulation Directive in 2015. Moreover, under its Capital Markets Union program, the Commission has proposed a business restructuring directive. If implemented, it would provide the tools to rescue viable businesses and give honest, albeit, bankrupt entrepreneurs a second chance (European Commission 2016; Stamegna 2018). Given the persistent variation in insolvency regulation across Europe, the Commission's reform agenda in this area is laudable.

Unfortunately, "fear of failure" cannot be eliminated by efficient and effective insolvency regulation alone. Such attitudes depend, in no small measure, on a cultural dimension that differs markedly across the EU. To the extent that reforms of formal institutions affect citizens' attitudes about entrepreneurial venturing, such effects will only materialize in the long run. Nevertheless, if policymakers signal to society that business failure is acceptable, cultural attitudes can gradually become more supportive (Sanders et al. 2018b).

Furthermore, while laggard countries must improve their insolvency regulation to become more innovative and entrepreneurial, this cannot be done in isolation. Policymakers must combine reforms in this direction with a strengthening of the rule of law, government effectiveness, and the security of property rights (Chap. 2); otherwise, reforms will prove ineffective or even facilitate abuse and fraudulence. An insolvency regulation such as Finland's—which strikes a sound balance between protecting and restructuring inherently healthy firms, discouraging rent seeking, and encouraging entrepreneurial risk-taking—may fail miserably in Romania or Greece. As such, forgiving insolvency regulation is only feasible when countries also rank highly on the most fundamental rules of the game. Portugal and Slovenia provide what may be a second-best solution in this respect: given their apparent success, it is probably a wise, low-risk strategy for countries with similar institutional configurations to undertake reforms akin to theirs, so as not to base their reform strategy on non-existing high-quality legal institutions.

Finally, we believe it would be a waste of resources not to draw lessons from failed ventures: much of this knowledge is tacit and hard to record and transmit, but that which can be saved should not go to waste. However, the transferrable knowledge generated by failed ventures is lost if entrepreneurs do not record or share it. Because private incentives to do so are absent, it makes sense to publicly fund the collection, curation, and diffusion of such knowledge. The creation of entrepreneurial knowledge observatories would help to diffuse such knowledge to potential investors, would-be entrepreneurs and academic researchers alike, especially when combined with open access data on, for example, crowdfunding campaigns. Therefore, and in line with our principle of transparency, we propose the following:

> Proposal 40: Set up publicly funded "entrepreneurial knowledge observatories" where knowledge accumulated in the entrepreneurial process is collected, curated, and freely diffused.

Because the generated knowledge is typically highly context dependent and firm specific, it makes sense to create the observatories in the ecosystems or collaborative innovation blocs where entrepreneurial entry and exit rates are high. For example, it would be valuable to locate an observatory in London, since the UK's entrepreneurial venturing is highly concentrated there, to further strengthen the ecosystem. In countries such as Italy or Germany, where start-up activity is much less geographically concentrated, the strategic formation of a few observatories could help create clusters that can grow into national hotbeds for new firm formation.

## 6.3   Summary

Contestability ensures progress in an entrepreneurial society: Only when new entrants can challenge the status quo and selection takes place on merit will the market's evolutionary process yield the kind of creative destruction that drives innovation and growth (Schumpeter 1934 [1911]). To achieve contestability, entry and exit barriers must be low, transparent, and functional. Moreover, vital infrastructure must be accessible to challengers and incumbents alike. Finally, the knowledge generated in the entrepreneurial process must, to the extent that it is possible, be shared and used, even when—or perhaps especially when—a venture fails. Table 6.1 provides a summary of our proposals regarding contestable markets for entry and exit, specifying the level in the governance hierarchy that should make the necessary decisions.

The EU has extensive competencies in regard to the regulation of product markets and ensuring the mobility of capital, labor, goods, and services in the single market. These instruments should be used to ensure that challengers can compete on a level playing field with incumbents. EU competencies are also strong in regard to competition regulation and supervision as well as state aid and public procurement, but here, in view of the political backlash of the financial crisis, it is probably wise to allow the member states themselves to experiment with new governance models and allow for more contestability in public service provision. Once experimentation has provided an evidence base that can be used to formulate specific reforms, the EU should become involved opening up public sector services for more competition.

In regard to the resolution of insolvency and the management of highly region-specific knowledge, the Union does not seem to be the most appropriate level for policymaking; regional and local policymakers are probably better placed to combine the proposed knowledge observatories with their current policies on regional and local business development.

**Table 6.1** Summary of proposals regarding contestable markets for entry and exit, specifying the level in the governance hierarchy where the necessary decisions should be made

| No. | Principle(s) | Policy area | Proposal | Policy level[a] |
|---|---|---|---|---|
| 32 | Contestability | Entry barriers | Excessive barriers to new business formation and new entry should be lifted where possible. | EU, MS, REG, LOC |
| 33 | Contestability, transparency, and justifiability | Entry barriers | Create transparent and open systems of occupational certification, such that people can easily move across occupations and in and out of new ventures. | EU, MS |
| 34 | Contestability and justifiability | Entry barriers | Continue to harmonize and liberalize product and service markets in the Union by setting functional and transparent minimum requirements and limiting the influence of lobbyists. | EU |
| 35 | Contestability | Entry barriers | Undertake the responsible deregulation of publicly provided services to introduce contestability into these growing areas of the economy. | EU, MS |
| 36 | Contestability and justifiability | Entry barriers | Allow experiments with private actors providing public services in carefully designed markets and learn from these experiments. | MS |
| 37 | Contestability and transparency | ICT | Invest in excellent, open access digital infrastructure for European citizens and businesses. | EU, MS, REG, LOC |
| 38 | Transparency | ICT | Develop open but responsible standards and open regulation for the many digital platforms that emerge to facilitate peer-to-peer and business-to-business trade, services, and finance. | EU |
| 39 | Justifiability | Insolvency | Insolvency regulation should protect ventures that are inherently healthy and promising and allow for a quick and ex ante transparent liquidation of those that are not. | EU, MS |
| 40 | Transparency | Insolvency | Set up publicly funded "entrepreneurial knowledge observatories" where knowledge accumulated in the entrepreneurial process is collected, curated, and freely diffused. | REG, LOC |

[a]*EU* federal level, *MS* member state level, *REG* regional government level, *LOC* local/municipal level

# 7

# Mobilizing Human Capital for Entrepreneurship

## 7.1 General Principles

The creative potential of the human brain has led researchers to label it the ultimate resource (Simon and Kahn 1981; Simon 1996; Naam 2013). Indeed, the mainstream growth literature finds strong support for the notion that human capital—knowledge, skills, and social and personal attributes—matter fundamentally for economic growth (Lucas 1988; Mankiw et al. 1992; Barro 2001). Because an entrepreneurial society requires a broad variety of skills and knowledge, a key challenge lies in accumulating sufficient human capital and matching it to a sophisticated demand. This accumulation starts in school but continues throughout the working life, whether on production floors or in dedicated R&D labs.

The specific public good nature of knowledge (Arrow 1962) and the positive network externalities involved in basic human capital accumulation (reading, writing, arithmetic, shared culture and history, socialization, etc.) mean that private incentives and social returns rarely coincide. Therefore, public policy intervention is called for to create incentives to acquire, maintain, and diffuse skills and knowledge. In this chapter, we discuss proposals for institutional reform that will ensure that a sufficient level and quality of human capital is available to entrepreneurs and their ventures.

The roles of formal education and on-the-job training have shifted over time. In the early industrialization phase in the West, leading innovators seldom had much formal education; their innovations emanated from practical experience in workshops and production plants. This gradually changed when specialized engineering schools were established in late nineteenth century

© The Author(s) 2019
N. Elert et al., *The Entrepreneurial Society*, International Studies in Entrepreneurship 98,
https://doi.org/10.1007/978-3-662-59586-2_7

Europe and the USA, followed by the formation of R&D departments in large engineering firms in the early twentieth century (Rosenberg and Birdzell 1986; Mowery and Rosenberg 1998). Today, exceptional cases notwithstanding, most innovation emanates from team efforts that bring together skills and knowledge from different sources. The EOE perspective illustrates this through its emphasis on the need for several actors and competencies to realize the benefits of innovation. A new idea is only the first step in a knowledge-intensive innovation and commercialization process, and if new knowledge is to translate into economic growth, entrepreneurs must exploit it by introducing new methods of production or new products in the marketplace (Schumpeter 1934 [1911]; Michelacci 2003; Bhidé 2008).

In Chap. 2, we discussed reforms in the system of IPR that would increase the access to and availability of new ideas. Here, we once more embrace the principle of justifiability, since it is necessary to carefully balance private and public interests when discussing reforms to address the positive externalities involved in the accumulation of human capital and the availability of a broad and diversified pool of high-quality knowledge in collaborative innovation blocs. The principle of neutrality helps us safeguard the European value of universal access to high-quality education, whereas the principle of contestability ensures that challengers can compete for knowledge, skills, and skilled employees on a level playing field.

We should note that proposals referring to educational systems will usually be directed at EU member states, since the Union's competencies regarding education are limited (Suse and Hachez 2017, pp. 73–74). In contrast, policies supporting R&D and on-the-job human capital accumulation already make up a substantial share of the EU annual budget and have been well situated within the competencies of the EU since the Lisbon Treaty. As to innovation, the European Commission is looking into how existing regulatory frameworks in a host of relevant areas affect innovation, striving "to collect further suggestions on the relationship between innovation and regulation, indications of regulatory barriers to innovation and suggestions for simpler, clearer and more efficient regulation supporting growth and jobs" (Suse and Hachez 2017, p. 76).[1] The role and competencies of local and regional policymakers in this area are typically found at the base of the educational institutional framework in European member states.

---

[1] The EU may also influence member states' educational policies through coordination processes, such as the open method of coordination (OMC), recommendations, and incentive measures.

## 7.2   Proposals

In all likelihood, an excellent educational system from kindergarten through and including the university level would provide entrepreneurial ventures with a rich and diverse pool of human capital. Casual observation suffices to conclude that there is significant variation across the EU in how educational systems are set up, financed, and managed—as well as in how they perform. Given this diversity, one-size-fits-all reforms, such as allocating more public funds to the educational system, are not the answer.

Consider the evidence provided in internationally comparable tests of pupils' abilities and skills, the most important of which are the Programme for International Student Assessment (PISA; OECD 2016b) and the Trends in Mathematics and Science Study (TIMSS; Mullis et al. 2016). Human capital, as measured in these tests, is of crucial importance for economic growth (Hanushek and Woessman 2015), but the link between educational expenditures and test scores is far from homogenous. While high educational spending accompanies good results in Finland (especially at the beginning of the twenty-first century), it is associated with weak results in Sweden.[2] Whereas pupils in Poland and Estonia achieve excellent results despite relatively low educational spending, Romania and Bulgaria spend little and do poorly (see Table A.5 in the Appendix for details). An immediate implication is that naïvely implemented increases in educational budgets are unlikely to promote a more entrepreneurial society.

Undoubtedly, teacher quality is critical for pupil achievement on these tests (Goe and Stickler 2008), but still more critical factors are a detailed, coherent, and carefully sequenced curriculum organized around subject disciplines (Hirsch 2016b; Christodoulou 2014) and external exit exams ensuring that schools are held accountable for their performance (Woessman 2016). The exam content governs the content of teaching, provides adequate guidance to developers and publishers of textbooks and other teaching materials, and makes it possible to benchmark schools. That said, centralized exams and curricula limit diversity and possibly creativity almost by definition. As such, they may tempt teachers and pupils to "teach to the test," possibly forgetting about the cultivation of other useful skills and the preservation of a critical

---

[2] Granted, measuring inputs and outputs and comparing the quality of education across and even within educational systems is notoriously difficult. We focus on measures that ensure international comparability. PISA is done every 3 years and measures 15-year-old pupils' knowledge in mathematics, science, and reading. TIMSS is done every 4 years and measures the knowledge of fourth- and eighth-graders in mathematics and science. In 2015, 72 countries participated in the PISA tests and 57 countries in the TIMSS test.

attitude. Moreover, personality traits and family background matter for the performance of individual pupils (Johnson et al. 1983; Downey 1995; Magnusson et al. 2006), blurring the relationship between educational inputs and outputs and eventual success in the labor market (Winding et al. 2013). Consequently, the link from national performance in international tests to economic growth may be positive, but strong causality is hard to establish. The link to successful entrepreneurial venturing is even less evident.

The USA is a case in point. Though commonly believed to be the most innovative and entrepreneurial of all countries, government spending on education is intermediate, while private spending is substantial (2% of GDP compared to an EU average of 0.5% of GDP; see OECD 2018b, p. 207). Despite this high total spending, US pupils perform poorly in all three PISA knowledge areas, particularly in mathematics, yet they do exceptionally well in entrepreneurial venturing. The USA may be the exception that confirms the rule—or an indication that supporting an entrepreneurial mindset in education is not a matter of spending more resources or inserting business model canvassing into the national curriculum. A strong knowledge base is essential, but evidence also suggests that entrepreneurship is best taught in an experiential, learning-by-doing manner (Elert et al. 2015).

The essence of entrepreneurship is trial and error and learning from failure, hinting at the importance of fostering a positive attitude towards learning among pupils. To achieve this goal, it is important that the early stages of an educational career are characterized by positive learning experiences (Illeris 2006; Sanders et al. 2015) and that they instill a tolerance for failure and an appreciation of trial and error (Clifford 1984; Clifford et al. 1988; Metcalfe 2017). Therefore, we propose the following:

> Proposal 41: Reforms in primary and secondary education should provide pupils with a solid and coherent knowledge base and promote initiative, creativity, and willingness to experiment.

We do not propose, as some have (Griffin and Care 2014; Lazonder and Harmsen 2016), that the actual acquisition of knowledge be neglected in favor of skills training or purely curiosity-driven learning. Entrepreneurship is so broad, diverse, and uncertain that it is impossible to predict the specific knowledge that entrepreneurial ventures need. The educational focus should, therefore, be on broad and generic bodies of knowledge, rather than on highly specialized topics and fields.

Moreover, pupils and students should be challenged, not pleased: human capital of a mathematical and natural science orientation, for example, has been shown to be important for science-based entrepreneurship (Shavinina 2013; Dilli and Westerhuis 2018). Indeed, this type of entrepreneurship typically delivers the most scalable and growth-enhancing innovations, and the most successful entrepreneurs in the world tend to have advanced technical degrees from international universities (Henrekson and Sanandaji 2014). It would seem, therefore, that an educational system that makes it easy for students to avoid challenging topics such as science, technology, engineering, and mathematics (STEM) would do the entrepreneurial society no favors. As Dilli and Westerhuis (2018) argue, early efforts to promote STEM (not least among young girls) would be a way to promote more ambitious entrepreneurship in the long run.

Similarly, because scaling a venture in Europe also often implies crossing national borders, there is a clear case for training effective international communication skills at early stages of the educational career, when such skills are relatively easy to train (Krashen et al. 1979; Collier 1995; Flege et al. 1999). In line with our principles of neutrality and justifiability, we therefore propose the following:

Proposal 42: Promote STEM education and English as a (mandatory) second language early on and then throughout students' educational careers.

The proposal aligns well with the European Commission's Entrepreneurship 2020 Action Plan, including measures that induce students to be more entrepreneurial and encourage a focus on STEM fields. Bringing an entrepreneurial spirit to European curricula is a key ingredient in almost any strategy to create an entrepreneurial society. We stress that this should start early (Jayawarna et al. 2014), but a great deal can be done to make students in tertiary education more entrepreneurial as well.

Students typically make a crucial human capital decision at the end of secondary school when they decide whether to work or pursue tertiary education. In light of this fact, it is notable that tertiary enrolment has exploded in recent decades, which is evident from the first column of Table 7.1. The fact that the enrolment rate is high in many of the poorest EU countries, notably Greece, Bulgaria, and the Baltic countries, suggests that high enrolment rates per se are no guarantee that university studies have a high social rate of return, especially not in an entrepreneurial society.

The educational quality at the earlier levels largely determines how much one can expect and demand from students at the tertiary level. If their earlier education has been deficient, fewer students will be willing or able to choose more demanding lines of study, notably science and engineering. The second

**Table 7.1** Tertiary enrolment and graduates in science and engineering in EU countries and the USA, 2016

| Country | Tertiary enrolment (%) | Graduates in S&E (%) | Country | Tertiary enrolment (%) | Graduates in S&E (%) |
|---|---|---|---|---|---|
| Greece | 117.4 | 29.9 | Portugal | 62.9 | 27.9 |
| Finland | 87.0 | 29.5 | Czech Rep. | 64.0 | 23.2 |
| USA | 85.8[a] | 17.4 | Italy | 62.9 | 23.3 |
| Spain | 91.2 | 23.9 | Sweden | 62.3 | 26.0 |
| Slovenia | 80.0 | 25.7 | France | 65.3 | 25.3 |
| Denmark | 81.1 | 20.5 | Croatia | 67.5 | 25.3 |
| Austria | 83.5 | 30.3 | Germany | 66.3 | 36.4[b] |
| Netherlands | 81.8 | 14.1 | Hungary | 48.0 | 22.8 |
| Ireland | 83.5 | 24.9 | UK | 57.3 | 26.1 |
| Estonia | 72.0 | 26.5 | Slovakia | 52.7 | 21.1 |
| Belgium | 74.6 | 17.4 | Cyprus | 60.1 | 15.9 |
| Lithuania | 66.0 | 23.8 | Romania | 48.0 | 28.8 |
| Poland | 66.6 | 22.9 | Malta | 48.8 | 18.0 |
| Bulgaria | 71.2 | 19.7 | Luxembourg | 19.7 | 13.8 |
| Latvia | 68.2 | 20.5 | | | |

Note: The ratio of total tertiary enrolment, regardless of age, to the population of the age group that officially corresponds to the tertiary level of education. Tertiary education, whether or not aiming at an advanced research qualification, normally requires, as a minimum condition of admission, the successful completion of education at the secondary level. The share of graduates in science and engineering is defined as the share of all tertiary graduates in science, manufacturing, engineering, and construction over all tertiary graduates
Source: UNESCO Institute for Statistics, UIS online database (2010–2017)
[a]2015
[b]Data from http://data.uis.unesco.org/index.aspx?queryid=163 measuring "graduates from Science, Technology, Engineering and Mathematics programmes in tertiary education". In addition, Germany had 22.0% "graduates from tertiary education graduating from Engineering, Manufacturing and Construction programmes" in 2016

column in Table 7.1 confirms that such education matters more in European countries than in the USA (see also Fig. A.4 in the Appendix).

The demonstrated importance of engineering skills for entrepreneurship notwithstanding, more technical graduates in no way equates to more successful entrepreneurs. Nevertheless, universities can teach students entrepreneurial skills even when they are learning about other topics by making academic research and teaching more action-oriented and aimed at real-world experience; a mindset of trial and error and learning from failure is, after all, something all pupils should embrace (Sanders et al. 2018c). Moreover, to the extent that there are specific courses in entrepreneurship, they should be taught by people who have been involved in entrepreneurial venturing (rather than by tenured university researchers lacking hands-on experience, as is all too often the case; see, e.g., Sanders et al. 2018a).

European educational systems differ from the USA in a fundamental respect: the private rates of return to education and analytical skills are much lower (see Table A.6 in the Appendix). Consequently, Europe cannot finance its university systems through high tuition fees that students subsequently recover by means of a highly paid job after graduation. Since their expected lifetime incomes are not high enough, we believe the EU should not opt for the American model of high private (out of pocket) investments. Instead, the Union should strive for accessibility to ensure an adequate supply of well-trained technical personnel. Given the niches in which the EU competes in global markets, such a supply is crucial for its entrepreneurial society.

Proposal 43: Invest in high-quality tertiary level technical education by attracting excellent teaching staff and students and by strengthening Europe's strong tradition of vocational training.

This general recommendation translates into different interventions depending on the member state. For example, the UK's educational system provides world-class university education, but vocational and on-the-job training falls short of the country's needs (Sanders et al. 2018c). Thus, its brilliant new start-ups struggle to hire and retain the human capital required to compete on quality in global markets. In contrast, the German university system fails to provide excellence, while the vocational training and apprentice systems support a world-class manufacturing apparatus (Sanders et al. 2018b). In Italy, curricula are challenging and people may be well educated, but traditional curricula are a poor match for dynamic market demand (Sanders et al. 2018a).

When discussing tertiary education, it is necessary to emphasize the importance of university campuses. Evidence shows that campuses can be hotbeds of entrepreneurial venturing (Audretsch 2014), and some of the Europe's campuses have already realized that potential (e.g., Chalmers in Gothenburg, Sweden: Jacob et al. 2003; Dahlstrand 2007; Lundqvist 2014). If others are to follow, policymakers need to take measures that enable several university-level links to function efficiently. Notably, for knowledge-based entrepreneurship to flourish, universities must have incentives to align subject areas with business sector demand and to facilitate knowledge transfer from academia to the entrepreneurial sector. The USA may serve as an important role model here.

That said, the US system of granting property rights for patentable research findings to universities is unlikely to be beneficial in Europe, given that

European universities are typically government owned.[3] Existing research shows that abolishing the "professor's privilege" (i.e., the university researcher's rights to acquire IPR by patenting ideas stemming from their own research) has negative effects on patenting and knowledge commercialization in countries where universities are state owned (Hvide and Jones 2018; Färnstrand Damsgaard and Thursby 2013; Goldfarb and Henrekson 2003).

The fact that Continental Europe operates just behind the global technology frontier (Acemoglu et al. 2017) suggests that its prevalence of vocational education and on-the-job-training compensates for a lack of innovative, entrepreneurial campuses. In addition, semi-public knowledge institutes (such as the Fraunhofer Institut and Max Planck Society in Germany, the CNRS in France, and TNO and ECN in the Netherlands) complement the European university system, diffusing scientific knowledge into commercial activity and society at large (Agrawal 2001; Bergman 2010; Perkmann et al. 2013).[4] To be sure, incumbent firms are often the partners of choice in this more institutionalized European system of knowledge diffusion. By also supporting students and researchers striving to creating new and competing ventures, European universities could aid in the transition to an entrepreneurial society.

However, most European systems of higher education are currently ill equipped to take on such a role. For one thing, they are too centralized; European universities tend to be government owned and tax financed, with the entry of private universities being disallowed or highly restricted (Aghion et al. 2007, 2008; Jongbloed 2010). The Union's universities should be given more flexibility to respond to the needs of regional collaborative innovation blocs, where demanding customers serve as crucial sources of information regarding consumer needs and preferences (von Hippel et al. 2011). Here, academic entrepreneurs can show how to commercialize new knowledge and research. Furthermore, it is important to actively engage with societal partners outside of academia, such as corporations, governments, NGOs, and civil society organizations. Reaching out more to such external stakeholders would expose students and staff to more opportunities for useful application of new knowledge in social or commercial ventures.

---

[3] Much research examines the effects of the Bayh-Dole Act that established this incentive in the USA (Popp Berman 2008; Leydesdorff and Meyer 2010). The EU's and many European countries' efforts to emulate its success have met mixed results (Siepmann 2004; Mowery and Sampat 2004), likely because the same institutional reform works out very differently in different national contexts.

[4] *Wikipedia* lists 106 such institutes in France, 173 in Germany, and 64 in the Netherlands. The US total is 405, suggesting that they are far more prevalent in Europe.

Proposal 44: The link between universities and external stakeholders should be strengthened by encouraging universities to stimulate entrepreneurial initiatives and university spinoffs.

There are already successful examples of such collaborations, bringing business to science and science to business (Jacob et al. 2003; Hommen et al. 2006; Castillo and Meyer 2018). Successful incubators managed by European universities ranking in the global top 20 include Bath in the UK, Politechnico di Milano in Italy, Chalmers ventures in Gothenburg, Sweden, and London's South Bank University. More European incubators are affiliated with and collaborating with universities (Castillo and Meyer 2018). Such joint efforts may be especially crucial in high-technology fields; for example, universities and their faculties have encouraged local economic development by improving the ability of new and incumbent firms to use biotech research (Zucker et al. 1998; McKelvey et al. 2003; Okubo and Sjöberg 2000; Link and Swann 2016; Amoroso et al. 2018). If they learn from such examples, European policymakers will be better placed to stimulate academic entrepreneurship and accelerate the commercialization of university-developed inventions of great potential value (Goldfarb and Henrekson 2003; Kauffman Foundation 2007; Link and Swann 2016; Amoroso et al. 2018).

A shift towards excellence is also required if academic entrepreneurship is to flourish. European universities already pay lip service to excellence (Vogel 2006; Corradi 2009; Hallonsten and Silander 2012; Wolfensberger 2015), but the reality is that few of them rank among the top universities globally.[5] Europe's strategy of providing a high-quality university education to the average student worked very well in the age of "the managed society" (Audretsch and Thurik 2000) when the rapid adoption of new knowledge in multinational industrial firms was sufficient to maintain a viable competitive position (Acemoglu et al. 2006; Audretsch et al. 2017). Following the rise of Asia, this strategy must now be complemented with policies allowing Europe's best and brightest to excel.

The challenge is to turn (some of) the EU's universities into world-class institutions while safeguarding the distinct inclusive character of university education (Aghion et al. 2008). A sensible way to reach higher is to broaden the base. Europe's university research and education systems are still nationally organized and fragmented. Differences are often deeply rooted, which

---

[5] Whereas seven UK universities can be found among the 50 highest ranked universities, only five universities from the rest of the EU appear (three from Germany, one from Belgium, and one from Sweden) (Times Higher Education 2018).

complicates efforts to create an integrated European Research Area (European Commission 2012). Indeed, the Union respects member states' prerogatives in this area. For example, EU leadership acknowledges the existence of 28 national research systems funded from national tax revenues and states that these member state-specific systems "will remain distinct in so far as this benefits the EU and individual Member States, allowing Europe to capitalize on its scientific, cultural and geographical diversity" (European Commission 2012, p. 3). This obliging attitude sometimes hampers the exchange and mobility of both students and academic staff and may be a chief reason why so little actual progress has been made. Most students still study in their country of birth, and only the most productive and innovative researchers are truly mobile (Karamanis and Economidou 2018).

A push for more openness in the national science foundations could strengthen the integration of the EU's knowledge base. National borders and nationality should, after all, be irrelevant in regard to basic research. Therefore, it is worth pondering whether all EU researchers should be eligible for funding by all member states' national research funding agencies. Such a change would be relatively easy to implement, but it entails a non-negligible risk that the already strong universities and knowledge centers will be the big winners, further concentrating world-class research in leading countries at the expense of laggards.

Of course, the top-ranked universities in the USA and elsewhere maintain their position precisely by attracting the best and brightest from a large population of students. Today, these institutions compete for the best and brightest from all over the world. Perhaps geographical concentration is simply the price we have to pay for academic excellence, and as long as all Europeans have equal access, the problem may be tolerable. Before considering a reform in this direction, however, policymakers should strive to ensure that all countries develop an intellectual environment capable of identifying and honing citizens' talents, absorbing research findings and applying them commercially. To level the playing field before introducing healthy competition, there is a need to nurture a sound academic environment in all member states, thereby paving the way for a much needed top-level European research environment (Aghion et al. 2008).

Proposal 45: Both the EU and its member states should create healthy, well-funded, academic institutions that allow Europe's most talented academics to pursue their research interests.

The specifics matter for the implementation of such a proposal, and they differ across countries. In Germany, for example, this proposal may be interpreted as a call for increased public funding for universities, which despite their strong educational focus have seen a steep decline in their spending per student (Füller 2017; Sanders et al. 2018b). By contrast, Italy should first take measures to open up academic institutions characterized by deeply entrenched vested interests and gilded contracts; before such structural issues are addressed, it makes little sense to spend much money (Sanders et al. 2018a).

Competition on excellence among universities will inevitably create regional knowledge concentration, especially given the importance of networks in academic research and economies of agglomeration. This concentration should be considered as normal and acceptable between member states as it is between regions within countries. Likewise, successful entrepreneurial ecosystems and industrial clusters follow an economic logic that is not necessarily politically convenient. There is little doubt that geographic proximity facilitates knowledge spillover and knowledge transfer among networks and collaborations (Jaffe et al. 1993; Sorenson and Stuart 2001; Ponds et al. 2007; Arzaghi and Henderson 2008; Rosenthal and Strange 2008).

These findings hint at a potential role for governments, national and local, in promoting urbanization, local networks, and clusters (Andersson and Henrekson 2015). Today, clusters are considerably more common in Western European countries, but they could help facilitate entrepreneurship in Eastern and Mediterranean Europe as well if policymakers enable a greater transfer of knowledge between businesses and knowledge-creating organizations (Moretti 2012; Moretti and Thulin 2013). Strong, dynamic clusters are bottom-up phenomena that can emerge anywhere (Klepper 2016) and should be allowed to form endogenously. However, policy and institutional reforms can improve initial conditions. For one thing, they can reform real estate markets so that housing prices reflect scarcity and preferences; where appropriate, they should also liberalize zoning laws and remove any red tape that could curb cluster development (Glaeser 2008, 2011). Local policymakers should also provide an infrastructure that allows smooth transportation and commuting.

> Proposal 46: Liberalize, where possible, spatial planning regulations to allow the endogenous clustering of business activity rather than trying to plan clusters from the top down.

Furthermore, policymakers should keep in mind the late Steven Klepper's (2016) persuasive findings that industry clusters can gain momentum through entrepreneurial spinoffs from existing firms. In the USA, it seems that many spinoffs and spinouts result from conflict and strategic disagreement between R&D workers and their managers (e.g., Klepper 2002, 2009; Klepper and

Thompson 2010). In the more consensual European context, a system of collaborative, open innovation characterized by intrapreneurship and consensual spinouts may well serve a similar function; at least in the UK, spin-off ventures are on average more innovative and successful than those started without industry experience (Sanders et al. 2018c; Wennberg et al. 2011). The same is probably the case elsewhere in the Union. Currently, however, incumbent firms likely shelve many potentially valuable R&D projects because they do not fit these firms' strategies and interests.

It may be worthwhile to encourage entrepreneurial R&D workers to spin off and develop such projects as independent ventures. Another option would be to promote intrapreneurship—entrepreneurship by employees. Judging by the evidence to date, intrapreneurship seems well aligned with the Nordic welfare state and the Rhineland consensus model (Henrekson and Roine 2007; Bosma et al. 2010), perhaps because intrapreneurship depends crucially on management practices and employee autonomy in the workplace, phenomena that, in turn, stem from a high level of generalized trust (Elert et al. 2019; Ljunge and Stenkula 2018). While trust is not easily stimulated through institutional reforms, policymakers should permit the many European firms that already experiment with intrapreneurship (Bosma et al. 2013, 2014) to keep doing so. Hopefully, careful study of intrapreneurship can teach us how to develop more targeted interventions in the future.

Returning to the role that knowledge plays in an entrepreneurial society, we should note that scientific knowledge is a pure public good (Nelson 1959; Romer 1990; Salter and Martin 2001; Pavitt 1991)—channeling more money to basic research that provides positive knowledge spillovers throughout the Union would therefore seem like a no-regrets policy. Furthermore, R&D spending is positively associated with a greater patenting rate (Elert et al. 2017). However, it does not follow from these facts that a policy of increased government R&D spending or subsidies will result in more economically valuable knowledge.[6] Public R&D can crowd out private R&D: the share of R&D in the business sector that is directly or indirectly funded by the government tends to be lower in countries with high R&D spending by business enterprises and higher in countries with low R&D spending by businesses (Table A.7 in the Appendix). Furthermore, patenting and R&D are inputs in the production process; the desired output—higher value creation—depends on many more steps along the way.

---

[6] Da Rin et al. (2006) examined 14 European countries between 1988 and 2001, without finding any positive relationship between public R&D spending and the rate of innovation (defined as the share of high-tech and early-stage venture capital investments).

For these reasons, it is probably better to promote R&D—and ultimately, scientific knowledge—through the pull of demand rather than through the push of supply. A broad policy program conducive to innovative entrepreneurial venturing will likely spontaneously increase R&D spending and allocate it efficiently as a side effect. Conversely, if a well-functioning entrepreneurial ecosystem is not already in place, a government push to increase R&D becomes a waste of resources, directing focus and resources towards factors that would have found better use elsewhere in the European economy. Spontaneous, demand-driven increases in R&D expenditures should be preferred over any top-down designed alternatives, as it is next to impossible for a bureaucracy to "pick the winners." Instead, policies and reforms should aim to mobilize and incentivize the available resources to flow to their most productive use, including R&D.

People always create knowledge; policymakers should, therefore, begin by increasing the pool of talented and highly motivated individuals able to dedicate time to research. As such, educational reforms must aim to increase the stock and quality of home-grown human capital. The aging European economy would also do well not to ignore the pool of talent available abroad. In this respect, the European Commission's Blue Card Directive, while laudable, is problematic because it remains reserved exclusively for highly qualified *employees* (Eisele 2013). The Directive explicitly refers to this group as "managers and specialists" who are required to have (and hold) a formal labor contract with a minimum salary that may differ per member state but that is invariably high. In its current guise, therefore, the Blue Card system has little to offer entrepreneurial start-ups in Europe. It certainly does not promote the immigration of entrepreneurs, who are typically not specialists with high salaries but "jacks-of-all-trades" possessing a broad and balanced skill mix (Lazear 2005). A college drop-out with a wild idea (like Bill Gates when he founded Microsoft) would currently not qualify for a Blue Card. In line with our principle of neutrality, we therefore propose to reform the Blue Card system in a direction that makes it more conducive to an entrepreneurial society.

Proposal 47: Reform the European Blue Card system to also include nonemployees and people lacking high formal educational credentials provided they have a plan to support themselves and the requisite equity to start a viable business.

Furthermore, entrepreneurship should not be promoted by picking winners but by creating an environment in which winners thrive. To that end, policy initiatives should support firms that experiment with a clear market focus in mind, much like the US Small Business and Innovation Research Program (SBIR), a highly competitive program encouraging domestic small businesses to engage in federal research and development with the potential for commercialization. However, whereas SBIR by and large has been successful in stimulating innovation (Lerner 1999; Wessner 2008), similar initiatives by EU member states have thus far had mixed and limited success (Camerer and van Eijl 2011; Apostol 2017).

Hopefully, that track record can improve: according to Apostol (2017), a key success factor for such programs is that they predominantly tender high-risk R&D projects to small and young firms, and public program managers play a critical role by carefully selecting these projects based on a sound understanding of market and technological trends. Moreover, a tolerance for failure is essential, and an EU equivalent to the US SBIR program should not be a backdoor to protecting local and domestic firms from foreign competition. It seems, therefore, that SBIR-type programs are best suited for countries with high-quality public sectors, low risk of corruption, and a strong tradition of small industrial firm R&D. Strict enforcement of nondiscrimination clauses is also essential. Thus, in line with the principle of contestability, we propose:

Proposal 48: Develop highly competitive programs encouraging small businesses to engage in research and development with the potential for commercialization.

Of course, IPR are essential to ensure strong incentives for knowledge creation and diffusion. In Chap. 2, we made several proposals to improve the balance between just rewards and positive externalities in the IPR system. These reforms are relevant here as well. As we noted in Chap. 2, a core issue is to weigh the interests of inventors against the positive spillover effects of knowledge diffusion. We would add that although bureaucrats should not try to pick winners, policymakers may have a legitimate role to play in formulating challenges for entrepreneurs (Montalvo and Leijten 2015; Mazzucato 2018). SBIR-like programs would be one way for political bodies to support and direct the activities of entrepreneurs. By challenging entrepreneurs to develop innovative solutions to well-defined social challenges, such programs provide clear market signals, even if the customer is the taxpayer. Such targeted support can also be justified if one expects strong positive externalities; in the European setting, this would be the case for international partnerships for innovation, in which public and private parties cooperate to address specific innovation challenges.

Proposal 49: Support international partnerships for innovation through specific innovation challenges.

The European Commission's Horizon 2020 program already has this structure. For the most part, it sets clear innovation challenges and invites international consortia to enter an open competition for the funds. The solution to the problem articulated in a call is rarely the only positive outcome of such grants, as lasting collaborations across the Continent are established in the process. In an interim evaluation, the European Commission (2017c) reported that some 75% of Horizon 2020 funding benefited international collaborations, which, in nine cases out of ten, benefited EU-28 research institutes and researchers. It is too early to tell if the connections forged in European projects will have lasting impact and sustain a more integrated European Research Area, but we believe that incentivizing researchers to collaborate across borders is an effective way to make progress in this area.

Horizon 2020 and similar public R&D programs typically select a few proposals on a predefined call before commissioning the research. By contrast, in the eighteenth and nineteenth centuries, the use of innovation challenges often took the specific form of prizes. Such challenge-based prizes yielded substantial progress in such varied fields as navigation, air voyage, and food preservation (Abramowicz 2003; Shavell and van Ypersele 2001). The competitions are specific, in the sense that they stipulate a clear goal to be achieved— say, the development of a climate-neutral technology for transportation—but can be formulated in an open-ended way in regard to matters of technology. Furthermore, technology inducement prizes are exempt from the welfare loss that comes from the monopoly rents associated with patents (Adler 2011) and do not require an extensive bureaucracy that assesses and evaluates proposals and credentials *ex ante*.[7] While a social loss due to duplication of effort is likely to occur, a prize does imply that the public pays a clear and pre-set amount only when the problem gets solved.

The prize philosophy currently guides the XPRIZE Foundation, a nonprofit organization that designs and manages public competitions intended to encourage technological development that could benefit humanity. The same is the case for Sir Richard Branson's Virgin Earth Challenge, awarding 25 million dollars to "a commercially viable design which results in the removal of anthropogenic, atmospheric greenhouse gases so as to contribute materially

---

[7] An evaluation of the web page *Innocentive*, where firms and organizations announce rewards to problem-solvers, reveals that the best solutions often originate with outsiders who are neither researchers nor work in the relevant field (Lakhani et al. 2007).

to the stability of Earth's climate." Though huge, that prize sum is small in comparison to what governments throughout the world spend annually on energy- and climate-related research, as well as in comparison to the projected costs should humanity fail to stop climate change. European countries could easily emulate the same philosophy, combining a minimal risk to taxpayers with innovation encouragement that does not commit to specific firms or a particular technology. Moreover, a prize can be made transparent, neutral, and contestable by design. We therefore propose the following:

> Proposal 50: Institute technology inducement prizes to further the development of commercially applicable knowledge in socially important areas, such as climate change, health care, and education.

Obviously, it is always possible that collaborations emanating from publicly funded knowledge creation have spillover effects that benefit third-party countries or private parties and might be perceived as free riding on European funds (e.g., Mazzucato 2015). From the point of view of an entrepreneurial society, however, it would be wise to allow private firms, even from third-party countries, to use publicly generated knowledge at zero marginal cost.

The problem is not that they use "our" knowledge but that the knowledge in question is sometimes used to secure socially inefficient rents for the benefit of the few. Ultimately, it is a good thing that a firm like Apple uses vast amounts of knowledge—even if some of that knowledge was initially developed with public funds in European university labs. The act of taking the risk and putting all that knowledge together in a well-designed and functional smartphone entitles the firm to a handsome reward. This emphatically does not mean that Apple should be allowed to patent some design features and use those patents to prevent competitors from entering the same market.[8] Unfortunately, such practices do occur, but they do not justify a stop on promoting publicly funded research *ex ante*, nor should policymakers seek to recover such public funds *ex post* through taxation or the exclusion of foreign partners. Instead, the goal should be to maximize the social benefits and consumer surplus by enforcing full disclosure and contestability, in IPR as well.

---

[8] See https://en.wikipedia.org/wiki/Apple_Inc._v._Samsung_Electronics_Co. for an entertaining description of the Smartphone War in which Samsung and Apple have been engaged since 2011. Burnick (2017) offers a more academic account of the Supreme Court Ruling.

## 7.3   Summary

The European entrepreneurial society will bring inclusive and innovative growth only if its citizens are educated and able to act on the opportunities that arise. Educational reform tailored to national preconditions is essential in equipping Europeans for a productive and fulfilling future in that society. Knowledge and innovation clustering will inevitably result in regional disparities but should not be considered a problem as long as Europeans can participate and benefit from such clustering regardless of their place of birth. The principles of neutrality and contestability ensure that the entrepreneurial society will be inclusive at all levels, whereas a clear focus on excellence and societal challenges through public procurement, prizes, and public research programs can ensure the innovativeness and sustainability of growth.

In Table 7.2, we list the proposals made in this chapter. As seen, the appropriate level of policymaking differs quite a bit: For the reforms in the educational system, member states or even regional and local authorities possess the necessary legal competencies, but the EU can and should support their actions. Likewise, the policies and institutions supporting local and regional knowledge and entrepreneurship clusters will typically take shape in the interaction between universities and local authorities. In contrast, the European Commission should be able to address innovation policy, as the Lisbon Treaty gave it the budget and legal competencies necessary to do so.

**Table 7.2** Summary of proposals regarding mobilizing human capital for entrepreneurship, specifying the level in the governance hierarchy where the necessary decisions should be made

| No. | Principle(s) | Policy area | Proposal | Policy level[a] |
|---|---|---|---|---|
| 41 | Neutrality and contestability | Education system | Reforms in primary and secondary education should provide pupils with a solid and coherent knowledge base and promote initiative, creativity and a willingness to experiment. | MS, REG, LOC |
| 42 | Neutrality and contestability | Education system | Promote STEM education and English as a (mandatory) second language early on and then throughout educational career. | EU, MS |
| 43 | Justifiability and neutrality | Education system | Invest in high-quality tertiary level technical education by attracting excellent teaching staff and students and by strengthening Europe's strong tradition of vocational training. | MS |

(continued)

**Table 7.2** (continued)

| No. | Principle(s) | Policy area | Proposal | Policy level[a] |
|---|---|---|---|---|
| 44 | Justifiability and contestability | Universities/entrepreneurial clusters | The link between universities and external stakeholders should be strengthened by encouraging universities to stimulate entrepreneurial initiatives and university spinoffs. | MS, LOC |
| 45 | Justifiability and contestability | Universities/entrepreneurial clusters | Both the EU and its member states should create healthy, well-funded, academic institutions that allow Europe's most talented academics to pursue their research interests. | EU, MS |
| 46 | Justifiability and contestability | Entrepreneurial clusters | Liberalize, where possible, spatial planning regulations to allow the endogenous clustering of business activity rather than trying to plan clusters from the top down. | MS, REG, LOC |
| 47 | Neutrality and contestability | Immigration | Reform the European Blue Card system to also include nonemployees and people lacking high formal educational credentials provided they have a plan to support themselves and the requisite equity to start a viable business. | EU |
| 48 | Justifiability and contestability | Innovation policy | Develop highly competitive programs encouraging small businesses to engage research and development with the potential for commercialization. | EU, MS |
| 49 | Justifiability and contestability | Innovation policy | Support international partnerships for innovation through specific innovation challenges. | EU |
| 50 | Justifiability and contestability | Innovation policy | Institute technology inducement prizes to further the development of commercially applicable knowledge in especially important areas, such as climate change. | EU |

[a]*EU* federal level, *MS* member state level, *REG* regional government level, *LOC* local/municipal level

# 8

# Making Entrepreneurship Policy or Entrepreneurial Policymaking

Europe faces what some have dubbed an innovation emergency. Following the global financial crisis, the Union's challenge has been to return to a path of inclusive, sustainable, and innovative growth. This challenge, we believe, can only be overcome by a strategy acknowledging the importance of entrepreneurship, especially the type of Schumpeterian entrepreneurship that introduces new products and technologies and serves as a conduit of new knowledge to generate innovation and progress. To understand how to promote an entrepreneurial society, policymakers must recognize the crucial importance of collaborative innovation blocs, their agents, the roles these agents play, and how the blocs interact with the institutional framework that surrounds them. Indeed, tracing these components of the entrepreneurial ecosystem helped us identify the institutional areas in need of reform if Europe is to transform into a more entrepreneurial society.

We argued that an entrepreneurship-friendly reform strategy, to be coherent, must be informed by a set of common principles, which we identified for each area under discussion. In total, the result was a list of six principles: *neutrality, transparency, moderation, contestability, legality*, and *justifiability*. When tailored to local, regional, and national conditions, a reform strategy inspired by these principles is Europe's best chance to maintain its position in the global world order given the challenges we face in a globalized world increasingly steeped in digitalization.

To illustrate how these principles might be enshrined in Europe's diverse institutional landscape, we have proposed institutional reforms pertaining to six broad areas:

© The Author(s) 2019
N. Elert et al., *The Entrepreneurial Society*, International Studies in Entrepreneurship 98,
https://doi.org/10.1007/978-3-662-59586-2_8

1. *The rule of law and the protection of property rights*: The rule of law and secure property rights are fundamental to any market economy. To understand how they can be strengthened in an entrepreneurship-friendly manner across the EU, we first emphasize the principle of *legality*, i.e., considering de facto rather than de jure institutions. In regard to the protection of property rights, however, these cannot be absolute; property rights applying to intangibles and intellectual property in particular require a careful balancing of public and private interests to ensure *justifiability*. A clear and actionable reform agenda presents itself here given the European Commission's competencies in international negotiations on these issues.

2. *Taxation*: Taxation shapes and biases the incentives for corporations, individuals, and organizations in a multitude of ways, which are often detrimental to entrepreneurial venturing. Sometimes, reforms that explicitly favor entrepreneurship yield strong positive external effects, in line with the principle of *justifiability*. More often, we argue for a level playing field to ensure *neutrality* and *moderate* taxation to restore or maintain market incentives. The EU's limited competencies in this area mean that tax reforms in support of a more entrepreneurial society are chiefly the domain of member states.

3. *Savings, finance, and capital*: Europe's history has left most EU member states with a largely bank-based, highly regulated system of financial markets that predominantly "locks up" savings in professionally managed funds and assets. In such a system, entrepreneurial investees without collateral, strong balance sheets or long track records are fighting an uphill battle for credit and financial resources. We propose to aim for *neutrality* and *transparency* and level the financial playing field to restore *contestability*. Of course, there is a fundamental public interest in financial stability, especially in the payment and store-of-value functions of money. In line with the principle of *justifiability*, these valid considerations must be acknowledged but not allowed to prevent well-designed public interventions that enable the financial sector to mobilize more of Europe's ample financial resources for entrepreneurial ventures. Proposals are mostly addressed at the EU level, as competencies for reform are increasingly delegated to the European level.

4. *Labor markets and social security systems*: These institutions largely determine the allocation of human resources, notably skilled labor, to entrepreneurial ventures. Systems are typically tilted in favor of large, stable incumbent firms, which implies that experimental, innovative ventures are at a disadvantage. Our proposed reforms aim to improve the situation for entrepreneurs in Europe by making rights more *transparent* and portable

and security more universal and unconditional. Such portability and unconditionality ensure *neutrality* and *contestability* for human resources, whereas flexibility for entrepreneurs must be balanced against security for employees, according to the principle of *justifiability*. We primarily address proposals to the member states, as they retain most legal competencies in this area.

5. *Contestable markets for entry and exit*: An area of strong and extensive EU competencies is the single market. Under that heading, Europe can do more to ensure that a vibrant entrepreneurial society can bloom across the Union. Lowered entry barriers are key to this reform area, and this is particularly true for services: especially in the semi-public and public domains of health, education, and similar services, there is room for productive venturing under appropriate constraints. Finally, to facilitate entry in many sectors, exit must also be well arranged, which motivates our proposals in the area of bankruptcy law and the smooth liquidation of outdated and failed ventures. The proposals in this chapter are addressed at national and European policymakers alike, as the EU has extensive competencies in regulating markets and competition, whereas health and education are the domain of member states.

6. *Mobilizing human capital for entrepreneurship*: Since the Treaty of Lisbon, knowledge policy is firmly part of the Commission's competencies, but we are yet to see institutional reforms aimed at building a truly European knowledge space. If realized, such a knowledge space would permit useful knowledge to flow freely to the benefit of incumbents and challengers alike. The large positive externalities *justify* public policy at the local, national, and European levels, whereas *neutrality* and *contestability* inevitably lead to an endogenous clustering of knowledge and innovation across the Union.

Throughout the six chapters, we make no fewer than 50 reform proposals, the lion's share of which are highly concrete. We hope that they will inspire policymakers, practitioners, and other readers of this book and provide a firm and principled idea of how a European reform agenda could look. Of course, policymakers will need to tailor most proposals to specific national and regional contexts; others may need to be reformulated or reconsidered. We see this as demonstrating the robustness of our approach and not as a weakness. There are already enough books where unquestionably talented economists present statistical inference and econometrics to support proposals that, ultimately, amount to an if-it-works-on-average-it-will-work-everywhere approach to reforms (see, e.g., Colander and Freedman 2018). As Rodrik

(2015) argues, no one model can be applied everywhere. All judicious policy advice is context dependent.

Benchmarking is useful, of course, as is learning from success elsewhere. However, one must always dig deep and uncover the full causal chain that explains success before naïvely starting to implement partial reforms. As no two institutions are built upon the same bedrock, it is better to identify the functions that a healthy entrepreneurial ecosystem needs and then build institutions that perform those functions, perhaps differently in different places, but fitting in the local context.

That is not the same as saying "it all depends" and giving up on offering guidance. As long as reforms are informed by the core principles that enabled us to derive our proposals in the first place, reform adjustments and reformulations are, in our view, a feature rather than a bug of our approach. The devil is in the details, and policymaking itself must therefore be an entrepreneurial process. Institutional reforms should go through rapid cycles of experimentation, learning, and pivoting until policymakers find suitable and satisfactory solutions. Ultimately, these solutions may end up looking different from what we have proposed above, but the general principles should still shine through. Below, we identify several points to which followers of our strategy should adhere.

First, a European reform agenda striving to create an entrepreneurial society needs sophistication. It falls to reformers and other practitioners to package the proposed principles into institutional designs sensitive to local constraints and opportunities. The identification of best-practice institutions is a *sine qua non* for any reform agenda to be successful, but so is the recognition that a first-order economic principle such as market competition does not map onto one single policy package. No unique correspondence exists between functionally good institutions and the form that such institutions take; in fact, policymakers must choose between several institutional bundles, each with the potential to achieve the desired economic and social ends. The bundle that is the most appropriate will depend upon the context. At best, misguided reforms that ignore this fact do not work, plain and simple. At worst, a thoughtless introduction of supposedly first-class institutions can backfire, undermining existing domestic institutions instead of taking hold (Rodrik 2008).

Second, a reform agenda must be appropriately concrete. Most historical and econometric studies of institutions and growth tend to remain at a high level of generality and do not provide much policy guidance (Besley and

Burgess 2003; Rodrik 2008).[1] Here, we have attempted to go beyond abstract reasoning, drilling down to the specific effects of particular measures. Much more work is required in this respect before an entrepreneurial reform agenda is realized, but we hope to have proceeded further down the ladder of concreteness than most other books and articles with similar aims.

Third, a reform agenda must prioritize. The EOE and VoC perspectives are valuable for understanding how. The EOE perspective identifies which institutions matter the most for the key actors in collaborative innovation blocs, whereas the VoC perspective groups countries with respect to their institutional frameworks, hinting at the institutional complementarities within a particular cluster of countries (Dilli et al. 2018). Here, an essential part of future work is to identify and suggest the removal of the so-called institutional bottlenecks (Acs et al. 2014). Doing so will make it possible for researchers and policymakers to assess the problems that should be the top priority within a cluster. Furthermore, countries in a cluster can be more or less successful, and their relative rank within the cluster has important informational and practical value for any reform process. Rather than trying to leapfrog directly to a point of institutional bliss, a laggard country should try to become more like the leader in its cluster in the short and medium term. This goal is likely to be attainable by virtue of its relative modesty and because the reforming country then aspires to something that has been tried before in a similar institutional context.

Fourth, the reform process should be incremental and leave room for experimentation rather than imitation without reflection. From a Schumpeterian (and, arguably, Popperian) perspective, the quest to develop an optimal set of legal rules ignores a central feature of successful economic development, namely, the fact that institutions and organizations in a competitive environment continuously contest, innovate, and adapt. Reforms that are tailor-made to a country's specific constraints and opportunities through experimentation during a discovery process will likely be more beneficial than reforms based on mere imitation (Hausmann and Rodrik 2003; Sabel and Reddy 2007). Nevertheless, given the complexities involved, it is important to keep in mind that simple legal principles are often preferable to a detail-oriented case-by-case approach. Indeed, one possibility is to strive for the sort of "simple rules for a complex world" advocated by Epstein (2009).

---

[1] For instance, although it is very useful to know that inclusive institutions introduced in colonies in the sixteenth century persist to this day and can be instrumented with settler mortality in that era (Acemoglu et al. 2001), that leaves us with preciously little actionable policy advice.

Finally, a reform agenda should dig into the local context. An offshoot of the FIRES project is presently conducting urgent work in this direction that will culminate in the book *The Entrepreneurial Society: Tailoring a Reform Strategy to Local Institutions*, edited by Axel Marx, Mark Sanders, and Mikael Stenkula. If the reform proposals in this book form a menu of options, this second book will show how to assess an entrepreneurial ecosystem and how that assessment should be used to select those proposals that are most relevant to a particular local, regional, and national context. Together, the two volumes help reformers address the most urgent and pressing problems and choose specific designs that achieve the goal and fit the context. Our explicit formulation of our reform agenda's underlying principles gives direction to that exercise, while our proposals may inspire policymakers to look beyond the limits of traditional entrepreneurship policy.

The EU needs a new and appealing narrative. By offering real opportunities for all, the entrepreneurial society provides an urgently needed optimistic answer to the stifling populist conservatism that has swept across Europe and put the European project in jeopardy. The recipes of neoliberal reformers have failed to deliver for significant parts of Europe's constituency, and the current debate simply cannot support another round of "structural reforms" naïvely liberalizing product, service, labor, and capital markets. Instead, the EU needs to start building an institutional environment that brings appealing opportunities to all of its citizens. By directing its citizens' abundant creativity, talent, and resources towards new venturing, Europe can return to socially inclusive, ecologically sustainable, and innovation-driven growth. This will not turn the *gilets jaunes* into a happy and docile electorate. But it will provide the defenders of an open European society with more ammunition to turn the populist, nationalist tide and goes a long way towards protecting the European project that has brought peace and prosperity to most of the Continent for the past 70 years.

# Appendix

N. Elert et al., *The Entrepreneurial Society*, International Studies in Entrepreneurship 98,
https://doi.org/10.1007/978-3-662-59586-2

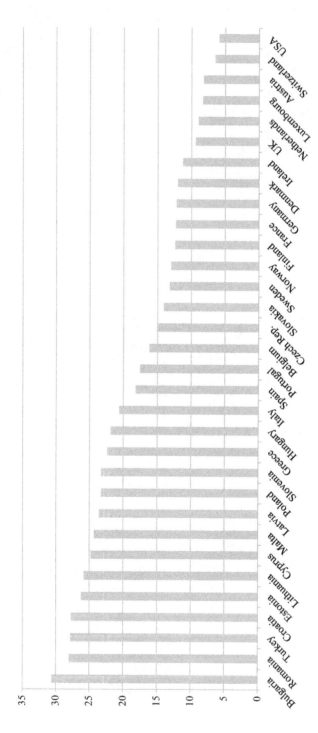

**Fig. A.1** The size of the shadow economy in European countries and the USA in 2015 (in % of official GDP). Source: Schneider (2015a)

Single, average wage, 6 months, excl. housing benefits

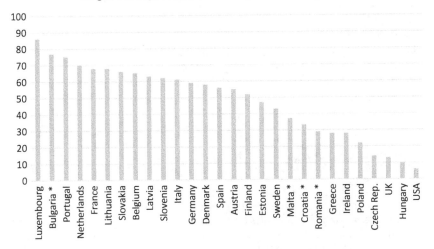

Couple, 2 children, average wagefor both, 6 months, incl. housing benefits

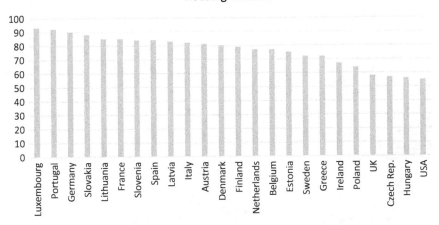

**Fig. A.2** The net replacement rates of unemployment benefits in EU countries and the USA, 2018. Source: OECD and European Commission

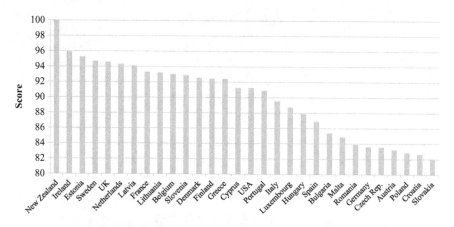

**Fig. A.3** Ease of starting a business in EU countries, the USA, and the leading country, 2019. Note: The ranking of economies on the ease of starting a business is determined based on their distance to frontier scores for starting a business. These scores are the simple average of the distance to frontier scores for each of the component indicators. Source: World Bank, *Ease of Doing Business Index 2019*

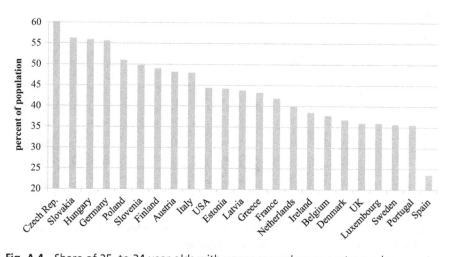

**Fig. A.4** Share of 25- to 34-year olds with upper secondary or postsecondary non-tertiary education in EU countries and the USA, 2017. Source: OECD, *Education at a Glance 2018*, p. 55

**Table A.1** European countries with wealth taxation, 2019

| Country | Tax rate, % | Top rate applies or exempted amount | Comments |
| --- | --- | --- | --- |
| France | 0.5–1.5 | Above €10 million | Exempted amount: €1.3 million (per household) |
| Italy | 0.2/0.76 | No exemption | 0.2% on financial assets held abroad and 0.76% on real estate held abroad except if primary residence |
| Liechtenstein | 0.1–1.12 | CHF 200,000 | 2.5–2.8% income tax on 4% on net wealth (= a net wealth tax of 0.1–1.12%) |
| Luxembourg | 0.5 | | Only applies for corporations |
| Moldova | 0.8 | MDL 1.5 mio exempted | For real estate (except land) |
| Netherlands | 1.2 | | 30% income tax on a fictitious return of 4% on financial assets (= a net wealth tax of 1.2%) |
| Norway | 0.85 | NOK 1.48 mio p.p. exempted | |
| Spain | 0.2–2.5 | Exemption € 700,000; top rate above € 10.7 million | Habitual dwellings exempt up to €300,000 |
| Switzerland | 0.007–0.963 | Above CHF 10 mio | Exemption of CHF 75,000, but varies between cantons |

Sources: https://www.oldmutualinternational.com/other/Adviser/technical-centre/knowledge-direct/international/europe/european-inheritance-gift-and-wealth-tax/ and the respective national tax agencies websites

**Table A.2** Inheritance taxation (for spouse and children) in European countries and the USA, 2019

| Country | Tax rate, % | Exempted amount | Top rate on amount > | Comments |
|---|---|---|---|---|
| USA[a] | 0–40 | $5.6 mio | $5.6 mio | Some states levy an additional inheritance tax |
| Austria | n/a | | | Abolished 2008 |
| Belgium[b] | 3–55 | 0 | €75,000 | |
| Bulgaria | 0.4–0.8 | €128,000 | | For direct descendants, up to 6.6% for others |
| Croatia | 0–5 | HRK 50,000 | n/a | HRK 50,000 ≈ €6700 |
| Cyprus | n/a | | | Abolished 2001 |
| Czech Rep. | n/a | | | Abolished 2014 |
| Denmark[a] | 15 | DKK 289,000 | Flat rate | DKK 289,000 ≈ €39,000 |
| Estonia | n/a | | | |
| Finland | 0–33 | €20,000 | €1 mio | |
| France | 5–60 | 0 | €1.8 mio | |
| Germany | 7–50 | 0 | €6 mio | |
| Greece | 10 | €400,000 | €220,000 | |
| Ireland | 33 | €325,000 | n/a | |
| Italy | 4 | €1 mio | n/a | |
| Latvia | n/a | | | |
| Lithuania | 0 | €3000 | €150,000 | n/a for family members |
| Luxembourg | 0–1.5 | €10,000 | €1.75 mio | |
| Malta | n/a | | | % stamp-duty for inherited immovable property |
| Netherlands | 10–20 | €19,868 | €117,214 | |
| Norway | n/a | | | Abolished 2014 |
| Poland | 0–20 | PLN 9637 | PLN 20,557 | PLN 20,557 ≈ €5000 |
| Portugal | n/a | | | Abolished 2004 |
| Romania | n/a | | | |
| Slovakia | n/a | | | |
| Slovenia | 5–39 | €5,000 | | Exemption applies to direct descendants |
| Spain | 7.65–34 | €15,957 | €797,555 | |
| Sweden | n/a | | | Abolished 2004 |
| Switzerland | 0/6 | | | Zürich/Geneva |
| UK[a] | 40 | £325,000 | £325,000 | If ≥10% to charity, rate 36% |

Note: In most cases the same tax rate applies to in vivo gifts
Source: Ernst and Young (2018), https://www.ey.com/Publication/vwLUAssets/ey-worldwide-estate-and-inheritance-tax-guide-2018/$FILE/ey-worldwide-estate-and-inheritance-tax-guide-2018.pdf and the respective national tax agencies websites
[a]The estate rather than the inheritance lot allocated to each heir is taxed; Denmark levies both estate and inheritance tax, depending on the relationship between deceased and recipient
[b]Flemish region

**Table A.3**  Rules limiting the deduction of interest expenses by firms in European countries and the USA, 2019

| Country | % of EBITDA | Min. allowed | Specifics |
|---|---|---|---|
| USA | 30 | n/a | |
| Austria | n/a | n/a | Claimed to have equally effective legislation; derogation denied by the EC |
| Belgium | 30 | €3 mio | |
| Bulgaria | 30 | €3 mio | |
| Croatia | 30 | €3 mio | |
| Cyprus | 30 | €3 mio | |
| Czech Rep. | 30 | CZK 80 mio | CZK 80 mio ≈ €3 mio |
| Denmark | 30 | DKK 22.3 mio | DKK 22.3 mio ≈ €3 mio |
| Estonia | 30 | €3 mio | |
| Finland | 25 | €3 mio | |
| France | 30 | €3 mio | |
| Germany | 30 | €3 mio | |
| Greece | 30 | €3 mio | |
| Ireland | n/a | | Claimed to have equally effective legislation. Derogation denied by the EC |
| Italy | 30 | n/a | |
| Latvia | 30 | €3 mio | |
| Lithuania | 30 | €3 mio | |
| Luxembourg | 30 | €3 mio | |
| Malta | 30 | €3 mio | |
| Netherlands | 30 | €1 mio | |
| Norway | 25 | NOK 25 mio | NOK 25 mio ≈ €1 mio |
| Poland | 30 | PLN 3 mio | PLN 3 mio ≈ €0.7 mio |
| Portugal | 30 | €1 mio | |
| Romania | 30 | RON 4.6 mio | RON 4.6 mio ≈ €1 mio |
| Slovakia | 25 | n/a | |
| Slovenia | n/a | n/a | Thin cap rule of debt-to-equity ratio of 4:1 |
| Spain | 30 | €1 mio | 30% of the calculation base (adjusted operating income) |
| Sweden | 30 | SEK 5 mio | SEK 5 mio ≈ €0.5 mio |
| Switzerland | n/a | n/a | Notional interest deduction on safety equity, i.e., equity which exceeds the average equity required for business operations |
| UK | 30 | GBP 2 mio | GBP 2 mio ≈ €2.2 mio |

Note: In implementing ATAD II, most countries have exercised their right to exclude financial undertakings. Among member states of the EU, only Greece, France, Slovakia, Slovenia, and Spain had legislation deemed by the European Commission to be equally effective to the interest limitation rule as specified in Article 4 of the Anti-Tax Avoidance Directive

Source:    https://www.ibfd.org/IBFD-Tax-Portal/News/New-Tables-Monitor-Anti-Tax-Avoidance-Directive-implementation and the websites of the various national tax agencies

**Table A.4** Effective tax rate on stock options in selected countries, 2012

| Country | Tax rate, % | Country | Tax rate, % |
|---|---|---|---|
| Australia | 24.8 | Japan | 50.5 |
| Canada | 31.9 | Netherlands | 25.0 |
| China | 45.0 | Norway | 50.8 |
| Denmark | 55.3 | Portugal | 56.5 |
| Finland | 51.3 | Singapore | 20.0 |
| France | 29.9 | South Korea | 61.5 |
| Germany | 47.5 | Spain | 52.0 |
| Hong Kong | 15.0 | Sweden | 54.3 |
| Ireland | 7.4 | Switzerland | 51.5 |
| Israel | 25.0 | UK | 28.0 |
| Italy | 72.2 | USA | 15.0 |

Sources: PricewaterhouseCoopers (PwC), Thomson One, and Henrekson and Sanandaji (2018a)

**Table A.5** Expenditure on education as a share of GDP in EU countries and the USA, 2014, and PISA results (in reading, mathematics, and science) in EU countries and the USA, 2015

| Country | Education spending | Country | PISA mathematics | Country | PISA science | Country | PISA reading |
|---|---|---|---|---|---|---|---|
| UK | 6.6 | Estonia | 520 | Estonia | 534 | Finland | 526 |
| Denmark | 6.5 | Netherlands | 512 | Finland | 531 | Ireland | 521 |
| USA | 6.2 | Finland | 511 | Slovenia | 513 | Estonia | 519 |
| Cyprus (2015) | 6.0 | Denmark | 511 | UK | 509 | Germany | 509 |
| Belgium | 5.8 | Slovenia | 510 | Germany | 509 | Poland | 506 |
| Portugal | 5.8 | Belgium | 507 | Netherlands | 509 | Slovenia | 505 |
| Finland | 5.7 | Germany | 506 | Ireland | 503 | Netherlands | 503 |
| Sweden | 5.4 | Ireland | 504 | Belgium | 502 | Denmark | 500 |
| Netherlands | 5.4 | Poland | 504 | Denmark | 502 | Sweden | 500 |
| France | 5.3 | Austria | 497 | Poland | 501 | Belgium | 499 |
| Estonia | 5.0 | Sweden | 494 | Portugal | 501 | France | 499 |
| Malta | 4.9 | France | 493 | USA | 496 | UK | 498 |
| Austria | 4.9 | UK | 492 | Austria | 495 | Portugal | 498 |
| Croatia (2015) | 4.8 | Portugal | 492 | France | 495 | USA | 497 |
| Ireland | 4.8 | Czech Rep. | 492 | Sweden | 493 | Spain | 496 |
| Latvia | 4.7 | Italy | 490 | Czech Rep. | 493 | Latvia | 488 |
| Poland | 4.7 | Spain | 486 | Spain | 493 | Czech Rep. | 487 |
| Slovenia | 4.6 | Luxembourg | 486 | Latvia | 490 | Croatia | 487 |
| Greece (2015) | 4.3 | Latvia | 482 | Luxembourg | 483 | Austria | 485 |
| Germany | 4.3 | Malta | 479 | Italy | 481 | Italy | 485 |
| Spain | 4.3 | Lithuania | 478 | Hungary | 477 | Luxembourg | 481 |
| Lithuania | 4.2 | Hungary | 477 | Lithuania | 475 | Lithuania | 472 |
| Italy | 4.0 | Slovakia | 475 | Croatia | 475 | Hungary | 470 |
| Bulgaria (2015) | 4.0 | USA | 470 | Malta | 465 | Greece | 467 |
| Czech Rep. | 3.9 | Croatia | 464 | Slovakia | 461 | Slovakia | 453 |
| Slovakia | 3.9 | Greece | 454 | Greece | 455 | Malta | 447 |

(Continued)

**Table A.5** (Continued)

| Country | Education spending | Country | PISA mathematics | Country | PISA science | Country | PISA reading |
|---|---|---|---|---|---|---|---|
| Hungary | 3.8 | Romania | 444 | Bulgaria | 446 | Cyprus | 443 |
| Luxembourg | 3.6 | Bulgaria | 441 | Romania | 435 | Romania | 434 |
| Romania (2015) | 3.1 | Cyprus | 437 | Cyprus | 433 | Bulgaria | 432 |

Note: The scores are calculated in each year so that the mean is 500 and the standard deviation 100

Source: *OECD Programme for International Student Assessment* (PISA) and OECD, *Education at a Glance 2018*. Education spending data for Romania, Bulgaria, Greece, Croatia, and Cyprus are from Eurostat → General government expenditure by function → Education

**Table A.6** Before tax educational premiums and return on analytical/numerical ability in EU countries and the USA

| Country | Educational premium | Country | Return on analytical/numerical ability |
|---|---|---|---|
| USA | 11.1 | USA | 27.9 |
| Poland | 10.1 | Ireland | 24.1 |
| Germany | 9.5 | Germany | 23.5 |
| Slovakia | 9.5 | Spain | 22.8 |
| Cyprus | 8.9 | UK | 22.5 |
| UK | 8.5 | Poland | 19.1 |
| Ireland | 8.5 | Netherlands | 18.3 |
| Netherlands | 8.2 | Austria | 17.9 |
| Spain | 7.9 | Slovakia | 17.9 |
| Austria | 7.7 | Estonia | 17.9 |
| Estonia | 7.4 | France | 17.4 |
| Finland | 6.8 | Belgium | 14.9 |
| Belgium | 6.2 | Finland | 14.2 |
| Czech Rep. | 5.9 | Cyprus | 13.8 |
| France | 5.5 | Denmark | 13.7 |
| Denmark | 5.5 | Italy | 13.2 |
| Italy | 5.3 | Czech Rep. | 12.4 |
| Sweden | 4.2 | Sweden | 12.1 |

Note: The educational premium is defined as the relative increase in the wage that can be attributed to an additional year of schooling. The return on analytical/numerical ability is defined as the relative increase in the wage that results from a one standard deviation increase in a person's PIAAC score for numeracy. All EU countries in the Hanushek et al. study are included in the table
Source: Hanushek et al. (2015)

**Table A.7** Direct government funding of business R&D and tax incentives for R&D, percentage of GDP 2017

| Country | Direct funding | Indirect support (through R&D tax incentives) | Direct and indirect funding | Government funding as % of total BERD |
|---|---|---|---|---|
| Austria | 0.13 | 0.14 | 0.27 | 8.8 |
| Belgium[a] | 0.11 | 0.28 | 0.39 | 15.7 |
| Czech Rep. | 0.08 | 0.06 | 0.14 | 8.3 |
| Denmark | 0.05 | 0.08 | 0.13 | 4.5 |
| Estonia | 0.06 | 0.00 | 0.06 | 4.7 |
| Finland | 0.07 | 0.00 | 0.07 | 2.6 |
| France[a] | 0.11 | 0.28 | 0.39 | 17.4 |
| Germany | 0.07 | 0.00 | 0.07 | 2.4 |
| Greece | 0.03 | 0.05 | 0.08 | 7.9 |
| Hungary | 0.20 | 0.15 | 0.35 | 29.0 |
| Ireland[a] | 0.07 | 0.29 | 0.36 | 30.6 |
| Italy | 0.04 | 0.04 | 0.08 | 6.2 |
| Netherlands | 0.02 | 0.15 | 0.17 | 8.4 |
| Poland | 0.05 | – | 0.05 | 5.2 |
| Portugal | 0.05 | 0.10 | 0.15 | 11.8 |
| Slovakia | 0.02 | 0.003 | 0.02 | 2.9 |
| Slovenia | 0.07 | 0.12 | 0.19 | 9.5 |
| Spain | 0.06 | 0.06 | 0.12 | 10.1 |
| Sweden[a] | 0.13 | 0.05 | 0.18 | 5.5 |
| UK[a] | 0.10 | 0.13 | 0.23 | 13.6 |
| USA[b] | 0.18 | 0.07 | 0.25 | 9.1 |

Source: *OECD Science, Technology and Industry Scoreboard 2017*
[a]2014
[b]2013

# References

Abramowicz, M. (2003). Perfecting patent prizes. *Vanderbilt Law Review, 56*(1), 115–236.

Acemoglu, D., Johnson, S., & Robinson, J. A. (2001). The colonial origins of comparative development: An empirical investigation. *American Economic Review, 91*(5), 1369–1401.

Acemoglu, D., Johnson, S., & Robinson, J. A. (2005). Institutions as a fundamental cause of long-run growth. In P. Aghion & S. Durlauf (Eds.), *Handbook of economic growth* (Vol. 1, pp. 385–472). Amsterdam: Elsevier.

Acemoglu, D., Aghion, P., & Zilibotti, F. (2006). Distance to frontier, selection, and economic growth. *Journal of the European Economic Association, 4*(1), 37–74.

Acemoglu, D., Robinson, J. A., & Verdier, T. (2017). Asymmetric growth and institutions in an interdependent world. *Journal of Political Economy, 125*(5), 1245–1305.

Acs, Z. J. (2006). A formulation of entrepreneurship policy. *Foundations and Trends in Entrepreneurship, 2*(3), 223–223.

Acs, Z. J., & Phillips, R. J. (2002). Entrepreneurship and philanthropy in American capitalism. *Small Business Economics, 19*(3), 189–204.

Acs, Z. J., & Sanders, M. (2012). Patents, knowledge spillovers, and entrepreneurship. *Small Business Economics, 39*(4), 801–817.

Acs, Z. J., & Sanders, M. (2013). Knowledge spillover entrepreneurship in an endogenous growth model. *Small Business Economics, 41*(4), 775–795.

Acs, Z. J., & Szerb, L. (2007). Entrepreneurship, economic growth and public policy. *Small Business Economics, 28*(2–3), 109–122.

Acs, Z. J., Desai, S., & Hessels, J. (2008). Entrepreneurship, economic development, and institutions. *Small Business Economics, 31*(3), 219–234.

Acs, Z. J., Audretsch, D. B., Braunerhjelm, P., & Carlsson, B. (2009). The knowledge spillover theory of entrepreneurship. *Small Business Economics, 32*(1), 15–30.

© The Author(s) 2019
N. Elert et al., *The Entrepreneurial Society*, International Studies in Entrepreneurship 98,
https://doi.org/10.1007/978-3-662-59586-2

Acs, Z. J., Autio, E., & Szerb, L. (2014). National systems of entrepreneurship: Measurement issues and policy implications. *Research Policy, 43*(3), 476–494.

Adler, J. (2011). Eyes on the climate prize: Rewarding energy innovation to achieve climate stabilization. *Harvard Environmental Law Review, 35*(1), 1–45.

Admati, A. R., DeMarzo, P. M., Hellwig, M., & Pfleiderer, P. (2010). *Fallacies, irrelevant facts, and myths in the discussion of capital regulation: Why bank equity is not expensive.* Bonn: Max Planck Institute for Research on Collective Goods.

Adnett, N., Bougheas, S., & Georgellis, Y. (2004). On the trade-off between work-related training and labor mobility: The role of firing and exit costs. *Journal of Economics, 82*(1), 49–70.

Aghion, P., & Howitt, P. (1992). A model of growth through creative destruction. *Econometrica, 60*(2), 323–351.

Aghion, P., Dewatripont, M., Hoxby, C., Mas-Colell, A., & Sapir, A. (2007). Why reform Europe's universities? *Bruegel Policy Brief, 4,* 1–8.

Aghion, P., Dewatripont, M., Hoxby, C., Mas-Colell, A., & Sapir, A. (2008). *Higher aspirations: An agenda for reforming European universities* (Bruegel blueprint series) (Vol. 5). Brussels: Bruegel.

Agrawal, A. K. (2001). University-to-industry knowledge transfer: Literature review and unanswered questions. *International Journal of Management Reviews, 3*(4), 285–302.

Alesina, A. F., Algan, Y., Cahuc, P., & Giuliano, P. (2015). Family values and the regulation of labor. *Journal of the European Economic Association, 13*(4), 599–630.

Amoroso, S., Audretsch, D. B., & Link, A. N. (2018). Sources of knowledge used by entrepreneurial firms in the European high-tech sector. *Eurasian Business Review, 8*(1), 55–70.

Andersen, T. M. (2005). The Danish labor market—from excess to shortage. In M. Werding (Ed.), *Structural unemployment in Western Europe: Reasons and remedies.* Cambridge, MA: MIT Press.

Anderson, A. R., & Starnawska, M. (2008). Research practices in entrepreneurship: Problems of definition, description and meaning. *International Journal of Entrepreneurship and Innovation, 9*(4), 221–230.

Andersson, M., & Henrekson, M. (2015). Local competitiveness fostered through local institutions for entrepreneurship. In D. B. Audretsch, A. N. Link, & M. Walshok (Eds.), *Oxford handbook of local competitiveness* (pp. 145–190). Oxford, UK: Oxford University Press.

Apergis, N., Fafaliou, I., & Polemis, M. L. (2016). New evidence on assessing the level of competition in the European Union banking sector: A panel data approach. *International Business Review, 25*(1), 395–407.

Apostol, R. (2017). *Trials and tribulations in the implementation of pre-commercial procurement in Europe.* The Hague: TMC Asser Press.

Arcand, J-L., Berkes, E., & Panizza, U. (2012). Too much finance? IMF working paper no. 12/161. Washington DC: International Monetary Fund. http://www.imf.org/external/pubs/ft/wp/2012/wp12161.pdf

Armour, J., & Cumming, D. (2006). The legislative road to Silicon Valley. *Oxford Economic Papers, 58*(4), 596–635.

Arrow, K. (1962). Economic welfare and the allocation of resources for invention. In *The rate and direction of inventive activity: Economic and social factors* (A report of the National Bureau of Economic Research) (pp. 609–626). Princeton, NJ: Princeton University Press.

Arthur, W. B. (1989). Competing technologies, increasing returns, and lock-in by historical events. *Economic Journal, 99*(394), 116–131.

Arzaghi, M., & Henderson, J. V. (2008). Networking off Madison Avenue. *Review of Economic Studies, 75*(4), 1011–1038.

Aschauer, D. (2000). Public capital and economic growth: Issues of quantity, finance and efficiency. *Economic Development and Cultural Change, 48*(2), 391–406.

Åslund, A., & Djankov, S. (2017). *Europe's growth challenge.* Oxford, UK: Oxford University Press.

Astarita, C., ed. (2014). *Taxing wealth: Past, present, future. Proceedings of the workshop organised by the Directorate General for Economic and Financial Affairs held in Brussels on 13 November 2014.* Brussels: European Commission Directorate-General for Economic and Financial Affairs.

Athanassiou, E., Kanellopoulos, N., Karagiannis, R., & Kotsi, A. (2015). *The effects of liberalisation of professional requirements in Greece.* Athens: Centre for Planning and Economic Research (KEPE).

Audretsch, D. B. (2014). From the entrepreneurial university to the university for the entrepreneurial society. *Journal of Technology Transfer, 39*(3), 313–321.

Audretsch, D. B., & Fritsch, M. (2002). Growth regimes over time and space. *Regional Studies, 36*(2), 113–124.

Audretsch, D. B., & Thurik, A. R. (2000). Capitalism and democracy in the 21st century: From the managed to the entrepreneurial economy. *Journal of Evolutionary Economics, 10*(1), 17–34.

Audretsch, D. B., Keilbach, M. C., & Lehmann, E. E. (2006). *Entrepreneurship and economic growth.* New York: Oxford University Press.

Audretsch, D. B., Sanders, M., & Zhang, L. (2017). International product life cycles, trade and development stages. *Journal of Technology Transfer,* published online.

Auerswald, P., & Acs, Z. J. (2009). Defining prosperity. *American Interest Magazine,* May/June, pp. 4–13.

Auerswald, P., & Branscomb, L. M. (2003). Valleys of death and Darwinian seas: Financing the invention to innovation transition in the United States. *Journal of Technology Transfer, 28*(3–4), 227–239.

Autio, E. (2016). *Entrepreneurship support in Europe: Trends and challenges.* Technical report. London: Imperial College.

Autio, E., Kronlund, M., & Kovalainen, A. (2007). *High-growth SME support initiatives in nine countries: Analysis, categorization, and recommendations.* Ministry of Trade and Industry: Helsinki.

Bachmann, R., & Burda, M. C. (2010). Sectoral transformation, turbulence and labor market dynamics in Germany. *German Economic Review, 11*(1), 37–59.

Barrdear, J., & Kumhof, M. (2016). *The macroeconomics of central bank issued digital currencies*. Bank of England working paper no. 605. https://ssrn.com/abstract=2811208 or https://doi.org/10.2139/ssrn.2811208

Barrios, J. M. (2018). Occupational licensing and accountant quality: Evidence from the 150-hour rule. *Working paper no. 2018–32*. Chicago, IL: Becker Friedman Institute for Research in Economics at the University of Chicago.

Barro, R. J. (2001). Human capital and growth. *American Economic Review, 91*(2), 12–17.

Bastiat, F. (1850). What is seen and what is not seen. In *Selected essays on political economy*. Irvington-on-Hudson, NY: Foundation for Economic Education.

Baumol, W. J. (1968). Entrepreneurship in economic theory. *American Economic Review, 58*(2), 64–71.

Baumol, W. J. (1990). Entrepreneurship: Productive, unproductive, and destructive. *Journal of Political Economy, 98*(5), 893–921.

Baumol, W. J. (2010). *The microtheory of innovative entrepreneurship*. Princeton, NJ: Princeton University Press.

Baumol, W. J. (2012). *The cost disease: Why computers get cheaper and health care doesn't*. New Haven, CT: Yale University Press.

Baumol, W. J., Litan, R. E., & Schramm, C. J. (2007). *Good capitalism, bad capitalism and the economics of growth and prosperity*. New Haven, CT: Yale University Press.

Bebchuk, L. A., & Roe, M. J. (2004). A theory of path dependence in corporate ownership and governance. In J. N. Gordon & M. J. Roe (Eds.), *Convergence and persistence in corporate governance* (pp. 69–113). Cambridge, UK: Cambridge University Press.

Becker, B., & Josephson, J. (2016). Insolvency resolution and the missing high yield bond markets. *Review of Financial Studies, 29*(10), 2814–2849.

Benes, J., & Kumhof, M. (2012). *The Chicago plan revisited*. Washington, DC: International Monetary Fund.

Bentivogli, C., & Pagano, P. (1999). Regional disparities and labour mobility: The Euro-11 versus the USA. *Labour, 13*(3), 737–760.

Benz, M., & Frey, B. S. (2004). Being independent raises happiness at work. *Swedish Economic Policy Review, 11*(2), 95–134.

Bergman, E. M. (2010). Knowledge links between European universities and firms: A review. *Papers in Regional Science, 89*(2), 311–333.

Besley, T., & Burgess, R. (2003). Halving global poverty. *Journal of Economic Perspectives, 17*(3), 3–22.

Besley, T., & Ghatak, M. (2010). Property rights and economic development. In D. Rodrik & M. R. Rosenzweig (Eds.), *Handbook of development economics* (Vol. 5, pp. 4525–4595). Amsterdam: North Holland.

Bezemer, D. J. (2014). Schumpeter might be right again: The functional differentiation of credit. *Journal of Evolutionary Economics, 24*(5), 935–950.

Bezemer, D. J., & Hudson, M. (2016). Finance is not the economy: Reviving the conceptual distinction. *Journal of Economic Issues, 50*(3), 745–768.

Bhidé, A. (2008). *The venturesome economy: How innovation sustains prosperity in a more connected world.* Princeton, NJ: Princeton University Press.

Bingham, T. (2011). *The rule of law.* London: Penguin.

Binmore, K. (2005). *Natural justice.* Oxford, UK: Oxford University Press.

Birch, D. (2006). What have we learned? *Foundations and Trends in Entrepreneurship, 2*(3), 57–62.

Bjørnskov, C., & Foss, N. J. (2013). How strategic entrepreneurship and the institutional context drive economic growth. *Strategic Entrepreneurship Journal, 7*(1), 50–69.

Blanchflower, D. G., & Oswald, A. J. (1998). What makes an entrepreneur? *Journal of Labor Economics, 16*(1), 26–60.

Block, J. H., Colombo, M. G., Cumming, D. J., & Vismara, S. (2018). New players in entrepreneurial finance and why they are there. *Small Business Economics, 50*(2), 239–250.

Bloom, N., Sadun, R., & van Reenen, J. (2009). Do private equity-owned firms have better management practices? In A. Gurung & J. Lerner (Eds.), *The globalization of alternative investments working papers volume 2: The global economic impact of private equity report 2009* (pp. 25–43). Geneva: World Economic Forum.

Boadway, R., Chamberlain, E., & Emmerson, C. (2010). Taxation of wealth and wealth transfers: Dimensions of tax design. In *Dimensions of tax design: The Mirrlees review* (pp. 737–814). Oxford, UK: Oxford University Press.

Boettiger, S., & Burk, D. L. (2004). Open source patenting. *Journal of International Biotechnology Law, 1*(6), 221–231.

Bordo, M. D., & Levin, A. T. (2017). *Central bank digital currency and the future of monetary policy.* NBER working paper no. 23711. Cambridge, MA: National Bureau of Economic Research.

Bordo, M. D., & Levin, A. T. (2019). *Digital cash: Principles and practical steps.* NBER working paper no. 25455. Cambridge, MA: National Bureau of Economic Research.

Bosma, N., Stam, E., & Wennekers, S. (2010). *Intrapreneurship—an international study.* EIM scales research report H201005. Zoetermeer, NL: EIM.

Bosma, N., Stam, E., & Wennekers, S. (2013). *Institutions and the allocation of entrepreneurship across new and established organizations.* EIM scales research reports H201213. Zoetermeer, NL: EIM.

Bosma, N., Stam, E., & Wennekers, S. (2014). Intrapreneurship versus entrepreneurship in high- and low-income countries. In R. Blackburn, F. Delmar, A. Fayolle, & F. Welter (Eds.), *Entrepreneurship, people and organisations: Frontiers in European entrepreneurship research* (pp. 94–115). Cheltenham, UK: Edward Elgar.

Bottazzi, L., & Da Rin, M. (2002). Venture capital in Europe and the financing of innovative companies. *Economic Policy, 17*(34), 229–270.

Bowblis, J. R., & Smith, A. (2018). Occupational licensing of social services and nursing home quality: A regression discontinuity approach. https://papers.ssrn.com/sol3/papers.cfm?abstract_id=3096268

Bowles, S. (2016). *The moral economy: Why good incentives are no substitute for good citizens.* New Haven, CT: Yale University Press.

Braguinsky, S., Branstetter, L. G., & Regateiro, A. (2011). *The incredible shrinking Portuguese firm.* NBER working paper no. 17265. Cambridge, MA: National Bureau of Economic Research.

Braunerhjelm, P. (2011). Entrepreneurship, innovation and economic growth: Interdependencies, irregularities and regularities. In D. B. Audretsch, O. Falck, & S. Heblich (Eds.), *Handbook of research on innovation and entrepreneurship* (pp. 161–213). Cheltenham, UK: Edward Elgar.

Braunerhjelm, P., & Henrekson, M. (2016). An innovation policy framework: Bridging the gap between industrial dynamics and growth. In D. B. Audretsch & A. N. Link (Eds.), *Essays in public sector entrepreneurship* (pp. 95–130). New York, NY: Springer.

Braunerhjelm, P., Acs, Z. J., Audretsch, D. B., & Carlsson, B. (2010). The missing link: Knowledge diffusion and entrepreneurship in endogenous growth. *Small Business Economics, 34*(2), 105–125.

Bredgaard, T. (2013). Flexibility and security in employment regulation: Learning from Denmark. In K. V. W. Stone & H. Arthurs (Eds.), *Rethinking workplace regulation: Beyond the standard contract of employment* (pp. 213–233). New York, NY: Russell Sage Foundation.

Bruton, G., Khavul, S., Siegel, D., & Wright, M. (2015). New financial alternatives in seeding entrepreneurship: Microfinance, crowdfunding, and peer-to-peer innovations. *Entrepreneurship Theory and Practice, 39*(1), 9–26.

Burke, A., van Stel, A., Hartog, C., & Ichou, A. (2014). What determines the level of informal venture finance investment? Market clearing forces and gender effects. *Small Business Economics, 42*(3), 467–484.

Burnick, S. (2017). The importance of the design patent to modern day technology: The Supreme Court's decision to narrow the damages clause in Samsung v. Apple. *North Carolina Journal of Law & Technology, 18*(5), 283–315.

Busenitz, L. W., Plummer, L. A., Klotz, A. C., Shahzad, A., & Rhoads, K. (2014). Entrepreneurship research (1985–2009) and the emergence of opportunities. *Entrepreneurship Theory and Practice, 38*(5), 981–1000.

Caballero, R. J., & Jaffe, A. B. (1993). How high are the giants' shoulders: An empirical assessment of knowledge spillovers and creative destruction in a model of economic growth. *NBER Macroeconomics Annual* (Vol. 8, pp. 15–74). Cambridge, MA: MIT Press.

Calcagno, P. T., & Sobel, R. S. (2014). Regulatory costs on entrepreneurship and establishment employment size. *Small Business Economics, 42*(3), 541–559.

Camerer, E., & van Eijl, E. (2011). Demand-side innovation policies in the European Union. In *Demand-side innovation policies*. Paris: OECD. https://doi.org/10.178 7/9789264098886-18-en.

Carbó, S., Humphrey, D., Maudos, J., & Molyneux, P. (2009). Cross-country comparisons of competition and pricing power in European banking. *Journal of International Money and Finance, 28*(1), 115–134.

Carone, G., Eckefeldt, P., Giamboni, L., Laine, V., & Pamies, S. (2016). *Pension reforms in the EU since the early 2000's: Achievements and challenges ahead*. European economy discussion paper no. 042. https://papers.ssrn.com/Sol3/papers. cfm?abstract_id=2964933

Case, S., & Harris, D. (2012). The startup uprising: Eighteen months of the startup America partnership. Kansas City, MO: Ewing Marion Kauffman Foundation.

Castillo, J., & Meyer, H. (2018). *The world rankings 17/18 report*. Stockholm: UBI Global. https://ubi-global.com/rankings/.

Chandler, A. D. (1990). *Scale and scope: The dynamics of industrial capitalism*. Cambridge, MA: Harvard University Press.

Chetty, R., & Saez, E. (2005). Dividend taxes and corporate behavior: Evidence from the 2003 dividend tax cut. *Quarterly Journal of Economics, 120*(3), 791–833.

Chetty, R., Looney, A., & Kroft, K. (2009). Salience and taxation: Theory and evidence. *American Economic Review, 99*(4), 1145–1177.

Christodoulou, D. (2014). *Seven myths about education*. London: Routledge.

Clifford, M. M. (1984). Thoughts on a theory of constructive failure. *Educational Psychologist, 19*(2), 108–120.

Clifford, M. M., Kim, A., & McDonald, B. A. (1988). Responses to failure as influenced by task attribution, outcome attribution, and failure tolerance. *Journal of Experimental Education, 57*(1), 17–37.

Colander, D., & Freedman, C. (2018). *Where economics went wrong: Chicago's abandonment of classical liberalism*. Princeton, NJ: Princeton University Press.

Cole, R. A., & Sokolyk, T. (2018). Debt financing, survival, and growth of start-up firms. *Journal of Corporate Finance, 50*(C), 609–625.

Collier, V. P. (1995). *Acquiring a second language for school*. Washington, DC: National Clearinghouse for Bilingual Education.

Commissie Evaluatie Risicoverevening ZVW (2012). *Evaluation risk equalization health care insurance act*. https://www.eumonitor.nl/9353000/1/j4nvgs5kjg-27kof_j9vvik7m1c3gyxp/vj0be75kk7zz/f=/blg171977.pdf.

Corradi, F. (Ed.) (2009). *Alla Ricerca dell'Eccellenza: Le Politiche per l'Eccellenza nell'Istruzione Superiore in Quattro Paesi Europei*. Milan, IT: LED Edizioni Universitarie.

Cosgel, M., & Klamer, A. (1990). Entrepreneurship as discourse. Mimeo. Storrs, CN: University of Connecticut.

Craig, B. R., Jackson, W. E., III, & Thomson, J. B. (2007). Small firm finance, credit rationing, and the impact of SBA-guaranteed lending on local economic growth. *Journal of Small Business Management, 45*(1), 116–132.

Crowdfunding Insider (2017). German real estate crowdfunding market booms. https://www.crowdfundinsider.com/2017/06/102443-german-real-estate-crowd-funding-market-booms/

Csíkszentmihályi, M. (1990). *Flow: The psychology of optimal experience*. New York, NY: Harper & Row.

Cumming, D. (2005). Agency costs, institutions, learning, and taxation in venture capital contracting. *Journal of Business Venturing, 20*(5), 573–622.

Cumming, D. (2012). Venture capital financial contracting: An overview of the international evidence. In H. Landström & C. Mason (Eds.), *Handbook of research on venture capital* (Vol. 2). Cheltenham, UK: Edward Elgar.

Cumming, D. J., Grilli, L., & Murtinu, S. (2017). Governmental and independent venture capital investments in Europe: A firm-level performance analysis. *Journal of Corporate Finance, 42*(C), 439–459.

Cumming, D., & Groh, A. P. (2018). Entrepreneurial finance: Unifying themes and future directions. *Journal of Corporate Finance, 50*(C), 538–555.

Da Rin, M., Nicodano, G., & Sembenelli, A. (2006). Public policy and the creation of active venture capital markets. *Journal of Public Economics, 90*(8–9), 1699–1723.

Dahlstrand, Å. L. (2007). Technology-based entrepreneurship and regional develop-ment: The case of Sweden. *European Business Review, 19*(5), 373–386.

Dahmén, E. (1970). *Entrepreneurial activity and the development of Swedish industry 1919–1939* (trans: Dahmén's Doctoral Dissertation published in Swedish in 1950). Homewood, IL: Richard D. Irwin for the American Economic Association.

Darnihamedani, P., Block, J. H., Hessels, J., & Simonyan, A. (2018). Taxes, start-up costs, and innovative entrepreneurship. *Small Business Economics, 51*(2), 355–369.

Davies, R., & Tracey, B. (2014). Too big to be efficient? The impact of implicit sub-sidies on estimates of scale economies for banks. *Journal of Money, Credit and Banking, 46*(s1), 219–253.

Davis, S. J., & Henrekson, M. (1999). Explaining national differences in the size and industry distribution of employment. *Small Business Economics, 12*(1), 59–83.

de Mooij, R. A., & Devereux, M. P. (2016). *Alternative systems of business tax in Europe: An applied analysis of ACE and CBIT reforms*. Oxford, UK: Oxford University Centre for Business Taxation.

de Soto, H. (2000). *The mystery of capital: Why capitalism triumphs in the west and fails everywhere else*. New York: Basic Books.

Degryse, C. (2016). *Digitalization of the economy and its impact on labour markets*. ETUI research paper-working paper 2016.02. Brussels: European Trade Union Institute.

Desai, M., Gompers, P., & Lerner, J. (2003). *Institutions, capital constraints and entre-preneurial firm dynamics: Evidence from Europe*. NBER working paper no. 10165. Cambridge, MA: National Bureau of Economic Research.

Desai, S., Acs, Z. J., & Weitzel, U. (2013). A model of destructive entrepreneurship: Insight for conflict and post-conflict recovery. *Journal of Conflict Resolution, 57*(1), 20–40.

Dilli, S., & Westerhuis, G. (2018). How institutions and gender differences in education shape entrepreneurial activity: A cross-national perspective. *Small Business Economics, 51*(2), 371–392.

Dilli, S., Elert, N., & Herrmann, A. M. (2018). Varieties of entrepreneurship: Exploring the institutional foundations of different entrepreneurship types through 'varieties-of-capitalism' arguments. *Small Business Economics, 51*(2), 293–320.

DNB (2018). *DNBulletin: Aandeel pinbetalingen aan de kassa overschrijdt 60%-grens.* https://www.dnb.nl/nieuws/nieuwsoverzicht-en-archief/DNBulletin2018/dnb379598.jsp

Dolado, J. J. (2016). European Union dual labour markets: Consequences and potential reforms. In L. Matyas et al. (Eds.), *Economics without borders: Economic research for European policy challenges.* Cambridge, UK: Cambridge University Press.

Dopfer, K., & Potts, J. (2009). On the theory of economic evolution. *Evolutionary and Institutional Economic Review, 6*(1), 23–44.

Dosi, G., & Nelson, R. (2010). Technical change and industrial dynamics as evolutionary processes. In B. H. Hall & N. Rosenberg (Eds.), *Handbook of the economics of innovation* (Vol. 1, pp. 51–127). Amsterdam: North-Holland.

Downey, D. B. (1995). When bigger is not better: Family size, parental resources, and children's educational performance. *American Sociological Review, 60*(5), 746–761.

Du Rietz, G., & Henrekson, M. (2015). Swedish wealth taxation (1911–2007). In M. Henrekson & M. Stenkula (Eds.), *Swedish taxation: Developments since 1862* (pp. 267–302). New York: Palgrave Macmillan.

Dufey, G. (1998). The changing role of financial intermediation in Europe. *International Journal of Business, 3*(1), 49–68.

Duruflé, G., Hellmann, T. F., & Wilson, K. E. (2017). *From start-up to scale-up: Examining public policies for the financing of high-growth ventures.* Saïd business school working paper 2017-05. Oxford, NY: Oxford University Press.

Dyson, B., Hodgson, G., & van Lerven, F. (2016). *Sovereign money: An introduction.* London: Positive Money. https://positivemoney.org/wp-content/uploads/2016/12/SovereignMoney-AnIntroduction-20161214.pdf.

Ebbinghaus, B. (Ed.). (2011). *The varieties of pension governance: Pension privatization in Europe.* Oxford, UK: Oxford University Press.

Ebbinghaus, B. (2015). The privatization and marketization of pensions in Europe: A double transformation facing the crisis. *European Policy Analysis, 1*(1), 56–73.

ECB (2017). *Report on financial structures.* Frankfurt: European Central Bank. https://www.ecb.europa.eu/pub/pdf/other/reportonfinancialstructures201710.en.pdf.

ECB (2019). *Payment statistics.* Frankfurt: European Central Bank. https://sdw.ecb.europa.eu/reports.do?node=1000001966.

Eichhorst, W., Marx, P., & Wehner, C. (2017). Labor market reforms in Europe: Towards more flexicure labor markets? *Journal for Labour Market Research, 51*(1), 3.

Eisele, K. (2013). *Why come here if I can go there? Assessing the 'attractiveness' of the EU's blue card directive for 'highly qualified' immigrants.* CEPS paper in liberty and security in Europe papers no. 60. Brussels: Centre for European Policy Studies.

Elert, N., & Henrekson, M. (2019). The collaborative innovation bloc: A new mission for Austrian economics. *Review of Austrian Economics,* https://doi.org/10.1007/s11138-019-00455-y

Elert, N., Andersson, F. W., & Wennberg, K. (2015). The impact of entrepreneurship education in high school on long-term entrepreneurial performance. *Journal of Economic Behavior & Organization, 111*(March), 209–223.

Elert, N., Henrekson, M., & Stenkula, M. (2017). *Institutional reform for innovation and entrepreneurship: An agenda for Europe.* Cham, CH: Springer.

Elert, N., Stam E., & Stenkula, M. (2019). "Intrapreneurship and trust." IFN working paper no. 1280. Stockholm: Research Institute of Industrial Economics.

Eliasson, G. (1996). *Firm objectives, controls and organization: The use of information and the transfer of knowledge within the firm.* Dordrecht: Kluwer.

Eliasson, G. (2000). Industrial policy, competence blocs and the role of science in economic development. *Journal of Evolutionary Economics, 10*(1–2), 217–241.

Ellen MacArthur Foundation (2013). Towards the circular economy: Economic and business rationale for an accelerated transition. Cowes, UK: Ellen MacArthur Foundation. https://www.ellenmacarthurfoundation.org/assets/downloads/publications/Ellen-MacArthur-Foundation-Towards-the-Circular-Economy-vol.1.pdf

Epstein, R. (2009). *Simple rules for a complex world.* Cambridge, MA: Harvard University Press.

Erixon, F., & Weigel, B. (2016). The innovation illusion: How so little is created by so many working so hard. New Haven, CT: Yale University Press.

Erixon, L. (2011). Development blocks, malinvestment and structural tensions—the Åkerman-Dahmén theory of the business cycle. Journal of Institutional Economics, 7(1), 105–129.

Ernst & Young (2018). *Worldwide estate and inheritance tax guide 2018.* https://www.ey.com/Publication/vwLUAssets/ey-worldwide-estate-and-inheritance-tax-guide-2018/$FILE/ey-worldwide-estate-and-inheritance-tax-guide-2018.pdf

Estrin, S., Gozman, D., & Khavul, S. (2018). The evolution and adoption of equity crowdfunding: Entrepreneur and investor entry into a new market. *Small Business Economics, 51*(2), 425–440.

European Banking Authority (2019). *The single rulebook.* London: European Banking Authority. https://eba.europa.eu/regulation-and-policy/single-rulebook.

European Banking Federation (2017). *High level principles on feedback given by banks on declined SME credit applications.* https://www.ebf.eu/wp-content/uploads/2017/06/High-level-principles-on-feedback-given-by-banks-on-declined-SME-credit-applications.pdf

European Commission (2007). *Towards common principles of flexicurity: More and better jobs through flexibility and security.* COM/2007/0359. Brussels: European

Commission. https://eur-lex.europa.eu/legal-content/EN/TXT/PDF/?uri=CELE X:52007DC0359&from=EN

European Commission (2012). *A reinforced European research area partnership for excellence and growth.* Communication from the commission to the European Parliament, The Council, The European Economic and Social Committee and the Committee of the Regions. Brussels, 17.7.2012 COM/2012/392. https://ec. europa.eu/research/science-society/document_library/pdf_06/era-communica- tion-partnership-excellence-growth_en.pdf

European Commission (2014). *The EU explained: Digital agenda for Europe.* European Commission: Directorate-General for Communication, Brussels. https://europa. eu/european-union/file/1497/download_en?token=KzfSz-CR.

European Commission (2015a). *An investment plan for Europe.* COM/2014/0903. Brussels: European Commission.

European Commission (2015b). *Why do we need an innovation union?* Brussels: European Commission. http://ec.europa.eu/research/innovation-union/index_ en.cfm?pg=why

European Commission (2016). *Proposal for a directive of the European Parliament and of the Council on Preventive Restructuring Frameworks, second chance and measures to increase the efficiency of restructuring, insolvency and discharge procedures and amending directive 2012/30/EU.* Brussels: European Commission. https://eur-lex. europa.eu/legal-content/EN/TXT/?uri=COM:2016:0723:FIN

European Commission (2017a). *Commission proposal for a regulation on a pan-Euro- pean personal pension product (PEPP).* Brussels: European Commission. https:// ec.europa.eu/info/sites/info/files/170629-personal-pensions-factsheet_en.pdf

European Commission (2017b). *Towards common principles of flexicurity: More and better jobs through flexibility and security.* Communication from the Commission to the European Parliament, the Council, the European Economic and Social committee and the committee of the regions. Brussels: European Commission. https://eur-lex.europa.eu/legal-content/EN/ALL/?uri=CELEX:52007DC0359

European Commission (2017c). *Interim evaluation of Horizon 2020.* Brussels: European Commission, DG Research and Innovation. https://publications. europa.eu/en/publication-detail/-/publication/fad8c173-7e42-11e7-b5c6- 01aa75ed71a1/language-en/format-PDF/source-77918455.

European Commission (2018a). *Financing your business in the EU: Know your rights.* http://publications.europa.eu/webpub/grow/factsheets/financing-your- business/en/

European Commission (2018b). *Thematic factsheet active labour market policies 2017.* Brussels: European Commission. https://ec.europa.eu/info/sites/info/files/euro- pean-semester_thematic-factsheet_active-labour-market-policies_en_0.pdf.

European Commission (2019a). *Database of regulated professions.* http://ec.europa. eu/growth/tools-databases/regprof/index.cfm?action=regprofs.

European Commission (2019b). *Investment plan results.* Brussel: European Commission.    https://ec.europa.eu/commission/priorities/jobs-growth-and-investment/investment-plan-europe-juncker-plan/investment-plan-results_en#eu-wide-results-as-of-february-2019

European Council (2016). *Directive 2016/1164/EC of 12 July 2016 laying down rules against tax avoidance practices that directly affect the functioning of the internal market.* Brussels: European Council.

European Council (2018). *Pensions: Council agrees its stance on pan-European pension product.* Press release. Brussels: European Council. https://www.consilium.europa.eu/en/press/press-releases/2018/06/19/pensions-council-agrees-its-stance-on-pan-european-pension-product/

European Parliament and Council of the European Union (2013). Regulation (EU) 575/2013 of 26 June 2013 on prudential requirements for credit institutions and investment firms and amending regulation (EU) 648/2012. *Official Journal of the European Union.* https://eur-lex.europa.eu/legal-content/EN/TXT/?uri=celex:32013R0575

European Union (2018). *Your Europe: Working hours.* https://europa.eu/youreurope/business/human-resources/working-hours-holiday-leave/working-hours/index_en.htm

Fagereng, A., Guiso, L., Malacrino, D., & Pistaferri, L. (2016). *Heterogeneity and persistence in returns to wealth.* NBER working paper no. 22822. Cambridge, MA: National Bureau of Economic Research.

Färnstrand Damsgaard, E., & Thursby, M. C. (2013). University entrepreneurship and professor privilege. *Industrial and Corporate Change, 22*(1), 183–218.

Feld, L., & Voigt, S. (2003). Economic growth and judicial independence: Cross-country evidence using a new set of indicators. *European Journal of Political Economy, 19*(3), 497–527.

Fenn, G., Liang, N., & Prowse, S. (1995). *The economics of the private equity market.* Washington, DC: Board of Governors of the Federal Reserve System.

Ferrari, R. (2016). FinTech impact on retail banking: From a universal banking model to banking verticalization. In S. Chishti & J. Barberis (Eds.), *The FinTech book: The financial technology handbook for investors, entrepreneurs and visionaries* (pp. 248–252). New York: Wiley.

Fitzenberger, B., Licklederer, S., & Zwiener, H. (2015). Mobility across firms and occupations among graduates from apprenticeship. *Labour Economics, 34*(C), 138–151.

Flege, J. E., Yeni-Komshian, G. H., & Liu, S. (1999). Age constraints on second-language acquisition. *Journal of Memory and Language, 41*(1), 78–104.

Focarelli, D., & Pozzolo, A. F. (2016). Banking industry. In G. Jones (Ed.), *Banking crises* (pp. 25–27). London: Palgrave Macmillan.

Fogel, R. W. (1999). Catching up with the economy. *American Economic Review, 89*(1), 1–21.

Ford, D., & Nelsen, B. (2014). The view beyond venture capital. *Nature Biotechnology*, *32*(1), 15.

Foss, N. J. (1997). Austrian insights and the theory of the firm. In *Advances in Austrian economics* (Vol. 4, pp. 175–198). Bingley, UK: Emerald.

Fouarge, D., Schils, T., & de Grip, A. (2013). Why do low-educated workers invest less in further training? *Applied Economics, 45*(18), 2587–2601.

Fox, J. (2010). Banks took big risks because shareholders wanted them to. *Harvard Business Review*, June 10. https://hbr.org/2010/06/maybe-shareholders-were-to-bla.html

Frank, C., Sink, C., Mynatt, L., Rogers, R., & Rappazzo, A. (1996). Surviving the 'valley of death': A comparative analysis. *Journal of Technology Transfer, 21*(1–2), 61–69.

Frenken, K., van Waes, A. H. M., Smink, M. M., & van Est, R. (2017). *A fair share: Safeguarding public interests in the sharing and gig economy.* The Hague: Rathenau Institute.

Frey, B. S., Benz, M., & Stutzer, A. (2004). Introducing procedural utility: Not only what, but also how matters. *Journal of Institutional and Theoretical Economics, 160*(3), 377–401.

Fukuyama, F. (1989). The end of history? *The National Interest, 16*, 3–18.

Füller, C. (2017). Educational expenditure: More money for schools and universities. Munich: Goethe Institute. Retrieved April 16, 2018, from https://www.goethe.de/en/kul/wis/20925479.html

Gangl, M. (2003). Labor market structure and re-employment rates: Unemployment dynamics in West Germany and the United States. *Research in Social Stratification and Mobility, 20*, 185–224.

Garicano, L., Lelarge, C., & Van Reenen, J. (2016). Firm size distortions and the productivity distribution: Evidence from France. *American Economic Review, 106*(11), 3439–3479.

Gash, V. (2008). Bridge or trap? Temporary workers' transitions to unemployment and to the standard employment contract. *European Sociological Review, 24*(5), 651–668.

Gebel, M. (2010). Early career consequences of temporary employment in Germany and the UK. *Work, Employment and Society, 24*(4), 641–660.

Ghoshal, S., Moran, P., & Almeida-Costa, L. (1995). The essence of the megacorporation: Shared context, not structural hierarchy. *Journal of Institutional and Theoretical Economics, 151*(4), 748–759.

Gilson, R. J. (1999). The legal infrastructure of high technology industrial districts: Silicon Valley, Route 128, and covenants not to compete. *New York University Law Review, 74*(3), 575–629.

Gilson, R. J., & Schizer, D. M. (2003). Understanding venture capital structure: A tax explanation for convertible preferred stock. *Harvard Law Review, 116*(3), 874–916.

Glaeser, E. L. (2008). The rise of the sunbelt. *Southern Economic Journal,* *74*(3), 610–643.

Glaeser, E. L. (2011). *Triumph of the city: How our greatest invention makes us richer, smarter, greener, healthier, and happier.* New York: Penguin Press.

Goe, L., & Stickler, L. M. (2008). *Teacher quality and student achievement: Making the most of recent research.* TQ research & policy brief. Washington, DC: National Comprehensive Center for Teacher Quality.

Goldfarb, B., & Henrekson, M. (2003). Bottom-up versus top-down policies towards the commercialization of university intellectual property. *Research Policy,* *32*(4), 639–658.

Gompers, P. A., & Lerner, J. (1999). An analysis of compensation in the U.S. venture capital partnership. *Journal of Financial Economics, 51*(1), 3–44.

Gompers, P. A., & Lerner, J. (2001). *The money of invention: How venture capital creates wealth.* Cambridge, MA: Harvard Business Press.

Gompers, P. A., & Lerner, J. (2004). *The venture capital cycle.* Cambridge, MA: MIT Press.

Gompers, P. A., Lerner, J., & Kovner, A. (2009). Specialization and success: Evidence from venture capital. *Journal of Economics and Management Strategy,* *18*(3), 817–844.

Grant Thornton (2016). *Konkurrenskraften i svensk ägarbeskattning.* Stockholm: Confederation of Swedish Enterprise.

Griffin, P., & Care, E. (Eds.). (2014). *Assessment and teaching of 21st century skills: Methods and approach.* London: Springer.

Grilli, L., & Murtinu, S. (2014a). Government, venture capital and the growth of European high-tech entrepreneurial firms. *Research Policy, 43*(9), 1523–1543.

Grilli, L., & Murtinu, S. (2014b). New technology-based firms in Europe: Market penetration, public venture capital, and timing of investment. *Industrial and Corporate Change, 24*(5), 1109–1148.

Gropp, R., Gruendl, C., & Guettler, A. (2013). The impact of public guarantees on bank risk-taking: Evidence from a natural experiment. *Review of Finance, 18*(2), 457–488.

Grossman, G. H., & Helpman, E. (1991). *Innovation and growth in the global economy.* Cambridge, MA: MIT Press.

Gustafsson, A., Gustavsson Tingvall, P., & Halvarsson, D. (2018). *Subsidy entrepreneurs.* Ratio working paper no. 303. Stockholm: Ratio Institute.

Haas, W., Krausmann, F., Wiedenhofer, D., & Heinz, M. (2015). How circular is the global economy? An assessment of material flows, waste production, and recycling in the European Union and the World in 2005. *Journal of Industrial Ecology, 19*(5), 765–777.

Haldane, A. G., & Booth, P. (2014). On being the right size. *Journal of Financial Perspectives, 2*(1), 13–25.

Haldane, A. G., & May, R. M. (2011). Systemic risk in banking ecosystems. *Nature, 469*(7330), 351.

Hall, R. E., & Jones, C. I. (1999). Why do some countries produce so much more output per worker than others? *Quarterly Journal of Economics, 114*(1), 83–116.

Hall, P. A., & Soskice, D. (2001). *Varieties of capitalism: The institutional foundations of comparative advantage.* Oxford, UK: Oxford University Press.

Hallonsten, O., & Silander, C. (2012). Commissioning the university of excellence: Swedish research policy and new public research funding programmes. *Quality in Higher Education, 18*(3), 367–381.

Hanushek, E. A., & Woessman, L. (2015). *The knowledge capital of nations: Education and the economics of growth.* Cambridge, MA: MIT Press.

Hanushek, E. A., Schwert, G., Widerhold, S., & Woessmann, L. (2015). Returns to skills around the world: Evidence from PIAAC. *European Economic Review, 73*(January), 103–130.

Harford, T. (2011). *Adapt: Why success always starts with failure.* New York: Farrar, Strauss and Giroux.

Harrington, B. (2016). *Capital without borders: Wealth managers and the one percent.* Cambridge, MA: Harvard University Press.

Hassan, K., Sanchez, B., & Yu, J.-S. (2011). Financial development and economic growth: New evidence form panel data. *Quarterly Review of Economics and Finance, 51*(1), 88–104.

Hatfield, I. (2015). *Self-employment in Europe.* London: Institute for Public Policy Research.

Hausmann, R., & Rodrik, D. (2003). Economic development as self-discovery. *Journal of Development Economics, 72*(2), 603–633.

Hayek, F. A. (1945). The use of knowledge in society. *American Economic Review, 35*(4), 519–530.

Hechavarria, D. M., & Reynolds, P. D. (2009). Cultural norms & business start-ups: The impact of national values on opportunity and necessity entrepreneurs. *International Entrepreneurship and Management Journal, 5*(4), 417–437.

Held, L., Herrmann, A. M., & Polzin, F. (2018a). *Follow the money: The funding acquisition process of nascent ventures.* Financial and Institutional Reforms for an Entrepreneurial Society. http://www.projectfires.eu

Held, L., Herrmann, A. M., & van Mossel, A. (2018b). Team formation processes in new ventures. *Small Business Economics, 51*(2), 441–464.

Henrekson, M., & Johansson, D. (2009). Competencies and institutions fostering high-growth firms. *Foundations and Trends in Entrepreneurship, 5*(1), 1–80.

Henrekson, M., & Roine, J. (2007). Promoting entrepreneurship in the welfare state. In D. B. Audretsch, I. Grilo, & A. R. Thurik (Eds.), *Handbook of research on entrepreneurship policy* (pp. 64–93). Cheltenham, UK: Edward Elgar.

Henrekson, M., & Rosenberg, N. (2001). Designing efficient institutions for science-based entrepreneurship: Lessons from the US and Sweden. *Journal of Technology Transfer, 26*(3), 207–231.

Henrekson, M., & Sanandaji, T. (2014). Small business activity does not measure entrepreneurship. *Proceedings of the National Academy of Sciences (PNAS), 111*(5), 1760–1765.

Henrekson, M., & Sanandaji, T. (2016). Owner-level taxes and business activity. *Foundations and Trends in Entrepreneurship, 12*(1), 1–101.

Henrekson, M., & Sanandaji, T. (2018a). Stock option taxation and venture capital activity: A cross-country study. *Venture Capital, 20*(1), 51–71.

Henrekson, M., & Sanandaji, T. (2018b). Schumpeterian entrepreneurship in Europe compared to other industrialized regions. *International Review of Entrepreneurship, 16*(2), 157–182.

Henrekson, M., & Sanandaji, T. (2018c). Stock option taxation: A missing piece in European innovation policy? *Small Business Economics, 51*(2), 411–424.

Henrekson, M., & Sanandaji, T. (2019). Measuring entrepreneurship: Do established metrics capture Schumpeterian entrepreneurship? *Entrepreneurship Theory and Practice.* https://doi.org/10.1177/1042258719844500

Hernández-Cánovas, G., & Martínez-Solano, P. (2010). Relationship lending and SME financing in the continental European bank-based system. *Small Business Economics, 34*(4), 465–482.

Hervé, F., & Schwienbacher, A. (2018). Crowdfunding and innovation. *Journal of Economic Surveys, 32*(5), 1514–1530.

Hijzen, A., Upward, R., & Wright, P. W. (2010). Job creation, job destruction and the role of small firms: Firm-level evidence for the UK. *Oxford Bulletin of Economics and Statistics, 72*(5), 621–647.

Hinrichs, K. (2016). Pension reforms in Europe: Directions and consequences. In *Converging Europe* (pp. 109–132). London: Routledge.

Hirsch, B. (2016a). Dual labor markets at work: The impact of employers' use of temporary agency work on regular workers' job stability. *ILR Review, 69*(5), 1191–1215.

Hirsch, E. D. (2016b). *Why knowledge matters: Rescuing our children from failed educational theories.* Cambridge, MA: Harvard Education Press.

Ho, Y.-P., & Wong, P.-K. (2007). Financing, regulatory costs and entrepreneurial propensity. *Small Business Economics, 28*(2–3), 187–204.

Hofer, H. (2007). The severance pay reform in Austria ('Abfertigung Neu'). *CESifo DICE report 4/2007*, pp. 41–48.

Holmlund, B., & Söderström, M. (2011). Estimating dynamic income responses to tax reform. *B.E. Journal of Economic Analysis & Policy, 11*(1), 1–38.

Hommen, L., Doloreux, D., & Larsson, E. (2006). Emergence and growth of Mjärdevi Science Park in Linköping, Sweden. *European Planning Studies, 14*(10), 1331–1361.

Hornuf, L., & Schwienbacher, A. (2018). Market mechanisms and funding dynamics in equity crowdfunding. *Journal of Corporate Finance, 50*(June), 556–574.

Hudson, M., & Bezemer, D. J. (2012). Incorporating the rentier sectors into a financial model. *World Social and Economic Review, 1*, 1–12.

Hughes, J. P., & Mester, L. J. (1998). Bank capitalization and cost: Evidence of scale economies in risk management and signaling. *Review of Economics and Statistics, 80*(2), 314–325.

Huizinga, H., Laeven, L., & Nicodeme, G. (2008). Capital structure and international debt shifting. *Journal of Financial Economics, 88*(1), 80–118.

Hulten, C. (1996). *Infrastructure capital and economic growth: How well you use it may be more important than how much you have.* NBER working paper no. 5847. Cambridge, MA: National Bureau of Economic Research.

Hvide, H. K., & Jones, B. F. (2018). University innovation and the professor's privilege. *American Economic Review, 108*(7), 1860–1898.

Illeris, K. (2006). Lifelong learning and the low-skilled. *International Journal of Lifelong Education, 25*(1), 15–28.

Invest Europe. (2018). *2017 European private equity activity* https://www.investeurope.eu/media/711867/invest-europe-2017-european-private-equity-activity.pdf

Jacob, M., Lundqvist, M., & Hellsmark, H. (2003). Entrepreneurial transformations in the Swedish university system: The case of Chalmers University of Technology. *Research Policy, 32*(9), 1555–1568.

Jaffe, A. B., & Lerner, J. (2004). *Invention and its discontents: How our broken patent system is endangering innovation and progress, and what to do about It.* Princeton, NJ: Princeton University Press.

Jaffe, A. B., Trajtenberg, M., & Henderson, R. (1993). Geographic localization of knowledge spillovers as evidenced by patent citations. *Quarterly Journal of Economics, 108*(3), 577–598.

Jayawarna, D., Jones, O., & Macpherson, A. (2014). Entrepreneurial potential: The role of human and cultural capitals. *International Small Business Journal, 32*(8), 918–943.

Johansson, D. (2009). The theory of the experimentally organized economy and competence blocs: An introduction. *Journal of Evolutionary Economics, 20*(2), 185–201.

Johnson, J. E., & Kleiner, M. M. (2017). *Is occupational licensing a barrier to interstate migration?* NBER working paper no. 24107. Cambridge, MA: National Bureau of Economic Research.

Johnson, R. C., Nagoshi, C. T., Ahern, F. M., Wilson, J. R., DeFries, J. C., McClearn, G. E., & Vandenberg, S. G. (1983). Family background, cognitive ability, and personality as predictors of educational and occupational attainment. *Social Biology, 30*(1), 86–100.

Johnson, S., McMillan, J., & Woodruff, C. (2002). Property rights and finance. *American Economic Review, 92*(5), 1335–1356.

Jones, C. I. (1995). R&D-based models of economic growth. *Journal of Political Economy, 103*(4), 759–784.

Jones, C. I. (2005). Growth and ideas. In P. Aghion & S. Durlauf (Eds.), *Handbook of economic growth* (Vol. 1, pp. 1063–1111). Amsterdam: Elsevier.

Jongbloed, B. (2010). Funding higher education: a view across Europe. Brussels, ESMU. http://hdl.voced.edu.au/10707/252793

Kahn, L. M. (2009). Employment protection reforms, employment and the incidence of temporary jobs in Europe: 1996–2001. *Labour Economics, 17*(1), 1–15.

Kaplan, S. N., & Strömberg, P. (2003). Financial contracting theory meets the real world: Evidence from venture capital contracts. *Review of Economic Studies, 70*(2), 281–315.

Karamanis, D., & Economidou, C. (2018). *Mobility of highly skilled individuals and local innovation activity.* FIRES report D3.10, Financial and Institutional Reforms for an Entrepreneurial Society. http://www.projectfires.eu/wp-content/uploads/2018/03/d3.10-report.pdf

Kauffman Foundation (2007). *On the road to an entrepreneurial economy: A research and policy guide.* Kauffman Foundation working paper, July. Kansas City, MO: Ewing Marion Kauffman Foundation.

Kay, J. (2015). *Other people's money: The real business of finance.* London: Hachette.

Keuschnigg, C., & Nielsen, S. B. (2004a). Taxation and venture capital backed entrepreneurship. *International Tax and Public Finance, 11*(4), 369–390.

Keuschnigg, C., & Nielsen, S. B. (2004b). Start-ups, venture capitalists, and the capital gains tax. *Journal of Public Economics, 88*(5), 1011–1042.

King, M. A., & Fullerton, D. (Eds.). (1984). *The taxation of income from capital: A comparative study of the United States, the United Kingdom, Sweden and West Germany.* Chicago, IL: University of Chicago Press.

Klagge, B., Martin, R., & Sunley, P. (2017). The spatial structure of the financial system and the funding of regional business: A comparison of Britain and Germany. In R. Martin & J. Pollard (Eds.), *Handbook on the geographies of money and finance* (pp. 125–155). Cheltenham: Edward Elgar.

Kleiner, M. M. (2000). Occupational licensing. *Journal of Economic Perspectives, 14*(4), 189–202.

Kleiner, M. M., & Krueger, A. B. (2010). The prevalence and effects of occupational licensing. *British Journal of Industrial Relations, 48*(4), 676–687.

Kleiner, M. M., & Krueger, A. B. (2013). Analyzing the extent and influence of occupational licensing on the labor market. *Journal of Labor Economics, 31*(S1), S173–S202.

Kleinknecht, A., Oostendorp, R. M., Pradhan, M. P., & Naastepad, C. W. M. (2006). Flexible labour, firm performance and the Dutch job creation miracle. *International Review of Applied Economics, 20*(2), 171–187.

Klepper, S. (2002). The capabilities of new firms and the evolution of the US automobile industry. *Industrial and Corporate Change, 11*(4), 645–666.

Klepper, S. (2009). Spinoffs: A review and synthesis. *European Management Review, 6*(3), 159–171.

Klepper, S. (2016). *Experimental capitalism: The nanoeconomics of American high-tech industries.* Princeton, NJ: Princeton University Press.

Klepper, S., & Thompson, P. (2010). Disagreements and intra-industry spinoffs. *International Journal of Industrial Organization, 28*(5), 526–538.

König, W., & Müller, W. (1986). Educational systems and labour markets as determinants of worklife mobility in France and West Germany: A comparison of men's career mobility, 1965–1970. *European Sociological Review, 2*(2), 73–96.

Korpi, T., & Mertens, A. (2003). Training systems and labour mobility: A comparison between Germany and Sweden. *Scandinavian Journal of Economics, 105*(4), 597–617.

Kotha, R., & George, G. (2012). Friends, family, or fools: Entrepreneur experience and its implications for equity distribution and resource mobilization. *Journal of Business Venturing, 27*(5), 525–543.

Koumenta, M., & Humphris, A. (2015). The effects of occupational licensing on employment, skills and quality: A case study of two occupations in the UK. Mimeo. London: Queen Mary University of London.

Koumenta, M., & Pagliero, M. (2017). Measuring prevalence and labour market impacts of occupational regulation in the EU. Brussels: European Commission; Ref. Ares (2016) 6854283 – 08/12/2016. https://ec.europa.eu/growth/content/measuring-prevalence-and-labour-market-impacts-occupational-regulation-eu-0_en

Kraemer-Eis, H., Botsari, A., Gvetadze, S., Lang, F., & Torfs, W. (2017). *European small business finance outlook: December 2017.* EIF working paper no. 2017/46. Luxembourg: European Investment Fund.

Krashen, S. D., Long, M. A., & Scarcella, R. C. (1979). Age, rate and eventual attainment in second language acquisition. *TESOL Quarterly, 13*(4), 573–582.

Krenek, A., & Schratzenstaller, M. (2018). *A European net wealth tax.* WIFO working paper no. 561. Vienna: WIFO Institute.

Krippner, G. R. (2005). The financialization of the American economy. *Socio-Economic Review, 3*(2), 173–208.

Kumhof, M., & Noone, C. (2018). *Central bank digital currencies—design principles and balance sheet implications.* Bank of England working paper no. 725. https://ssrn.com/abstract=3180713 or https://doi.org/10.2139/ssrn.3180713

Kuran, T. (1988). The tenacious past: Theories of personal and collective conservatism. *Journal of Economic Behavior and Organization, 10*(2), 143–171.

Lagarde, C. (2018). Speech at Singapore FinTech Festival 19-11-2018. https://www.indianweb2.com/2018/11/19/imf-chief-advocates-considering-digital-currency-by-central-banks-globally/

Lakhani, K. R., Jeppesen, L. B., Lohse, P. A., & Panetta, J. A. (2007). *The value of openness in scientific problem solving.* Boston, MA: Division of Research, Harvard Business School.

Landström, H., & Mason, C. (Eds.). (2016). *Handbook of research on business angels.* Cheltenham, UK: Edward Elgar.

Lazear, E. P. (2004). Balanced skills and entrepreneurship. *American Economic Review: Papers & Proceedings, 94*(2), 208–211.

Lazear, E. P. (2005). Entrepreneurship. *Journal of Labor Economics, 23*(4), 649–680.

Lazonder, A. W., & Harmsen, R. (2016). Meta-analysis of inquiry-based learning: Effects of guidance. *Review of Educational Research, 86*(3), 681–718.

Le Grand, J., & Bartlett, W. (1993). The theory of quasi markets. In J. Le Grand & W. Bartlett (Eds.), *Quasi markets and social policy*. London: Palgrave Macmillan.

Lee, N., Sameen, H., & Cowling, M. (2015). Access to finance for innovative SMEs since the financial crisis. *Research Policy, 44*(2), 370–380.

Lerner, J. (1999). The government as venture capitalist: The long-run impact of the SBIR Program. *Journal of Business, 72*(3), 285–318.

Lerner, J., & Tåg, J. (2013). Institutions and venture capital. *Industrial and Corporate Change, 22*(1), 153–182.

Levine, R. (1997). Financial development and economic growth: Views and agenda. *Journal of Economic Literature, 35*(2), 688–726.

Leydesdorff, L., & Meyer, M. (2010). The decline of university patenting and the end of the Bayh–Dole effect. *Scientometrics, 83*(2), 355–362.

Libecap, G. D. (1993). *Contracting for property rights*. New York: Cambridge University Press.

Liebregts, W. J. (2016). *Institutional explanations for patterns of entrepreneurial activity: The case of the Dutch task market*. FIRES deliverable D5.3. Financial and Institutional Reforms for an Entrepreneurial Society. http://www.projectfires.eu/

Liikanen, E., et al. (2012). *High-level expert group on reforming the structure of the EU banking sector*. Final Report. Brussels: European Commission.

Lin, M., Hung, S. W., & Chen, C. J. (2009). Fostering the determinants of knowledge sharing in professional virtual communities. *Computers in Human Behavior, 25*(4), 929–939.

Lin, M., Prabhala, N. R., & Viswanathan, S. (2013). Judging borrowers by the company they keep: Friendship networks and information asymmetry in online peer-to-peer lending. *Management Science, 59*(1), 17–35.

Lindbeck, A. (1982). Tax effects versus budget effects on labor supply. *Economic Inquiry, 20*(3), 473–489.

Lindbeck, A., & Snower, D. J. (2001). Insiders versus outsiders. *Journal of Economic Perspectives, 15*(1), 165–188.

Link, A., & Swann, C. (2016). R&D as an investment in knowledge-based capital. *Economia e Politica Industriale: Journal of Industrial and Business Economics, 43*(1), 11–24.

Liu, S., & Chollet, D. (2006). *Price and income elasticity of the demand for health insurance and health care services: A critical review of the literature*. Washington, DC: Mathematica Policy Research.

Ljunge, M., & Stenkula, M. (2018). Fertile soil for intrapreneurship: Impartial institutions and human capital. Mimeo. Stockholm: Research Institute of Industrial Economics.

Lucas, R. E. (1988). On the mechanics of economic development. *Journal of Monetary Economics, 22*(1), 3–42.

Lundqvist, M. A. (2014). The importance of surrogate entrepreneurship for incubated Swedish technology ventures. *Technovation, 34*(2), 93–100.

Maarse, H., Jeurissen, P., & Ruwaard, D. (2016). Results of the market-oriented reform in the Netherlands: A review. *Health Economics, Policy and Law, 11*(2), 161–178.

Mackenzie, A. (2015). The FinTech revolution. *London Business School Review, 26*(3), 50–53.

Madrian, B. C., Herschfeld, H. E., Sussman, A. B., Bhargava, S., Burke, J., Huettel, S. A., Jamison, J., Johnson, E. J., Lynch, J. G., Meier, S., Rick, S., & Shu, S. B. (2017). Behaviorally informed policies for household financial decisionmaking. *Behavioral Science & Policy, 3*(1), 26–40.

Magnusson, P. K., Rasmussen, F., & Gyllensten, U. B. (2006). Height at age 18 years is a strong predictor of attained education later in life: Cohort study of over 950,000 Swedish men. *International Journal of Epidemiology, 35*(3), 658–663.

Mankiw, N. G., Romer, D., & Weil, D. N. (1992). A contribution to the empirics of economic growth. *Quarterly Journal of Economics, 107*(2), 407–437.

Mariathasan, M., & Merrouche, O. (2014). The manipulation of Basel risk-weights. *Journal of Financial Intermediation, 23*(3), 300–321.

Martin, J., & Scarpetta, S. (2012). Setting it right: Employment protection, labour reallocation and productivity. *De Economist, 160*(2), 89–116.

Marx, M., Strumsky, D., & Fleming, L. (2009). Mobility, skills, and the Michigan non-compete experiment. *Management Science, 55*(2), 875–889.

Marx, A., Sanders, M., & Stenkula, M. (Eds.). (2019). *Financial and institutional reforms for an entrepreneurial society in Europe part II: Tailoring a reform strategy to Germany, Italy and the UK.* Cham, CH: Springer.

Mazzucato, M. (2015). *The entrepreneurial state: Debunking public vs. private sector myths.* London: Anthem Press.

Mazzucato, M. (2018). Mission-oriented innovation policies: Challenges and opportunities. *Industrial and Corporate Change, 27*(5), 803–815.

McCloskey, D. N. (2010). *Bourgeois dignity: Why economics can't explain the modern world.* Chicago, IL: University of Chicago Press.

McCloskey, D. N. (2016). *Bourgeois equality: How ideas, not capital or institutions, enriched the world.* Chicago, IL: University of Chicago Press.

McCloskey, D. N., & Klamer, A. (1995). One quarter of GDP is persuasion. *American Economic Review: Papers & Proceedings, 85*(2), 191–195.

McKelvey, M., Alm, H., & Riccaboni, M. (2003). Does co-location matter for formal knowledge collaboration in the Swedish biotechnology–pharmaceutical sector? *Research Policy, 32*(3), 483–501.

Merrill, S. A., Levin, R. C., & Myers, M. B. (2004). *A patent system for the 21st century.* Washington, DC: National Academic Press.

Messenger, J. C., Lee, S., & McCann, D. (2007). *Working time around the world: Trends in working hours, laws, and policies in a global comparative perspective.* New York: Routledge.

Metcalfe, J. S. (1998). *Evolutionary economics and creative destruction*. London: Routledge.

Metcalfe, J. (2010). On Marshallian evolutionary dynamics, entry and exit. In H. Kurz & P. Samuelson (Eds.), *Value, growth and distribution: Essays in honour of Ian Steedman* (chapter 23). London: Routledge.

Metcalfe, J. S. (2017). Learning from errors. *Annual Review of Psychology, 68*, 465–489.

Meyer, D. (2019). Finland's basic income experiment kind of works, but not in employment terms. *Fortune*, February 19. http://fortune.com/2019/02/08/basic-income-finland-employment/

Michaelas, N., Chittenden, F., & Poutziouris, P. (1999). Financial policy and capital structure choice in UK SMEs: Empirical evidence from company panel data. *Small Business Economics, 12*(2), 113–130.

Michelacci, C. (2003). Low returns to R&D due to the lack of entrepreneurial skills. *Economic Journal, 113*(484), 207–225.

Miklaszewska, E. (2017). *Institutional diversity in banking: Small country, small bank perspectives*. Berlin: Springer.

Mills, K., & McCarthy, B. (2014). *The state of small business lending: Credit access during the recovery and how technology may change the game*. Harvard Business School General Management Unit working paper no. 15-004. https://ssrn.com/abstract=2470523

Mitter, C., & Kraus, S. (2011). Entrepreneurial finance—issues and evidence, revisited. *International Journal of Entrepreneurship and Innovation Management, 14*(2–3), 132–150.

Mollick, E., & Robb, A. (2016). Democratizing innovation and capital access: The role of crowdfunding. *California Management Review, 58*(2), 72–87.

Molyneux, P., Lloyd-Williams, D. M., & Thornton, J. (1994). Competitive conditions in European banking. *Journal of Banking & Finance, 18*(3), 445–459.

Montalvo, C., & Leijten, J. (2015). Is the response to the climate change and energy challenge a model for the societal challenges approach to innovation? *Intereconomics, 50*(1), 25–30.

Montes, M. F. (2018). Concealing wealth and ownership: Asset management and tax havens. *Development and Change, 49*(3), 893–906.

Moretti, E. (2012). *The new geography of jobs*. New York: Houghton Mifflin Harcourt.

Moretti, E., & Thulin, P. (2013). Local multipliers and human capital in the United States and Sweden. *Industrial and Corporate Change, 22*(1), 131–151.

Mowery, D. C., & Rosenberg, N. (1998). *Paths of innovation: Technological change in 20th-century America*. Cambridge, UK: Cambridge University Press.

Mowery, D. C., & Sampat, B. N. (2004). The Bayh-Dole act of 1980 and university–industry technology transfer: A model for other OECD governments? *Journal of Technology Transfer, 30*(1–2), 115–127.

Mullis, I. V. S., Martin, M. O., Foy, P., & Hooper, M. (2016). *TIMSS 2015 international results in mathematics*. Boston, MA: TIMSS & PIRLS International Study Center, Boston College.

Murphy, K. M., Shleifer, A., & Vishny, R. W. (1991). The allocation of talent: Implications for growth. *Quarterly Journal of Economics, 106*(2), 503–530.

My Community (2019). *Understanding the community right to challenge.* https://mycommunity.org.uk/resources/understanding-the-community-right-to-challenge/

Naam, R. (2013). *The infinite resource: The power of ideas on a finite planet.* Lebanon, NH: University Press of New England.

Nelson, R. R. (1959). The simple economics of basic scientific research. *Journal of Political Economy, 67*(3), 297–306.

Niebuhr, A., Granato, N., Haas, A., & Hamann, S. (2012). Does labour mobility reduce disparities between regional labour markets in Germany? *Regional Studies, 46*(7), 841–858.

Noorderhaven, N., Thurik, R., Wennekers, S., & Van Stel, A. (2004). The role of dissatisfaction and per capita income in explaining self-employment across 15 European countries. *Entrepreneurship Theory and Practice, 28*(5), 447–466.

Nordhaus, W. D. (2004). *Schumpeterian profits in the American economy: Theory and measurement.* NBER working paper no. 10433. Cambridge, MA: National Bureau of Economic Research.

North, D. C. (1990). *Institutions, institutional change, and economic performance.* Cambridge, UK: Cambridge University Press.

North, D. C. (1991). Institutions. *Journal of Economic Perspectives, 5*(1), 97–112.

North, D. C., & Weingast, B. R. (1989). Constitutions and commitment: The evolution of institutions governing public choice in seventeenth-century England. *Journal of Economic History, 49*(4), 803–832.

North, D. C., Wallis, J., & Weingast, B. R. (2009). *Violence and social orders: A conceptual framework for interpreting recorded human history.* Cambridge, UK: Cambridge University Press.

Nunn, N. (2009). The importance of history for economic development. *Annual Review of Economics, 1*(1), 65–92.

Nykvist, J. (2008). Entrepreneurship and liquidity constraints: Evidence from Sweden. *Scandinavian Journal of Economics, 110*(1), 23–43.

O'Connor, A., Stam, E., Sussan, F., & Audretsch, D. B. (Eds.). (2018). *Entrepreneurial ecosystems: Place-based transformations and transitions* (International studies in entrepreneurship) (Vol. 38). Cham, CH: Springer.

O'Rourke, A. (2003). A new politics of engagement: Shareholder activism for corporate social responsibility. *Business Strategy and the Environment, 12*(4), 227–239.

OECD (2010). *The OECD innovation strategy: Getting a head start on tomorrow.* Paris: OECD.

OECD (2013). *Indicators of employment protection legislation.* http://www.oecd.org/els/emp/oecdindicatorsofemploymentprotection.htm

OECD (2016a). *OECD employment outlook 2016.* Paris: OECD.

OECD (2016b). *PISA 2015 results (volume 1): Excellence and equity in education.* Paris: OECD.

OECD (2017). *Limiting base erosion involving interest deductions and other financial payments, action 4—2016 update: Inclusive framework on BEPS*. OECD/G20 base erosion and profit shifting project. Paris: OECD.

OECD (2018a). *Pension funds in figures*. Paris: OECD. https://www.oecd.org/daf/fin/private-pensions/Pension-Funds-in-Figures-2018.pdf.

OECD (2018b). *OECD education at a glance 2018*. Paris: OECD.

OECD (2019a). *OECD data portal*. Paris: OECD. https://data.oecd.org/natincome/saving-rate.htm.

OECD (2019b). *OECD data portal*. Paris: OECD. https://data.oecd.org/emp/part-time-employment-rate.htm.

Oh, I., Lee, J. D., Heshmati, A., & Choi, G. G. (2009). Evaluation of credit guarantee policy using propensity score matching. *Small Business Economics, 33*(3), 335–351.

Okubo, Y., & Sjöberg, C. (2000). The changing pattern of industrial scientific research collaboration in Sweden. *Research Policy, 29*(1), 81–98.

Olsson, M., & Tåg, J. (2017). Private equity, layoffs, and job polarization. *Journal of Labor Economics, 35*(3), 697–754.

Pagliero, M. (2015). The effects of recent reforms liberalising regulated professions in Italy. Mimeo. Turin: University of Turin & Carlo Alberto College.

Parker, S. C. (2018). *The economics of entrepreneurship*. Cambridge, MA: Cambridge University Press.

Pavitt, K. (1991). What makes basic research economically useful? *Research Policy, 20*(2), 109–119.

Pelikan, P. (1988). Can the imperfect innovation systems of capitalism be outperformed? In G. Dosi et al. (Eds.), *Technical change and economic theory*. London: Pinter Publishers.

PensionsEurope (2017). *Pension fund statistics 2017*. Brussels. https://www.pensionseurope.eu/system/files/PensionsEurope%20statistics%202017%20-%20Explanatory%20note.pdf

Perkmann, M., et al. (2013). Academic engagement and commercialisation: A review of the literature on university–industry relations. *Research Policy, 42*(2), 423–442.

Phelps, E. S. (2007). Macroeconomics for a modern economy: 2006 Nobel prize lecture in economics. *American Economic Review, 97*(3), 543–561.

Phelps, E. S. (2013). *Mass flourishing: How grassroots innovation created jobs, challenge, and change*. Princeton, NJ: Princeton University Press.

Philpot, J., Hearth, D., Rimbey, J. N., & Schulman, C. T. (1998). Active management, fund size, and bond mutual fund returns. *Financial Review, 33*(2), 115–125.

Piketty, T. (2014). *Capital in the twenty-first century*. Cambridge, MA: Belknap Press of Harvard University Press.

Piketty, T. (2015). About capital in the twenty-first century. *American Economic Review, 105*(5), 48–53.

Piketty, T., Saez, E., & Zucman, G. (2013). *Rethinking capital and wealth taxation.* Working paper. Paris School of Economics, UC Berkeley and London School of Economics.

Pilbeam, K. (2018). *Finance & financial markets.* London: Macmillan.

Pohl, M., & Tortella, T. (2017). *A century of banking consolidation in Europe: The history and archives of mergers and acquisitions.* London: Routledge.

Polzin, F. (2017). Mobilizing private finance for low-carbon innovation—a systematic review of barriers and solutions. *Renewable and Sustainable Energy Reviews, 77*(September), 525–535.

Polzin, F., Sanders, M., & Täube, F. (2017). A diverse and resilient financial system for investments in the energy transition. *Current Opinion in Environmental Sustainability, 28*(October), 24–32.

Polzin, F., Sanders, M., & Stavlöt, U. (2018a). Do investors and entrepreneurs match? Evidence from the Netherlands and Sweden. *Technological Forecasting and Social Change, 127*, 112–126.

Polzin, F., Toxopeus, H., & Stam, E. (2018b). The wisdom of the crowd in funding: Information heterogeneity and social networks of crowdfunders. *Small Business Economics, 50*(2), 251–273.

Ponds, R., Van Oort, F., & Frenken, K. (2007). The geographical and institutional proximity of research collaboration. *Papers in Regional Science, 86*(3), 423–443.

Pongracic, I. (2009). *Employees and entrepreneurship: Co-ordination and spontaneity in non-hierarchical business organizations.* Cheltenham, UK: Edward Elgar.

Popp Berman, E. (2008). Why did universities start patenting? Institution-building and the road to the Bayh-Dole act. *Social Studies of Science, 38*(6), 835–871.

Popper, K. R. (1945). *The open society and its enemies.* London: Routledge.

PwC (2019). *Paying taxes 2019.* PwC and World Bank Group. https://www.pwc.com/payingtaxes

Reher, D. S. (1998). Family ties in Western Europe: Persistent contrasts. *Population and Development Review, 24*(2), 203–234.

Reinhardt, U. E., Hussey, P. S., & Anderson, G. F. (2004). U.S. health care spending in an international context. *Health Affairs, 23*(3), 10–25.

Riksbanken (2018). *E-krona.* Stockholm: Central Bank of Sweden. https://www.riksbank.se/en-gb/payments%2D%2Dcash/e-krona/

Rodrik, D. (2007). *One economics, many recipes: Globalization, institutions, and economic growth.* Princeton, NJ: Princeton University Press.

Rodrik, D. (2008). Second-best institutions. *American Economic Review, 98*(2), 100–104.

Rodrik, D. (2015). *Economics rules: The rights and wrongs of the dismal science.* New York: Norton.

Rodrik, D., Subramanian, A., & Trebbi, F. (2004). Institutions rule: The primacy of institutions over geography and integration in economic development. *Journal of Economic Growth, 9*(2), 131–165.

Romer, P. M. (1986). Increasing returns and long-run growth. *Journal of Political Economy, 94*(5), 1002–1037.

Romer, P. M. (1990). Endogenous technological change. *Journal of Political Economy, 98*(5), S71–S102.

Rosenberg, N., & Birdzell, L. E. (1986). *How the west grew rich: The economic transformation of the industrial world.* New York: Basic Books.

Rosenthal, S. S., & Strange, W. C. (2008). The attenuation of human capital spillovers. *Journal of Urban Economics, 64*(2), 373–389.

Sabel, S., & Reddy, S. (2007). Learning to learn: Undoing the Gordian knot of development today. *Challenge, 50*(5), 73–92.

Salter, A. J., & Martin, B. R. (2001). The economic benefits of publicly funded basic research: A critical review. *Research policy, 30*(3), 509–532.

Sanders, J. M., Damen, M. A., & Van Dam, K. (2015). Are positive learning experiences levers for lifelong learning among low educated workers? In *Evidence-based HRM: A global forum for empirical scholarship 3*(3) (pp. 244–257). London: Emerald Group.

Sanders, M., & Weitzel, U. (2013). Misallocation of entrepreneurial talent in post-conflict environments. *Journal of Conflict Resolution, 57*(1), 41–64.

Sanders, M., Grilli, L., Herrmann, A., Latifi, G., Pager, B., Szerb, L., & Terragno Bogliaccini, E. (2018a). *FIRES-reform strategy for Italy.* FIRES-report D5.12a, Financial and Institutional Reforms for an Entrepreneurial Society. http://www.projectfires.eu

Sanders, M., Fritsch, M., Herrmann, A., Latifi, G., Pager, B., Szerb, L., Terragno Bogliaccini, E., & Wyrwich, M. (2018b). *FIRES-reform strategy for Germany.* FIRES-report D5.12b, Financial and Institutional Reforms for an Entrepreneurial Society. http://www.projectfires.eu/

Sanders, M., Dunstan, J., Estrin, S., Herrmann, A., Pager, B., Szerb, L., & Terragno Bogliaccini, E. (2018c). *FIRES-reform strategy for the UK.* FIRES-report D5.12c, Financial and Institutional Reforms for an Entrepreneurial Society. http://www.projectfires.eu/

Sautet, F. (2000). *An entrepreneurial theory of the firm.* New York: Routledge.

Scarpetta, S., Hemmings, P., Tressel, T., & Woo, J. (2002). *The role of policy and institutions for productivity and firm dynamics: Evidence from micro and industry data.* OECD Economics Department working paper no. 329. Paris: OECD.

Schäfer, W., Kroneman, M., Boerma, W., van den Berg, M., Westert, G., Devillé, W., & van Ginneken, E. (2010). The Netherlands: Health system review. *Health Systems in Transition, 12*(1), 1–229.

Scherer, S. (2004). Stepping-stones or traps? The consequences of labour market entry positions on future careers in West Germany, Great Britain and Italy. *Work, Employment and Society, 18*(2), 369–394.

Schich, S., & Aydin, Y. (2014). Measurement and analysis of implicit guarantees for bank debt. *OECD Journal: Financial Market Trends, 2014*(1), 39–67.

Schivardi, F., & Torrini, R. (2008). Identifying the effects of firing restrictions through size-contingent differences in regulation. *Labour Economics, 15*(3), 482–511.

Schmidt, R. H., & Spindler, G. (2002). Path dependence, corporate governance and complementarity. *International Finance, 5*(3), 311–333.

Schneider, F. (2015a). *Size and development of the shadow economy of 31 European and 5 other OECD countries from 2003 to 2015: Different developments.* Mimeo. Linz, AUT: Department of Economics, Johannes Kepler University.

Schneider, J. D. (2015b). Growth for Europe–Is the Juncker plan the answer? *European Policy Centre discussion paper.*

Schumpeter, J. A. (1934 [1911]). *The theory of economic development: An inquiry into profits, capital, credit, interest, and the business cycle.* New York: Routledge.

Schumpeter, J. A. (1989[1949]). Economic theory and entrepreneurial history. In R. V. Clemence (Ed.), *Essays on entrepreneurs, innovations, business cycles, and the evolution of capitalism* (pp. 253–271). New Brunswick, NJ: Transaction Publishers.

Schut, E., Sorbe, S., & Høj, J. (2013). *Health care reform and long-term care in the Netherlands.* Paris: OECD. https://www-oecd-ilibrary-org.proxy.library.uu.nl/economics/health-care-reform-and-long-term-care-in-the-netherlands_5k4dlw04vx0n-en.

Shakow, D., & Shuldiner, R. (1999). A comprehensive wealth tax. *Tax Law Review, 53*(4), 499–585.

Shane, S. A. (2008). *The illusions of entrepreneurship.* New Haven, CT: Yale University Press.

Shavell, S., & van Ypersele, T. (2001). Rewards versus intellectual property rights. *Journal of Law and Economics, 44*(2), 525–547.

Shavinina, L. (2013). How to develop innovators? Innovation education for the gifted. *Gifted Education International, 29*(1), 54–68.

Shiller, R. J. (2013). Capitalism and financial innovation. *Financial Analysts Journal, 69*(1), 21–25.

Siepmann, T. J. (2004). The global exportation of the US Bayh-Dole act. *University of Dayton Law Review, 30*(2), 209–243.

Signori, A., & Vismara, S. (2018). Does success bring success? The post-offering lives of equity-crowdfunded firms. *Journal of Corporate Finance, 50*(C), 575–591.

Simon, J. L. (1996). *The ultimate resource* (2nd ed.). Princeton, NY: Princeton University Press.

Simon, J. L., & Kahn, H. (1981). *The ultimate resource.* Oxford, UK: Martin Robertson.

Sinn, H. W. (1996). Social insurance, incentives and risk taking. *International Tax and Public Finance, 3*(3), 259–280.

Skedinger, P. (2010). *Employment protection legislation: Evolution, effects, winners and losers.* Cheltenham, UK: Edward Elgar.

Sobel, R. S. (2008). Testing Baumol: Institutional quality and the productivity of entrepreneurship. *Journal of Business Venturing, 23*(6), 641–655.

Sørensen, P. B. (2010). *Swedish tax policy: Recent trends and future challenges* (Report to the expert group on public economics 2010:4). Stockholm: Ministry of Finance.

Sorenson, O., & Stuart, T. E. (2001). Syndication networks and the spatial distribution of venture capital investments. *American Journal of Sociology, 106*(6), 1546–1588.

Spigel, B., & Harrison, R. (2018). Toward a process theory of entrepreneurial ecosystems. *Strategic Entrepreneurship Journal, 12*(1), 151–168.

Squires, D. A. (2012). Explaining high health care spending in the United States: An international comparison of supply, utilization, prices, and quality. *Issue brief no. 10.* New York, NY: Commonwealth Fund.

Stam, E. (2014). The Dutch entrepreneurial ecosystem. *SSRN Electronic Journal.* https://doi.org/10.2139/ssrn.2473475

Stam, E. (2015). Entrepreneurial ecosystems and regional policy: A sympathetic critique. *European Planning Studies, 23*(9), 1759–1769.

Stam, E., & Lambooy, J. (2012). Entrepreneurship, knowledge, space, and place: Evolutionary economic geography meets Austrian economics. In D. E. Andersson (Ed.), *The spatial market process: Advances in Austrian economics* (Vol. 16, pp. 81–103). Bingley, UK: Emerald.

Stamegna, C. (2018). *New EU insolvency rules give troubled businesses a chance to start anew. Members' Research Service PE 623.548—June 2018.* Brussels: European Parliamentary Research Service. http://www.europarl.europa.eu/RegData/etudes/BRIE/2018/623548/EPRS_BRI(2018)623548_EN.pdf

Stenholm, P., Acs, Z. J., & Wuebker, R. (2013). Exploring country-level institutional arrangements on the rate and type of entrepreneurial activity. *Journal of Business Venturing, 28*(1), 176–193.

Stevenson, R. M., Kuratko, D. F., & Eutsler, J. (2019). Unleashing main street entrepreneurship: Crowdfunding, venture capital, and the democratization of new venture investments. *Small Business Economics, 52*(2), 375–393.

Strategic Banking Corporation of Ireland (2019). *SME credit guarantee scheme (CGS).* Dublin. https://sbci.gov.ie/sme-credit-guarantee-scheme-cgs

Subramanian, N., & Gunasekaran, A. (2015). Cleaner supply-chain management practices for twenty-first century organizational competitiveness: Practice-performance framework and research propositions. *International Journal of Production Economics, 164,* 216–233.

Sull, D., & Eisenhardt, K. M. (2015). *Simple rules: How to thrive in a complex world.* New York: Houghton Mifflin Harcourt.

Suse, A., & Hachez, N. (2017). *Identification and assessment of the legal implications of an entrepreneurial reform agenda.* FIRES report 6.2, Financial and Institutional Reforms for an Entrepreneurial Society. http://www.projectfires.eu/wp-content/uploads/2018/02/D6.2-REVISED.pdf

Svensson, R. (2008). Growth through research and development—what does the research literature say? *Vinnova Report VR 2008:19.* Stockholm: Vinnova, Sweden's Innovation Agency.

Tåg, J. (2012). The real effects of private equity buyouts. In D. Cumming (Ed.), *Oxford handbook of private equity* (pp. 271–299). Oxford, UK: Oxford University Press.

Taylor, M. Z., & Wilson, S. (2012). Does culture still matter? The effects of individualism on national innovation rates. *Journal of Business Venturing, 27*(2), 234–247.

The Economist (2017). Inheritance tax: A hated tax but a fair one. *The Economist*, November 23. https://www.economist.com/leaders/2017/11/23/a-hated-tax-but-a-fair-one

Times Higher Education (2018). *World university rankings 2017–2018*. https://www.timeshighereducation.com/world-university-rankings/2018/world-ranking

Toader, O. (2015). Quantifying and explaining implicit public guarantees for European banks. *International Review of Financial Analysis, 41*(1), 136–147.

Tomasi, J. (2012). *Free market fairness*. Princeton, NJ: Princeton University Press.

Toxopeus, H. (2019). *Financing sustainable innovation: From a principal-agent to a collective action perspective*. Doctoral Dissertation. Rotterdam: Erasmus Research Institute of Management, Erasmus University.

Udell, G. F. (2015). Issues in SME access to finance. *European Economy, 2*, 61–74.

Uesugi, I., Sakai, K., & Yamashiro, G. M. (2010). The effectiveness of public credit guarantees in the Japanese loan market. *Journal of the Japanese and International Economies, 24*(4), 457–480.

Urbano, D., & Alvarez, C. (2014). Institutional dimensions and entrepreneurial activity: An international study. *Small Business Economics, 42*(4), 703–716.

van Rooij, M., Lusardi, A., & Alessie, R. (2011). Financial literacy and stock market participation. *Journal of Financial Economics, 101*(2), 449–472.

van Tilburg, R. (2009). *Finance for innovation: Policy options for improving the financial component of the Dutch innovation system*. The Hague: Advisory Council on Science and Technology Policy. https://www.awti.nl/binaries/awti/documenten/publicaties/2009/11/6/finance-for-innovation_achtergrondstudie-36/finance-for-innovation-achtergrondstudie-36.pdf.

Verdier, D. (2002). *Moving money: Banking and finance in the industrialized world*. Cambridge, MA: Cambridge University Press.

Verdier, E. (2009). European lifelong learning strategy and diversity of national devices: An interpretation in terms of public policy regimes. *Report presented at the European Consortium for Political Research, General Conference in Potsdam, Germany*. https://halshs.archives-ouvertes.fr/halshs-00436545/document

Vermeylen, G. (2008). Mapping flexicurity in the EU. In P. Ester, R. Muffels, J. Schippers, & T. Wilthagen (Eds.), *Innovating European labour markets* (pp. 191–214). Cheltenham, UK: Edward Elgar.

Vickers Commission (2013). *The independent commission on banking: The Vickers report*. https://researchbriefings.parliament.uk/ResearchBriefing/Summary/SN06171#fullreport

Vivarelli, M. (2013). Is entrepreneurship necessarily good? Microeconomic evidence from developed and developing countries. *Industrial and Corporate Change, 22*(6), 1453–1495.

Vogel, G. (2006). A German Ivy league takes shape. *Science, 314*(5798), 400.

von Hippel, E., Ogawa, S., & de Jong, J. P. J. (2011). The age of the consumer-innovator. *MIT Sloan Management Review, 53*(1), 27–35.

Vulkan, N., Åstebro, T., & Sierra, M. F. (2016). Equity crowdfunding: A new phenomenon. *Journal of Business Venturing Insights, 5*, 37–49.

WEF. (2013). *Entrepreneurial ecosystems around the globe and company growth dynamics.* Geneva: World Economic Forum.

WEF. (2015). *The global competitiveness report 2014–2015.* Geneva: World Economic Forum.

WEF. (2016). S. Baller, S. Dutta, & B. Lanvin (Eds.), *The global information technology report 2016 innovating in the digital economy.* Geneva: World Economic Forum. http://reports.weforum.org/global-information-technology-report-2016/networked-readiness-index/

Welter, F., Baker, T., Audretsch, D. B., & Gartner, W. B. (2017). Everyday entrepreneurship: A call for entrepreneurship research to embrace entrepreneurial diversity. *Entrepreneurship Theory & Practice, 41*(3), 311–321.

Welter, F., Baker, T., & Wirsching, K. (2019). Three waves and counting: The rising tide of contextualization in entrepreneurship research. *Small Business Economics, 52*(2), 319–330.

Wennberg, K., Wiklund, J., & Wright, M. (2011). The effectiveness of university knowledge spillovers: Performance differences between university spinoffs and corporate spinoffs. *Research Policy, 40*(8), 1128–1143.

Wessner, C. W. (2008). *An assessment of the small business innovation research program.* Washington, DC: National Research Council (U.S.) Committee for Capitalizing on Science, Technology, and Innovation.

Westerhuis, G. (2016). Commercial banking: The changing interaction between banks, markets, industry and state. In Y. Cassis, R. S. Grossman, & C. R. Schenk (Eds.), *Oxford handbook of banking and financial history.* Oxford, UK: Oxford University Press.

Winding, T. N., Nohr, E. A., Labriola, M., Biering, K., & Andersen, J. H. (2013). Personal predictors of educational attainment after compulsory school: Influence of measures of vulnerability, health, and school performance. *Scandinavian Journal of Public Health, 41*(1), 92–101.

Witt, U. (1996). Innovations, externalities and the problem of economic progress. *Public Choice, 89*(1–2), 113–130.

Woessman, L. (2016). The importance of school systems: Evidence from international differences in student achievement. *Journal of Economic Perspectives, 30*(3), 3–31.

Wolf, M. (2014). Strip private banks of their power to create money. Retrieved January 30, 2019, from https://www.ft.com/content/7f000b18-ca44-11e3-bb92-00144feabdc0

Wolfensberger, M. V. C. (2015). The Netherlands: Focus on excellence, honors programs all around. In *Talent development in European higher education*. Cham, CH: Springer.

Woodruff, C. (2006). Measuring institutions. In S.-R. Ackerman (Ed.), *International handbook on the economics of corruption*. Cheltenham, UK: Edward Elgar.

World Bank. (2018). *Ease of doing business index*. Washington DC: World Bank. http://www.doingbusiness.org/en/rankings

Zecchini, S., & Ventura, M. (2009). The impact of public guarantees on credit to SMEs. *Small Business Economics, 32*(2), 191–206.

Zucker, L. G., Darby, M. R., & Brewer, M. B. (1998). Intellectual human capital and the birth of U.S. biotechnology enterprises. *American Economic Review, 88*(1), 290–306.

Zucman, G. (2014). Taxing across borders: Tracking personal wealth and corporate profits. *Journal of Economic Perspectives, 28*(4), 121–148.

Zucman, G. (2015). *The hidden wealth of nations: The scourge of tax havens*. Chicago, IL: University of Chicago Press.

CPSIA information can be obtained
at www.ICGtesting.com
Printed in the USA
LVHW042301180819
628100LV00007B/93/P

9 783662 595855